STORYING WRITING CENTER LABOR FOR ANTI-CAPITALIST FUTURES

Practices & Possibilities

Series Editors: Aimee McClure, Kelly Ritter, Aleashia Walton, and Jagadish Paudel

Consulting Editor: Mike Palmquist

The Practices & Possibilities Series addresses the full range of practices within the field of Writing Studies, including teaching, learning, research, and theory. From Richard E. Young's taxonomy of "small genres" to Patricia Freitag Ericsson's edited collection on sexual harassment in the academy to Jessie Borgman and Casey McArdle's considerations of teaching online, the books in this series explore issues and ideas of interest to writers, teachers, researchers, and theorists who share an interest in improving existing practices and exploring new possibilities. The series includes both original and republished books. Works in the series are organized topically.

The WAC Clearinghouse and University Press of Colorado are collaborating so that these books will be widely available through free digital distribution and low-cost print editions. The publishers and the series editors are committed to the principle that knowledge should freely circulate and have embraced the use of technology to support open access to scholarly work.

Other Books in the Series

Asao B. Inoue, *Cripping Labor-Based Grading for More Equity in Literacy Courses* (2023)

Jessie Borgman and Casey McArdle (Eds.), *PARS in Charge: Resources and Strategies for Online Writing Program Leaders* (2023)

Douglas Hesse and Laura Julier (Eds.), *Nonfiction, the Teaching of Writing, and the Influence of Richard Lloyd-Jones* (2023)

Linda Adler-Kassner and Elizabeth Wardle, *Writing Expertise: A Research-Based Approach to Writing and Learning Across Disciplines* (2022)

Michael J. Faris, Courtney S. Danforth, and Kyle D. Stedman (Eds.), *Amplifying Soundwriting Pedagogies: Integrating Sound into Rhetoric and Writing* (2022)

Crystal VanKooten and Victor Del Hierro (Eds.), *Methods and Methodologies for Research in Digital Writing and Rhetoric: Centering Positionality in Computers and Writing Scholarship, Volumes 1 and 2* (2022)

Heather M. Falconer, *Masking Inequality with Good Intentions: Systemic Bias, Counterspaces, and Discourse Acquisition in STEM Education* (2022)

Jessica Nastal, Mya Poe, and Christie Toth (Eds.), *Writing Placement in Two Year Colleges: The Pursuit of Equity in Postsecondary Education* (2022)

Natalie M. Dorfeld (Ed.), *The Invisible Professor: The Precarious Lives of the New Faculty Majority* (2022)

STORYING WRITING CENTER LABOR FOR ANTI-CAPITALIST FUTURES

by Genie Nicole Giaimo and Daniel Lawson
with Chapters from 34 Colleagues

The WAC Clearinghouse
wac.colostate.edu
Fort Collins, Colorado

University Press of Colorado
upcolorado.com
Denver, Colorado

The WAC Clearinghouse, Fort Collins, Colorado 80523

University Press of Colorado, Denver, Colorado 80203

© 2024 by Genie Nicole Giaimo and Daniel Lawson. This work is released under a Creative Commons Attribution-NonCommercial-NoDerivatives 4.0 International license.

ISBN 978-1-64215-240-1 (PDF) | 978-1-64215-241-8 (ePub) | 978-1-64642-689-8 (pbk.)

DOI 10.37514/PRA-B.2024.2401

Library of Congress Cataloging-in-Publication Data

Names: Giaimo, Genie Nicole, author. | Lawson, Daniel, 1976– author.
Title: Storying Writing Center labor for anti-capitalist futures / by Genie Nicole Giaimo and Daniel Lawson ; with chapters from 34 colleagues.
Description: Fort Collins : The WAC Clearinghouse; University Press of Colorado, 2025. | Series: Practices & possibilities | Includes bibliographical references.
Identifiers: LCCN 2024041424 (print) | LCCN 2024041425 (ebook) | ISBN 9781646426898 (paperback) | ISBN 9781642152401 (adobe pdf) | ISBN 9781642152418 (epub)
Subjects: LCSH: Writing centers—Employees—United States. | Universities and colleges—Faculty—Employment—United States. | Work environment—United States.
Classification: LCC PE1405.U6 G528 2024 (print) | LCC PE1405.U6 (ebook) | DDC 808/.0420711—dc23/eng/20230215
LC record available at https://lccn.loc.gov/2024041424
LC ebook record available at https://lccn.loc.gov/2024041425

Copyeditor: Caitlin Kahihikolo
Designer: Mike Palmquist
Cover Images: Cover Images: "Work Promotes Confidence" by an unnamed artist (Library of Congress Item Number 98518393) and "Work with Care" by Nathan Sherman (Library of Congress Item Number 98517388). Public domain.
Series Editors: Aimee McClure, Kelly Ritter, Aleashia Walton, and Jagadish Paudel
Consulting Editor: Mike Palmquist

The WAC Clearinghouse supports teachers of writing across the disciplines. Hosted by Colorado State University, it brings together scholarly journals and book series as well as resources for teachers who use writing in their courses. This book is available in digital formats for free download at wac.colostate.edu.

Founded in 1965, the University Press of Colorado is a nonprofit cooperative publishing enterprise supported, in part, by Adams State University, Colorado School of Mines, Colorado State University, Fort Lewis College, Metropolitan State University of Denver, University of Alaska Fairbanks, University of Colorado, University of Denver, University of Northern Colorado, University of Wyoming, Utah State University, and Western Colorado University. For more information, visit upcolorado.com.

Citation Information: Giaimo, Genie & Daniel Lawson. (2024). *Storying Writing Center Labor for Anti-Capitalist Futures*. The WAC Clearinghouse; University Press of Colorado. https://doi.org/10.37514/PRA-B.2024.2401

Land Acknowledgment. The Colorado State University Land Acknowledgment can be found at https://landacknowledgment.colostate.edu.

Contents

Acknowledgments ix

Introduction 3

Act I. Where We've Been: Project Frame

Chapter 1. Writing Center Labor in the Neoliberal University: Where Have We Been (So Far)? 9

Chapter 2. Methodology: Counterstorying, Testimony, and Narrative as Research Work 21

Chapter 3. Key Concepts in the Book 29

Chapter 4. The Untold Stories, The Hard Truths 35

Act II. Where We Are: Stories and Interchapters

Chapter 5. Genie and Dan's Origin Stories 41

Theme 1. Career Trajectories and Labor 47

Chapter 6. Laboring to Grow an Academic Field 51
   Muriel Harris

Chapter 7. *Curriculum Vitae:* An Alternative History 55
   Neal Lerner

Chapter 8. My Writing Center Side Hustle 59
   Anonymous

Chapter 9. Why Write?: Writing Center Publishing as Labor 63
   Rebecca Hallman Martini

Chapter 10. Moving On to Move Up 67
   Joseph Cheatle

Chapter 11. The First Year: A New Director's Experience 71
   Allie Sockwell Johnston

Chapter 12. From Dream Job to Unsustainable 75
   Anonymous

Theme 2. Precarity and Failed Advocacy 79

Chapter 13. Writing Fellows; Fellow Students 83
   Eva Dunsky

Chapter 14. I've Got a Secret: I'm Contingent. (Wait, You're Contingent Too?)..................87
    Anonymous

Chapter 15. Into and Out of the Tutoring Center.......................91
    Anonymous

Chapter 16. Writing Center as Life Raft: The Fracturing of the Grand Narratives of Working in Higher Education.......................95
    Anonymous

Chapter 17. Counterstory: Ignored Labor with a Writing Center 99
    Lan Wang-Hiles

Theme 3. Advocacy Successes...................................103

Chapter 18. "... at least for now": A Story About Undergraduate Writing Centers and Labor Compensation in Five Parts 107
    Scott Whiddon

Chapter 19. Advocating for Equitable Tutor Pay with Campus Partners ...111
    Katherine E. Tirabassi

Chapter 20. Benefits and Drawbacks of Hiring Professional Academic Tutors...115
    Libby Anthony

Chapter 21. From the Archive of a Tutor Representative's Email Correspondences (Summer 2022)..............................119
    Anonymous

Chapter 22. "I Have No Idea What I'm Doing": Why Training Is An Essential Part of Labor Conversations in Writing Centers...........123
    Olivia Imirie

Chapter 23. Overloaded: Balancing the Ethics of WC Administration and Student Labor...127
    Megan Keaton

Theme 4. Identity and Labor....................................131

Chapter 24. Writing Center Exile: Third Gender as Third Class in a Third Space...133
    Silk Jade (Pseudonymous)

Chapter 25. Thank You for Carrying Me Through, Thank You for Your Labor..137
    Saurabh Anand

Chapter 26. Coaching Queerly: Healing in Writing Center Work 141
    Molly Ryan

Chapter 27. "Fucking Up" and Listening in the Writing Center. 145
    Ryan Witt

Chapter 28. Boundless 149
    Genie Nicole Giaimo

Theme 5. Trauma and the New Workplace Normal. 153

Chapter 29. A Story of Writing Center Labor in a Violent Age 157
    John Chadderdon, Maggie M. Herb, and Elijah Hundley

Chapter 30. Tragedy in the Writing Center 163
    Vincent Belkin (Pseudonymous)

Chapter 31. Boundaries and Labor During the COVID-19 Pandemic 167
    Anne McMurtrey

Chapter 32. Bearing Witness: The Emotional Labor of (Pandemic) Tutoring 171
    Margaret Lundberg

Theme 6. Care Work and Sustainability 175

Chapter 33. Care and Work/Spaces: Writing Center Labor During COVID-19 177
    Janine Morris

Chapter 34. Labor of Love: Managing the Writing Center and New Motherhood during the Pandemic 181
    Mary Elizabeth Skinner and Jaclyn Wells

Chapter 35. What the COVID-19 Pandemic Taught Us About Writing Center Work: The Joys of a Tutor at the Laboratory of Academic Literacy 185
    Oluwatosin Mariam Junaid

Chapter 36. Mike 189
    Jonathan M. Green

Chapter 37. Growing Like Moss: Theorizing the Labor of Writing Center Placemaking 193
    Candis Bond

Chapter 38. Disruptive Labor: The Transformational Work of Pushing Boundaries 197
    Tiffany-Anne M. Elliott

Chapter 39. Keep Writing Centers Weird 201
   James Donathan Garner

ACT III. WHERE WE'RE GOING: CONCLUSION AND CALL TO ACTION

Chapter 40. Reclaiming Metalabor 207

Chapter 41. What Can We Do? Adopting an Anti-capitalist Framework in Writing Center Work... 217

Concluding Thoughts 235

References 239

Appendix A. Email to Workshop Participants........................ 247

Appendix B. Letter to Accreditors 249

Appendix C. Playbook for Unionizing 251

Contributors 255

Acknowledgments

Every year that passes, I am further astounded by the generosity and depth of experience of colleagues in our field. In a lot of ways, we only have to ask and you respond again and again. Thank you to all the contributors who shared their stories. Collectively, we have hundreds (of years of experience in writing centers. The field needs to hear our voices.

Thank you to those who helped to shape the early (and also later) stages of this project. Stacia Moroski-Rigney for meeting with us to demystify college accreditation processes. Dana Driscoll for reading multiple drafts of the first and third sections of the book and pushing us both structurally and politically. And Jamie McCallum, Associate Professor of Sociology at Middlebury College, who, early in the proposal drafting process, generously shared his expertise and knowledge on labor and work issues, as well as organizing. Also, thank you to Mike Palmquist, Aimee Taylor McClure, Aleashia Walton, and Jagadish Paudel of the WAC Clearinghouse and Practices and Possibilities series. You took a chance on a multi-step, structurally unique, archival, behemoth of a text, for which we are very grateful. Thank you, also, to the reviewers of the proposal, full monograph, and revision—your feedback was invaluable to us.

I want to thank my students—past and present—and all the tutors I have worked with over the years. In particular, thank you to my fall 2023 Labor Rhetorics course (WRPR345); our class discussions were invaluable as we revised this book throughout the fall.

To my family, my ideas about labor and organizing come from growing up with proud dues-paying union members (IBEW and SEIU). Through watching you, I learned how to do a hard day's work and advocate for what I and other workers need. Through you, I learned the importance of living beyond work and always looking to the future. I love you.

To Katherine and Grav, you are everything. Without you, my writing would be full of typos and far less interesting. Thank you for years of co-working and shared intellectual pursuits.

Finally, to Dan: when we first met at ECWCA nearly a decade ago, I had no idea how our collaboration and friendship would grow. But, even then, I recognized your Midwest Punk Gen X-er DIY ethos and your desire to break it all down and build it all up again. Thank you for always being willing to read a draft or write a letter of support for me. Thank you for believing in the future of this profession and always putting your money where your mouth is when it comes time to get down to work. You always know "which side" you are on.

And with that, I want to acknowledge and honor the bloody and violent struggle for labor rights and a future of ethical and fair work in the United States and around the world. The activist Florence Reece wrote in a 1931 song about the bloody conflict of the Harlan County miners' strike:

> Come, all you good workers
> Good news to you I'll tell
> Of how the good old union
> Has come in here to dwell
> Which side are you on?

– *Genie Nicole Giaimo*

First, I'd like to express my deepest gratitude for the brave and diligent work done by the contributors to this project. Your stories have moved and inspired me—broken my heart but also given me hope. Second, I'd like to thank the associate directors with whom I have had the privilege of working: Cyndi Boertje, Lori Rogers, and Emily Pioszak. Without your labor, our shared vision of our centers could not be enacted. Our associate directors are all too often our unsung champions. Similarly, I want to thank the colleagues in MiWCA, ECWCA, and IWCA who've provided me with so much over the years—friendship, community, mentors, information, and more.

A special thanks to those who had a hand in shaping the book. The editors and reviewers at WAC Clearinghouse were incredibly kind, patient, and insightful. Mike Palmquist, Aleashia Walton, and Jagadish Paudel were wonderful to work with, and Aimee Taylor McClure has been extraordinarily helpful. Stacia Moroski-Rigney lent us valuable time and expertise by teaching us more about the accreditation process. I thank Dana Driscoll for her willingness to wade through drafts of Acts I and III. Your feedback was invaluable, and your insight and friendship mean the world to me. Jennifer Grouling-Snider has been an invaluable reading partner as well: you have shepherded me through many, many drafts. Thank you. I have been blessed with wonderful friends.

I would also like to thank my family for their patience and emotional support. As a somewhat extrinsically motivated person, I sometimes struggle to find it in myself to do what is necessary. You are my reasons. I love you and am so grateful for you.

But most of all, I want to thank Genie. We talk frequently in this book about not giving the job more than it requires without compensation, and for good reason. That said, I am ever humbled by your implacable work ethic, determination, and resilience. You work harder than anyone I know. I have learned so much while writing this with you. But more than that, I am proud to have befriended a fellow malcontent and watch them become recognized for the amazing scholar, public intellectual, and fierce advocate they are in the years since. I am better for having met you.

– *Daniel Lawson*

STORYING WRITING CENTER LABOR FOR ANTI-CAPITALIST FUTURES

Introduction

Recently, we got together with another writing center scholar to talk about research projects. What started out as a writing group of sorts quickly turned into a conversation about work. Reviewer feedback and revision plans were put aside as each of us, in turn, chatted about circumstances in our institutions and our centers. We talked about institutional austerity, the reasons why we got into writing center work, and the joys of working with students and of mentoring. Suddenly, we have become mid-career scholars, though there are not often major signs that accompany these transitions, even if some of us have tenure and have been promoted. A deeper thread in this conversation was existential: after a decade or two working in our field, did we recognize it anymore? Did we recognize the institutions where we have worked? As the current landscape in higher education changes rapidly due to COVID-19, AI, the enrollment cliff, and changes brought upon by neoliberalism and the managed university, we wonder where our profession and our careers are headed. We wonder, as part of the title of this section suggests, where we are going. This might seem like an individual existential concern—a kind of mid-career crisis—but this book argues it is also a communal concern shared by many in the field.

Of course, in looking forward, we need to look back: where have we been? In part, this project is about that, too. We later share our stories about our own educational journeys and some of the challenges of writing center work. Here, however, we share how we landed in this work in the first place, as well as some of the challenges and opportunities we see in writing center work and the future of the profession. The challenges and opportunities are relational as our connections to one another and to the field have grown and continue to grow.

As two first-generation college graduates, we each came into this field serendipitously. Dan needed to work extra hours to save for future semesters at his community college. That early opportunity shaped much of his later career. Genie studied psychology and English in college and later worked as a writing center tutor—and later a graduate administrator—as part of their assistantship (which, ultimately, was also for pay). It was intoxicating to get those one-on-one thunderbolt moments where everything seemed to coalesce around an activity or a concept, and Genie was immediately hooked on the rewards of tutoring work. As serendipity would have it, work (unpaid service work) also brought Genie and Dan into each other's orbit. In 2016, Genie and Dan met at ECWCA—a regional writing center organization—and commiserated about workload, the field, scholarship, and life in general. Year after year, we continued to orbit one another through conferences, service work, and, eventually, collaborations. But long before this project on labor, we both had our own labor crises that we worked through together. We have learned that others have had similar experiences: in conference bars, break rooms, Zoom Rooms, and other social and private spaces, practitioners like us found their way to one another as they tried to make meaning out of their work.

This is not something that only happens in writing centers—there are a lot of places where these "watercooler conversations" happen, but because of the highly individualized (and often idiosyncratic) nature of our work, we are frequently the only writing center administrator at the watercooler. Yet, it is often only in collective and larger-scale events that we find community around writing center labor. This book brings together dozens of practitioners to document their labor stories, and it also explores ways to move our field forward. This project represents a collective effort to bring out into the world the private and often hurried or secret conversations that we have about our work. These can often feel catastrophic or overwhelming, but they can also be triumphant, funny, and joyous. During and right after COVID-19, our labor—as well as the labor of millions—shifted in dramatic ways. But many workers have also shifted their relationship to their work and questioned what they want from their jobs. The time to create a field-wide conversation about writing center work in its vicissitudes is *now*. Because what we do is highly relational—and because we believe that there is power in collective action—it is critical for us to document these stories and learn from them as we take further action and advocate for ourselves and other writing center workers. Writing center work is joyful, but, as we explain momentarily, it is also under-researched from a labor studies perspective.

While we talk methodologically about the role of stories in restorative justice and equity and inclusion work—and the history of counterstorying in the legal field and for BIPOC rhetors—we believe storying serves many different and inclusive purposes. For one, stories slow us down; they ask us to ponder, to ruminate, and to linger, echoing Berg and Seeber's (2013; 2016) calls for the Slow movement in academia. Stories also prompt us to action. Stories are anti-capitalist: they do not optimize meaning; they do not get right to the point; they are not, in other words, part of the efficiencies we might otherwise gravitate towards in our research and in our lives. In these ways, stories and storytelling help to materially represent the futures we hope for—futures that are sustainable, slower, calmer, collectivist, equity-minded, and not always pushing towards optimization of production. We find that many of the themes emerging in the narratives in this project respond to the pervasive logic of late capitalism omnipresent in the current neoliberal climate of the American university, even as the method of storying resists this very logic.

We acknowledge here that framing our work as anti-capitalist may be unsettling for some readers. We urge those readers to bear in mind that capitalism, strictly defined, is an economic system wherein capital is privately (or corporately) owned, and decisions are thus driven by profit rather than by the common good. Education is a common good. As we will explain in detail, capitalism—especially in the context of the neoliberal university—has negative consequences, and we argue throughout the book for new paradigms in which to envision our work. To be clear, as Terkel (1974) found many decades ago, many of us love our work and the legacy of our production. In fact, *we* love *our* work. However, given the neoliberal structures informing our industry, among many others, we also believe the current labor model we function within is unsustainable. We need to forge a new way forward, which we believe can be found through self-examination, collective action, and a framework of eroding capitalism provided by Erik Olin Wright (2019).

The first Act of this project thus outlines the state of writing center research on work as well as how neoliberalism impacts labor in higher education. We then examine intersectionality and its relationship to writing center labor before presenting our counterstorying and testimony methodology. We document and discuss how the collected narratives for the project were developed: writing center practitioners participated in a larger meaning-making process that began with a call for stories, a collective writing workshop, and series of feedback sessions. We then share the key concepts of the project and offer ways to engage with the book, concluding with a call for clear-eyed optimism informed by data and the realities of current labor conditions in the field. Act II contains stories of labor conditions from 34 contributors. Act III proposes ways forward informed by the anti-capitalist writing of Erik Olin Wright (2019). There, we imagine anti-capitalist futures that include wall-to-wall organizing of academic workers and provide methods to unlearn internalized capitalism. Along the way, we offer frameworks, key terms, and discussion questions for readers.

In the end, we hope that this project will be used in many ways that we detail more specifically below. Personally, we wanted to capture a series of moments in the early 2020s when labor manifested in the zeitgeist in ways not seen in over a generation and when unions enjoyed broad popularity and support. As we write these words (in fall 2023) union actions like strikes and walkouts are only increasing across countless sectors such as car manufacturing, health care, casino work, entertainment and so on (Associated Press, 2023). Higher education is no stranger to union actions, either, with Rutgers winning a new contract (Burns, 2023) after a spring 2023 walk-out that included broad support (faculty of all ranks, graduate students, postdocs, staff, etc.) and the UC system winning a new contract under similar circumstances in fall 2022 (Associated Press, 2022). At the same time, while unions are enjoying a reputational renaissance and worker actions increase, our legislative landscape is such that union battles are hard fought but do not always result in contract ratification or good faith bargaining by management. We began this work hoping to extend the knowledge base of the field, to document the difficulties of current labor conditions, and to identify opportunities to organize. But serendipitously in the process, we found community and collectivity, and we rekindled our joy and hope. We believe that the way forward is in collective action, in labor organizing, and in imagining an anti-capitalist future. We also believe stories can unite us in common purpose and in empathy.

In Solidarity.

Genie and Dan

Act I. Where We've Been: Project Frame

Chapter 1. Writing Center Labor in the Neoliberal University: Where Have We Been (So Far)?

Neoliberalism in the 1970s-'80s (and continuing today) in the United States has had wide-spread ramifications for jobs across many sectors. Techniques of neoliberalism such as privatization, outsourcing, deskilling, deregulation, and globalization all but wiped out some industries (like manufacturing) while also deeply transforming state-supported or state-funded industries like education, medicine, utilities, etc. As whole industries previously controlled or owned by the government were privatized, revenue ballooned even as the costs of these services were largely passed onto the consumer (Cohen & Mikaelian, 2021). In public higher education, this process included de-funding educational institutions and selling off university resources like utilities or parking infrastructure to private companies, even as tuition costs have soared over the last 40 or so years. The concept of "the managed university" is not new—it has been around since the 1980s—and it encompasses a perfect storm of neoliberal practices coalescing around deregulation, deskilling, and privatization. The managed university often sees a rapid increase in student enrollment at a time of decreased funding for higher education. This results in "greater managerial control and a diminishing sphere of academic professional autonomy" (Parker & Jary, 1994). In public universities, the managed university can often take the form of heavy top-down management that includes punitive budgetary practices like responsibility centered management (RCM), where individual programs or "units" are responsible for generating all of their revenue (Giaimo, 2022). In a university, RCM can play out with departments, colleges, or other units under-cutting each other for student enrollments in all kinds of creative ways, such as through the creation of mega-courses or 100-person sections of first year writing supported by an army of underpaid TAs running 30–40 student discussion sections. It can also lead to universities merging, cutting, or outright removing entire programs of study, as is occurring during the time of this writing at West Virginia University (Quinn, 2023). Such practices are part of the corporatization of higher education and, as the COVID-19 pandemic drastically impacted student enrollments and therefore revenues, these and other neoliberal business practices have become even more commonplace, especially as schools experience falling enrollments and ever-more reliance on tuition dollars to remain in the black.

As neoliberalism has shaped the landscape of higher education, so, too, has it shaped the ways in which programs and departments within these institutions are run. Writing centers are no exception to these practices, and there are several examples of scholars grappling with the effects of neoliberalism on writing center work and doing more with less (Iantosca, 2020; Mahala, 2007; Monty, 2019). In composition studies, more broadly, the COVID-19 pandemic brought such issues to the fore, such as in the article "Drown[ing] a Little Bit All the Time" which identifies a similar set of shifts in increased work demands, especially in teaching writing online with no additional compensation (Wooten et al., 2022). And while many writing center workers have tried to resist neoliberal impulses, there is a trend within writing center scholarship that ironically embraces the logic of neoliberalism—such as through extolling assessment and data—even as it argues that such practices can serve as a buffer against some of the neoliberal practices detailed above. Corporate-education partnerships, conference sponsorships, outsourcing for scheduling, and more have become even more prominent in the last ten or so years, and these trends doubtlessly affect writing centers, as well. At the same time, part of the managed university includes using data (and other empirical markers of success like revenue) to justify budgets or to seek external privatized partnerships as a way to maintain funding, which scholars in our own field often highlight or write about.

So, while we may mean well through our scholarship, our corporate partnerships, and our assessment practices, neoliberalism and its logic inform, drive, and respond to our praxis. Neoliberalism also informs the ways in which our professional associations structure their support and resources, such as through workshops, institutes, and events that prepare a highly transient population for writing center administration. As we and others in our field have found through assessment, writing center practitioners often occupy precarious, non-tenure track positions. Many come from fields outside of rhetoric and composition. And many do not remain in their positions—or in the field—beyond five to seven years (IWCA-sponsored survey on social justice and working conditions, Giaimo et al., unpublished). At times, our organizations, our journals, and our profession may feel like they are recreating the wheel of writing center work to prepare a revolving set of workers.

Other research confirms the high rate of attrition in our profession. In *The Working Lives of New Writing Center Directors*, Caswell et al. (2016) traced the field's discussion of the "work" in the profession, finding its earliest instance in Healy's (1995) report of his survey of writing center directors, describing their demographics, institutional status, distribution of workload, pay. Caswell, McKinney, and Jackson also conducted their own ethnographic study of the working conditions of new writing center directors where they found that the majority of their participants left their jobs not long after taking them. Caswell et al. (2016) also found "advice narratives" to be especially (and troublingly) prevalent, contributing "to our fuzzy perspective on writing center labor" (p. 8), echoing Boquet's (1999) observation that narrative and lore seem to pervade even our historical understandings of the origins of our centers and programs. At the same time, empirical pockets of research have found that work in our profession is more complex and perhaps more mobile and tenuous than we might like to imagine.

Since Caswell et al.'s (2016) study, interest in understanding and examining how writing center and writing program practitioners experience their labor has grown. For instance, Wynn Perdue et al. (2017) examined writing center job advertisements between 2004 and 2014, finding that writing center work was often configured as an unstated "add-on" to the supposedly primary duties of teaching and research. They also found the descriptions to be missing crucial information about the nature of the work, believing "at least in some cases, that hiring committees know that advertising these aspects of their jobs will make the positions less appealing. It is quite possible that this information is omitted intentionally" (p. 284). Many of the narratives in the present collection confirm this finding. The narratives in the collection also extend Perdue et al.'s finding about the identity crises among writing center administrators (WCAs) in terms of balancing their writing center work and identity alongside their other (teacherly, scholarly) identities.

Several books focusing on WCA identity and work have also been published in recent years. For example, Denny et al.'s (2019) *Out in the Center* and Wooten et al.'s (2020) *The Things We Carry: Strategies for Recognizing and Negotiating Emotional Labor in Writing Program Administration* are both edited collections that explore different facets and qualities of writing center labor. *Out in the Center*, for example, focused on the sorts of labor writing center practitioners engage in while negotiating dimensions of their intersectional identities. *The Things We Carry* shared case studies and essays on navigating emotional labor in the center. These collections show the way that our work inflects and is inflected by identity and affect, and each includes calls for more research. Similar to Caswell et al.'s (2016) study, Webster's 2021 *Queerly Centered* is "about a job" (p. 3), but specifically examines what labor looks like when queer people direct writing centers, especially what local and disciplinary phenomena surface alongside queer writing center leadership" (p. 6), finding a distinct imbalance between the labor performed by queer practitioners compared to their straight counterparts. Giaimo's (2021) edited collection *Wellness and Writing Center Work* similarly situated writing center work around identity and wellness practices, problematizing the fact that the incorporation of wellness in workplace contexts tends to focus on optimizing tutor labor—extracting still more of that labor from an already exploited workforce.

So, work is definitely in the imaginary of our profession, and several projects in the field increasingly focus on different aspects of labor in writing centers and administration work such as the *Writing Center Journal* special issue on contingent writing center workers (Herb et al., 2023), the *Journal of Multimodal Rhetorics*'s special issue on care work during the COVID-19 pandemic (Manivannan et al, 2022), the call for submissions on reluctant supervision in the writing center (Azima et al.2022), and the edited collection *WPA Advocacy in a Pandemic: Lessons Learned* (Ruecker & Estrem, 2022). This is just to name a few collections and special issues about labor and the profession, many of which are at a particular moment impacted by the COVID-19 pandemic. Professional associations (like the Northeast Writing Center Association in spring 2022 and the 2022 International Writing Centers Association Summer Institute) are increasingly offering workshops on labor studies with a particular focus on burnout, workism (Giaimo, 2022), and emotional labor (Mannon, 2023).

Yet, self-care cannot solve larger field-specific issues that arise from neoliberalism like austerity, retrenchment, precarity, etc. Wellness has appealed to our discipline for a long time, represented in scholarship and praxis around Zen Buddhism (Gamache, 2003; Murray, 2003; Spohrer, 2008), as well as in well-being and contemplative praxis work that was produced more recently (Driscoll & Wells, 2020; Emmelhainz, 2020). We argue here that wellness is a stand-in for broader workplace issues. While some of the research on tutor (and student) well-being was touted as helping to make these groups more productive—and, in the case of tutors more effective at their job (Mack & Hupp, 2017; Johnson, 2018; Kervin & Barrett, 2018)—other related issues such as the mental health concerns that tutors bring into their work (Degner et al., 2015; Perry, 2016) are not. They represent a larger issue with the collision of worker well-being, workplace environment and expectations, and the broader societal challenges that we are all facing at this current moment (Giaimo, 2023). Tutors are not outside the world, just as their work is not divorced from the economic, political, and environmental realities of the 21st century, which include the destructive products of neoliberalism, such as climate change, school shootings, police brutality and racism, income inequity, and more. Our work, then, is far larger than addressing wellness and well-being in our centers; it requires a larger examination and critique of our workplaces, of our labor politics, and of the economic and political decisions that have led to our current moment.

Even prior to the COVID-19 pandemic, writing centers struggled with attrition and austerity. Half of the twelve people featured in *The Working Lives of New Writing Center Directors* left the field early in their careers. These departures occurred during the post-2008 ("Great Recession") climate of cuts and further neoliberalization in the university, marked by budget cuts, increased pressure on faculty and programs to "do more with less," and ever increasing scrutiny under the guise of accountability (Scott & Welch, 2016). In turn, these conditions have led to increasing instability and uncertainty in academic labor markets. These austerity measures—and the instability they bring—have accelerated during the COVID-19 pandemic era (2020-2023 and beyond). Entire programs, departments, and units have been cut across the country (Dickler, 2020); faculty have been released en masse (Cyr, 2021; Marcus, 2021; Rodriguez, 2021) or faced salary reductions (De Dios, 2020; Flaherty, 2021); while others face increased teaching and overall workloads (Marcus, 2021; Miami AAUP, 2021).

Accordingly, we feel that we are at a tipping point in our field in terms of how we labor. Because no job is safe in our post-pandemic reality, we believe that now is the time to collect narratives about our field before they are lost and before more people disappear from our professional pipeline. We have, through referencing the scholarship above, offered a macro-view of many of the effects of austerity in higher education and in writing centers, but the lived experiences—the *felt sense*—of those effects are often lost, which is why we turn to stories in Act II of this project. Given what we have learned from the stories collected, we also wish to pool advice for how to move forward with less extractive and precarious models for labor in our profession. Finally, we also know little about why people engage in writing center work in the first place. The serendipity invoked in our introduction might seem magical or otherwise happenstance, but it is imprecise in terms of what people get out of their work, why they do this work, why they stay in this work, etc. Accordingly, we paid careful attention to positive stories about the profession as well, asking "what sustains us in our labor?"

At times, however, a single story details *both* the positive and negative aspects of our labor; this duality, we believe, is also worth pondering. What forces give rise to our joy but, also, which ones give rise to despair? Neoliberalism has been linked to negative collective outcomes in well-being and health (Card & Hepburn, 2022), and austerity is a common byproduct of neoliberalism that likely caused a lot of the wide-spread systemic failures in the early days of the COVID-19 pandemic, particularly in our health field (Navarro, 2020). While we writing center workers are not on the front lines like hospitals, we, too, have our own professional bellwethers that show us how neoliberalism and its consequences impact our labor. As a profession, we have been circling around this topic for nearly two decades (Mahala, 2007), yet how and why we work is not exactly the same as developing frameworks of labor and resistance. Compositionist James Daniel (2021) distinguishes between work and labor, asserting that labor "is associated with production" whereas work "names the conditions and locations of labor." The present project is thus not only about work—in the sense of how we do what we do and why—but also about labor, the larger constellation of issues related to our profession, our workplaces, our jobs (and its joys and challenges) in the aggregate.

Tracing Invisible Work to Metalabor

Though in the previous section we followed strands of labor associated with academia and writing centers, here we look back specifically to the 1980s to trace the origins of the then-nascent theory of invisible work and update it for our current labor moment. We see it as inextricably linked to this project's emerging theme: metalabor. Many of the conversations from that period–when neoliberalism began encroaching in academia and other spheres—anticipate and mirror many of the discussions we see as (disappointingly) necessary now.

Indeed, it seems that for as long as writing centers have been around in their modern-day iteration (circa 1970), there has been debate about whether or not the model of writing center work is a sustainable and justifiable one (Kail, 1983).

While we read about arguments of optimization and growth in early research, we also see concerns about loss of administrative control and even backlash against writing center praxis. We also recognized a commonly occurring concern for student writers rather than for writing center workers. For example, in "From Factory to Workshop: Revising the Writing Center," Ann Moseley (1984) argues that "limiting the services of a writing center is paralleled by the danger of expanding too much or too quickly for existing or dwindling tutor resources" (p. 33). Dwindling tutor resources:

> threatens not just the existence of the center but its ultimate success with individual students. More specifically, the danger is that in our zeal to be accountable and cost efficient—to prove our success to faculty and administrators—we may be seduced into paying more attention to test scores and number of students than to the individual student and his or her writing process. (p. 33)

While Moseley (1984) gets a lot right about how the booms and busts of writing center resources significantly impact student writers, she pays little attention to how writing center workers are hurt by these same booms and busts. It seems we have always had conversations about our field's "worth," which is measured through only *some* of its production (i.e., supporting student writers) but not others (i.e., supporting student workers). Moseley notes that the writing center administrator, in their "zeal to be accountable and cost efficient—to prove our success to faculty and administrators," loses sight of the "true" impact of writing center work which is not measured in student grades or even number of people served but in individual (and likely incremental) changes to how students write (p. 33).

This focus on the individual student, to our minds, still misses the focus on the systemic and the collective. Kail rightly attends to the job expectations of peer writing tutors and questions whether a model of student-teacher collaborative learning is one that institutions will determine is worth investing in, or, as Kail puts it "whether or not it is worth the trouble" (p. 598). In place of a student-worker centered professionalization model of tutoring is what Kail describes as a deskilled model where "student tutors are used exclusively as quiz graders and exercise givers, lab aides who administer to but do not collaborate with other students who are classified as 'remedial' and in need of certain 'writing skills'" (p. 598). While Kail sees this alternative deskilled model of tutoring as one that preserves faculty autonomy and teaching authority—to the detriment of student writers, student workers, and a collaborative learning model—we see this as evidence of the material change in how tutoring work is understood in the constellation of academic support in a university. In this instance, student labor is intentionally limited in order to shore-up faculty autonomy and other elements of their material position at the university. It also impacts the future of sustainable writing center work.

In the 1980s, there was a lot of concern about how peer tutors might undermine or undercut faculty/teacher authority and, perhaps, even engage in work with student writers that transforms writing so much as to be considered plagiarized. Implicit within this panic around peer tutoring edging into the work of faculty who teach writing is a kind of class-based fight over who gets to do teaching work and what kinds of authority and resources each group is awarded to do so. The flip side of this, of course, which Kail (1983) also talks about, is how peer tutors and writing centers/labs teach faculty how to teach writing. But this, too, could be seen as an encroachment on academic freedom in the classroom even as it outsources faculty labor to underpaid student workers. Here, we see a model of labor replicated in the university that is common in a globalized economy (and which really picked up steam in the United States in the 1980s): outsourcing specialized labor to a less skilled, lower-paid, and more precarious workforce. These are laborers whose labor is seen as somehow less legitimate, which impacts the "industry" of writing center work more broadly and into the future.

Collaborative learning (and ethical writing center work), then, comes with anxieties centered on workers other than faculty taking over writing pedagogy work: who is qualified to teach, and in what modes? And, as Kail (1983) suggested, the resource-intensive and time-consuming model of tutor training and work might be replaced by a deskilled model to placate faculty. Of course, 40 years on, we know that this model continues to thrive in writing center spaces and even expand to other kinds of tutoring work both inside and outside the classroom and across disciplines. There are even peer mentor models for mental health and well-being, first-year experience, and other, more niche needs on campus. Yet, writing centers are still faced with a deskilling crisis (and one might argue that the proliferation of peer mentor and tutoring programs is evidence of deskilling labor more broadly as universities and colleges grew but failed to invest in fair wages and stable jobs). As many of the stories included in this book note, yearly budgets are cut, staff are reduced, student workers leave for better paying jobs, and quick "fixes" for labor and staffing crises abound. While peer tutoring has become more legitimized as a vital informal learning model, it is no less precarious. While writing center administrators in Act II of this book talk about their struggle to resist the factory model that institutions would like to impose upon them, the theme of optimization runs through many of these stories. As Moseley (1984) suggests, because we are "forced to take on more and more tasks with fewer tutor resources (p. 34), we try to find the middle ground between exploiting precarious labor and uplifting it. In this way, it seems, very little has changed in nearly half a century, though writing centers are perhaps even more ensconced in the neoliberal university today simply because academia has become increasingly corporatized and managed.

At the same time, this is *not* the 1980s. Writing centers have become academic and scholarly spaces in their own right and have continued to employ tutor workers as these field-wide conversations have developed. We have several professional conferences, organizations, and journals, and a deep commitment to peer training and mentorship, as well as peer-led scholarship and assessment. Many of the old insecurities have given way to newer ones, though we still can hear echoes of the past in them: organizational challenges, structural changes, resource limitations, limited legitimacy, and (implicit but very often left unarticulated) labor anxiety.

These issues with how we labor can also be traced back to the 1980s with what Arlene Kaplan Daniels (1987) formulated as *invisible work*. Daniels argued that work is often perceived as legitimate—as visible—only if it is public, compensated, and valued. As a field, we often search for legitimacy through overworking, working outside of our contracts and bounds, and through taking on volunteer service and care work. In short, an argument can be made that our field has been suffused with invisible work—work that might be visible to the field but not our institutions—ever since writing centers were first established. Created by contingent workers (adjuncts, graduate students, faculty wives) and supported by volunteer labor, writing centers *are* invisible workspaces. Since then, we have struggled to establish our legitimacy, but perhaps this is the very paradox that we find ourselves confronting: we are asking (demanding) others to recognize our invisible work when we might not even really note it ourselves.

For instance, Grutsch McKinney (2013) has explained the problems of coziness and comfort as part of the "grand narrative" around center work. Grutsch McKinney has also (2005) examined the problems of the governing metaphor of "home" for writing centers. This metaphor is problematic for several reasons: because homes are "culturally marked" (Grutsch McKinney, 2005, 6); because for some students, schools are an escape from home and because of the gendered assumptions informing notions of "home" in Western cultures and thus of writing center work (p. 17). Yet, homes also involve unpaid labor, which is disproportionately performed by women (Dugarova, 2020). Writing-center-as-home makes the workspace freighted with gendered, classed, and raced understandings of work and its value. Of course, Daniels (1987) had already discussed the problems of positioning unpaid labor, explaining that "[i]n short, a real pressure underlying the work of the homemaker is lack of validation" (p. 407). Because it is not seen as work but rather as a natural extension of gender roles, such work is invisible and thus not valued, though it props up the paid economy and fills gaps when social and government support fails. Writing centers are often perceived as (gendered) *care* work, and folk knowledge—common sense—around care work is that it is not *real* work. The connection to domestic spaces and, inevitably, unpaid labor has been considered in the field. However, a larger labor-focused study in our field has yet to be produced on this topic. In this project, we develop and extend Daniel's (1987) concept of invisible work, focusing on a particular type of invisible work we call *metalabor*: work for and about work.

This book thus extends a field-wide conversation currently taking place about our work, particularly work during and after (if we are even *after*) the COVID-19 pandemic. And, of course, with the Great Resignation (Sull et al., 2022), or Great Reshuffling, continuing across the United States, and the increase of unionization efforts in spaces like Apple, Starbucks, Amazon, Kaiser Permanente, CVS, and GM (among many others), we are in an exciting moment where workers in many different industries have more power than at any time since the 1970s. Higher education is due for a reckoning, as the strikes at Rutgers and the UC system over the last year and a half—2022–2023—indicate. We are excited to contribute to this body of research but also offer practical guidance on how to advocate for one's personal labor rights as well as the rights of others. This book and the stories it contains, then, are a bellwether for our profession. We ought to listen.

Race, Capitalism, and Labor Studies

While we collected many stories about work in this project, many of them were written by white people. BIPOC contributors do share their stories, but many of those stories focus more on labor and capitalism than on racial identity or the intersection between race and labor. Yet, many labor stories also talk about the intersection of work with gender and sexuality, which leads us to ask: who feels empowered to talk about their labor *and* their identity? And what can we do to encourage narratives about both race and labor?

Currently, as in the past, there seems to be a split between research and scholarship on race and on labor—a kind of bifurcation that has roots in overtly racist union tactics and the collapse of coalition politics of the latter half of the 21st century. In the field of composition studies, scholars have moved away from studying how capitalism impacts its labor, though such studies were more pervasive in the 1980s and '90s. Instead, as Daniel (2022) notes, "interest in this critique [of capitalism] have declined over recent decades, with scholars increasingly moving into other areas, often situating themselves within critiques of identity with nominal relation to capitalism" (p. 13). Yet, the exploitative nature of capitalism enables and encourages racism and other systems of oppression through both economic and social control. While counterstory research featuring BIPOC voices has increased, we hope to see more pieces exploring the intersections of how class, race, and other forms of marginalized identity develop, survive, and are impacted by capitalism. These issues are not mutually exclusive—far from it—and they warrant exploration that bridges these fields of study.

Of course, because rhetoric and composition and the subfield of writing center studies are largely white fields, it makes sense that BIPOC writing center workers might not want to share their stories because there might be consequences that accompany such sharing. This is, of course, just one reason among many not to share overtly racialized labor stories. But we look to stories featured elsewhere that show us the power of linking race and labor. We see it in "Dear Writing Centers: Black Women Speaking Silence into Language and Action," where Talisha M. Haltiwanger Morrison and Talia O. Nanton (2019) talk about oppressive "toxic positively" workplace practices that prioritize comfort over worker safety and the white fragility of writing center workers which led to the unfair treatment of a Black tutor and her subsequent dismissal/resignation from her position. This piece features the story of a fumbling and unfair manager, uncomfortable white tutors, and a workplace that could benefit from worker meditation, updated worker policies, and training on microaggressions and cultural differences in communication (among other things). We also see this in stories like that of Neisha-Anne Green in "Moving beyond Alright: And the Emotional Toll of This, my Life Matters Too, in the Writing Center Work" (2018), a speech at the International Writing Centers Association conference in 2017 and published in *Writing Center Journal* (2018), where she details the micro and macro aggressions she experienced as a Black female writing center director at a school where several racist incidents targeting Black students and workers occurred. She talks about her Blackness—her racial identity—alongside her labor. Race and work are intertwined as she shares stories of alienation and aggression in writing center work and in higher education as the first Black woman in all of her (highly visible) writing center jobs.

So little has been written about these taxes and tolls that BIPOC workers experience in writing center labor, though, as both Morrison and O. Nanton (2019) and Green (2018) pointedly note, racist writing center workspaces have profound negative effects on Black (female) workers. So, in addition to invisible work—which we all perform for one reason or another—our BIPOC colleagues are doubly or even triply "taxed" in their work. As researchers Travis and Thorpe-Moscon (2018) explain:

> Emotional Tax is the combination of feeling different from peers at work because of gender, race, and/or ethnicity and the associated effects on health, well-being, and ability to thrive at work. These experiences can be particularly acute for people of color who fear being stereotyped, receiving unfair treatment, or feeling like the "other" (i.e., set apart from colleagues because of some aspect of their identity such as gender, race, or ethnicity). While most experiences of otherness are detrimental, a lifetime of being marginalized can have uniquely potent effects, including on health and well-being. (n.p.)

Yet, we know little about Black or BIPOC approaches to confronting their WCA work. Though Green details learning how to "fill these positions . . . as myself" (p. 21), the philosophical and ideological approaches to being a BIPOC writing center administrator are only alluded to in her piece.

Sheila Carter-Tod's chapter "Administrating While Black: Negotiating the Emotional Labor of an African American Female WPA" (2020) provides an example of a piece that not only connects race and labor, but also a new Black administrative consciousness. Carter-Tod (2020) notes the need for support systems, and the need to collect stories from Black writing administrators. While Carter-Tod (2020) offers strategies for navigating emotional labor as a Black writing program administrator, she also recognizes that systemic oppression will not be solved by such individualistic practices. As Carter-Tod (2020) notes in her chapter, our field needs more BIPOC labor stories, and we also need to acknowledge the issues with collecting such stories from a small and potentially vulnerable population. So, in addition to methodological concerns around anonymity and protection, the fact that there are fewer BIPOC writing center administrators is also concerning. This is yet another issue our field needs to confront: we need to make our profession more deeply welcoming rather than rhetorically welcoming, as Morrison and O. Nanton discuss (2019).

In all the stories that we detail in this section, one throughline is the mental health concerns that BIPOC (particularly Black) workers experience due to micro and macro aggressions stemming from implicit or overt racism. These experiences, which come along with being in highly visible positions—such as directing writing centers and programs—create a dual issue: not only is the labor itself devalued, but so is the BIPOC WCA's selfhood. So, while many writing center administrators contend with reduced budgets, or being forced to work for free, there are additional historical and political contexts for Black female writing administrators who experience this kind of exploitation. Green (2018) references a Black Lives Matter (BLM) activist's contemplation of suicide. O. Nanton (2019) discusses emotional anguish, crying, and withdrawing from work. Carter-Tod (2020) talks about self-doubt and hypervigilance in workplace encounters:

> While explanations of these decisions exist outside of race or gender bias, the burden comes with finding ways to work in an environment that requires that you solve the needed administrative problem (functioning without sufficient support or funding) while wrestling with the reading of the situation and further having to regulate your reactions, responses, and decisions. (p. 204)

The invisible work that we alluded to earlier is only further compounded by the kind of scrutiny that accompanies the racialized aspects of each and every interaction that this project's contributors detail in their workplace experiences.

The majority of BIPOC contributions for this project were either anonymous or did not feature explicit discussion about race in relation to labor. A collection featuring a lot of visible white voices on labor is a kind of cliche in labor studies and in labor movements. We recognize this limitation and acknowledge the need for more scholarship that bridges race, class, and labor studies, and we hope that this book can help to foreground some of this necessary future work even as we call attention to the dangers of sharing explicit stories that include race and labor.

In Act III, we argue that to ameliorate so much of the metalabor seemingly inherent in writing center work (we will explain this key concept momentarily), we must adopt an anti-capitalist framework for our labor. So much of the contemporary iteration of neoliberalism is bound up in Max Weber's Protestant work ethic: gig work, workism, and the fetishization of the grind. This is, of course, a raced, bodied, and gendered conception of what ought to be valued in a culture. As disability advocate Talila A. Lewis (2019) conceives it, ableism is:

> A system that places value on people's bodies and minds based on societally constructed ideas of normalcy, intelligence and excellence. These constructed ideas of normalcy, intelligence and excellence are deeply rooted in anti-Blackness, eugenics and capitalism. This form of systemic oppression leads to people and society determining who is valuable or worthy based on people's appearance and/or their ability to satisfactorily produce, excel & "behave." Importantly, you do not have to be disabled to experience ableism. (n.p.)

Ableism is thus informed by the same sorts of normative values that inevitably exert pressure on other forms of identity in order to extract ever more productivity from its subjects, thus narrowly constructing notions of "normalcy, intelligence, and excellence" (Lewis, 2019, n.p.). within the contexts of a capitalist, patriarchal, cisgendered society. We hope that the stories and work in this project can help make more visible the ways in which laborers in the current epoch of academic capitalism are interpellated and thus create more solidarity among various intersectionalities of identity. In short, we assert that anti-capitalist work is also antiracist, antisexist, anti-classist, anti-heteronormative, and anti-ableist.

Chapter 2. Methodology: Counterstorying, Testimony, and Narrative as Research Work

Before we talk about the methods (i.e., what we did to collect the stories featured in Act II of this project), we want to talk about the guiding methodology that shaped the broader project. The stories featured in this collection rely on a number of storying traditions, most particularly counterstorying. Counterstorying is a "critical race methodology [that] offers space to conduct and present research grounded in the experiences and knowledge of people of color" (Solórzano & Yosso, p. 23, 2002). Counterstories "can be used as theoretical, methodological, and pedagogical tools to challenge racism, sexism, and classism and work toward social justice" (Solórzano & Yosso, p. 23, 2002). Although writing center studies have discussed anti-racism and inclusion work for decades (the first anti-racism special interest group dates back to the early 2000s), research featuring the lived experiences (and counterstories) of BIPOC writing center administrators and tutors has become much more prominent in the last half decade or so (Faison & Condon, 2022; Green, 2018; Haltiwanger Morrison & Nanton, 2019; Martinez, 2016). Furthermore, scholars have centered the lived experiences of queer directors and writing center workers (Denny, 2005; Denny et al., 2019; Webster, 2021). While researchers in education and critical race studies have talked about counterstories and counterstorying for several decades (Delgado, 1989), writing centers are relative newcomers to this methodology of meaning making, though it is quickly becoming a popular research methodology in the field.

Many earlier references to narrative, however, also seemed to predict the move towards counterstory as it is a powerful and more inclusive approach to writing center scholarship. With McKinney's (2005) research on "cozy homes" and the ongoing interrogation of "lore" in our field (Driscoll & Perdue, 2012; Greenfield & Rowan, 2011; Kjesrud, 2015; McKinney, 2013), researchers understood clearly that narrative and stories pervade how we talk about writing centers. Yet, these stories often assume white, middle-class, and female-identifying administrators, as well as monolingual white tutors. These stories leave little space for heterogeneity in writing center workers' identities, backgrounds, and experiences (to say nothing of race, class, sexuality, gender expression, etc.). The reliance on lore to drive writing center tutoring practices has also created orthodoxies that have been challenged in an ongoing manner for decades (Clark, 1993; Thompson et al., 2009). So, while exchanging stories about writing center practices and work was critical to the early scholarly development of the field, the turn towards narrative interrogation and challenging lore has now moved the field to the incorporation of counterstory as a powerful and necessary methodology and praxis for our work. Unlike lore, narrative inquiry, or storying—as we see featured in Caswell et al.'s (2016) work—counterstories deconstruct the "givens" we have about writing centers and the experiences of workers in them. They also, as Faison and Condon (2022) and others note, constitute a critical research methodology that moves away from the obsession with data-driven methodologies meant to dispel that old lore-focused approach to writing center praxis.

Recent studies also aim to center storying outside of the Western epistemologies that drive both our field's scholarship and our administration processes. As Wang (2022) rightly notes, the work of writing center workers is often lonesome and nomadic; academics often work in places they are not originally from (p. 55). This kind of dislocation can cause all kinds of issues, such as under-serving or poorly serving community members (including ones outside the institution), and lacking cultural context for the center and its workers and writers. It also weakens labor activism, which so heavily relies on informal networks of community members. Storying, then, can help us to center our local contexts and do work outside of academic contexts while moving away from Westernized notions of what liberation looks like (p. 51). As Wang (2022) argues:

> To develop centers that are truly just, we must also work to decenter Western epistemologies and create definitions of justice which are rooted in local and Indigenous epistemologies. I believe that we can move towards these local definitions through storying our own positionality, receiving stories from others, and being deeply imbedded in communities outside the academic context of writing center work. (p. 55)

Wang (2022) thus broadens the scholarship and praxis of counterstorying to include non-Western, Indigenous, and place-based storying.

The existing research on writing center administration studies details profound levels of stress and lack of support (Caswell et al., 2016; Geller & Denny, 2013), which we know that writing center practitioners face broadly and often in addition to other challenges in their institutions. Anecdotally, we know of a lot more traumatic, disruptive, and toxic work experiences in our field that have not been shared publicly. These stories are often shared only informally—as we've often characterized it, over cocktails at conferences—because of fear of retaliation among other job-related concerns. This project provides insight into these and other work-related experiences, including what drew practitioners to writing center work and what joys/pleasures they have in doing such work. Without some form of instantiation, these stories become lost, and that loss contributes "to our fuzzy perspective" (Caswell et al., 2016, p. 8).

Featuring many different forms of stories about writing centers—personal and unofficial institutional histories, testimonies about the experience of laboring, stories of resistance and activism, stories of excitement and joy, and stories about place (Wang, 2022)—contributors rely on the autobiographical and engage in counter-historical narrative work. And, as the important work of our colleagues (Faison & Condon, 2022; Martinez, 2020) demonstrates their need, we ask you to share counterstories, too, in your writing centers, in your staff training, in your own scholarship, and among colleagues. As Suze Berkhout (2013) explains, "As an epistemic activity, testimony is a kind of first-person evidence that has the potential, under certain circumstances, to disrupt dominant metaphors, figurations, and ways of understanding the world—the so-called 'common sense' that belongs primarily to the imaginings of privilege" (p. 29). Our book seeks to disrupt commonplaces, lore, and otherwise taken-for-granted discussions about writing center work. We also see so few stories that take up labor as their main focus, so this is a reclamation process, too. The absence of labor counterstories indicates to us a kind of common sense element: that our work need not be theorized, complicated, or upended. Writing center labor thus becomes largely invisible and left unexamined except in very specific circumstances such as research on new directors, research on under-represented directors, or research on specific types of work (like emotional labor).

From this literature review, and in our own research, we recognize the growing interest in how personal experience and challenging dominant stories have become critical elements of writing center scholarship. Yet, even in this turn towards more anti-racist and inclusive scholarship, gaps in our understanding of how practitioners in writing centers and writing programs experience work and understand their labor—especially place-based labor and labor outside of U.S. contexts—persist. For example, many of the texts about writing center work that we mention above engage in ethnography. These accounts, however, are filtered through the interview methodology which necessarily comes with editing and far less detail from individuals. Another methodology, oral history, comes from legal and historical research, and it centers on the past lived experience of the speaker, but it is often also mediated and not as commonly used in our field's scholarship. While originating in different disciplines, counterstory, storying, and testimony center first-person experience and the disruption of dominant narratives (or lore) through direct engagement with the narrator/subject. In this book, we center first-person experiences that are structured (and mediated by external factors like word count) but that are not edited or otherwise filtered through our analysis.

Contributors to this book disrupt epistemic bias in ethnographic research (Code, 2006) wherein some forms of experience are counted as evidence while others are seen as mere anecdotes. As Robillard (2021) and Micciche (2018) have noted, the label "gossip" can often be used as a form of punishment against women for trying to identify and rupture patriarchal norms. However, gossip can serve as a way for women and other vulnerable populations to protect themselves, and to freely circulate information about environments that are often hostile to them. Here, then, we want to foreground and honor these lived experiences and call attention to how stories are often viewed through gendered, heteronormative, and racialized lenses when they are ascribed more or less authority. Interestingly, the turn away from lore very much follows this pattern of gating shared knowledge. At the same time, we also acknowledge that lore and storying can perpetuate non-inclusive, simple, and otherwise unhelpful narratives about our field. Turning to labor, and considering that less than a third of writing center directors are afforded the protection of a tenure-line (National Census of Writing, 2017), we feel that direct—at times anonymous—testimony is the best way to disrupt many of our current understandings around the conditions of their labor. This book, we hope, facilitates this necessary conversation about labor while recognizing that our profession includes scholars who have engaged in storying our work in other intersectional ways (Haltiwanger Morrison & Evans Garriott, 2023; Webster, 2021; Faison & Condon, 2022; Hallman-Martini, 2022; Caswell et al., 2016).

Methods

The Call for Stories

When we put the call out to listservs, social media, and direct colleagues, we described the objectives of the book and the central topics of labor, material needs and conditions, joys and frustrations in the work, student and contingent labor, advocacy and reform, joining and leaving the field, and more. We wanted to collect as many narratives as possible, recognizing that we may not have space for all of them in a traditionally conceived academic monograph. We worked to try to accept *all* submissions for Act II, only disqualifying a couple that did not quite identify the task in the call and would have to have been completely rewritten. Accordingly, after publication of this project, we are collaborating with *WAC Clearinghouse* to develop an archive that includes future labor narratives.

Inspired by the oral historian and radio broadcaster Studs Terkel and his book *Working* (1974), which collected oral histories of a broad range of workers across the United States, we wanted to capture what we saw as the essence of the lived experiences of workers in our field. Yet, we also realized that the hundred-plus stories that Terkel featured in his book were highly excerpted and edited. We also recognized that, sadly, our publishing landscape does not really allow for *Working's* unorthodox publication approach (10 books of stories on related themes clocking in at over 750 pages). This book—along with a digital archive—will allow the stories to live beyond our purposes and expand this project's scope and reach. We imagine, for example, practitioners who might seek narratives echoing their own experiences and find comfort, commiseration, and possibly solutions. We also hope these stories provide a corpus for other researchers who seek to better describe and understand our field in more nuanced ways. And, of course, we hope you and your colleagues will contribute stories to the archive to help this project grow and change over time.

The Feedback Process

From the beginning, feedback and community engagement were critical elements to story development. Ahead of the call, we held a virtual writing collective where we invited prospective contributors to workshop their ideas. In fact, the labor story heuristic that we include below and the resource in Appendix A were originally developed out of these workshops as guidance for contributors who were trying to "story" their labor experiences and who were getting hung up on the "laundry list" approach to writing about work that we commonly see in our field. Then, stories were collected through a Google Form with other information such as contributor(s) name, institutional affiliation, position, and attribution structure (i.e., anonymous or with name attribution). Once the stories were submitted, we worked with the writers—through multiple rounds of feedback and, in some cases, additional meetings—to ensure that they were telling their stories in an accessible way, honoring the word limit (to ensure as many submissions as possible), and conveying themes directly related to the book. We also wanted mostly unadulterated stories—ones that were not heavily excerpted, edited, or otherwise mediated, as can happen when collecting stories using interview methodologies like Terkel or even like some of our colleagues in the field.

However, we must acknowledge our own editorial and researcher roles in mediating these narratives. As Chase (2011) explained, "When narrative researchers interpret narratives . . . they begin with narrators' voices and stories, thereby extending the narrator-listener relationship and the active work of listening into the interpretive process" (p. 424). We hoped to reconceive notions of narrative agency and the typical researcher-subject dynamic by simply offering a topic—labor in the writing center—and enabling workers to tell their story rather than guide them with questions. In turn, however, we needed to make sure that these stories would meet the needs of their audience, exercising and negotiating another form of agency.

In the process of collecting stories and assembling the book, we also worked with participants who wanted to write anonymously or de-identify themselves and their institutions. Indeed, part of what motivated us to collect stories in this way was inspired by the conundrums of anonymity. For example, in describing her research in rural Ireland, ethnographer Nancy Scheper-Hughes (2000) outlined some of the problems with representing others' accounts. In particular, many of her participants took offense at her interpretation of them and what they had tried to convey to her. Much of this happened through her efforts to anonymize them. At this time, faculty in higher education are experiencing many different kinds of challenges to their academic freedom, from what they are able to teach to how they can present their identities in the classroom to retaliation for detailing an institution's negative treatment of workers (AAUP, 2022). Accordingly, we asked contributors to provide their own accounts of their work experiences and work histories with the option to publish their work anonymously or with attribution. Several contributors who chose to remain anonymous cited the compounding challenges that BIPOC, queer, disabled, and other intersectional academic workers face, especially when in non-tenured positions. We wish to hold space for colleagues who are in such positions and who want to contribute to this collection about work: their voices are necessary. At the same time, we recognize that freedom of speech and other rights related to academic freedom are under unprecedented threat by activist legislative bodies and school boards. In short, it makes sense that many of our more precarious contributors—many of whom are also historically marginalized in academia and our field—want to remain anonymous.

We thus acknowledge that this collection cannot provide completely unmediated, unfiltered, accounts of writing center laborers' experiences. Storytelling is always mediated at a number of levels. Nor is what we offer a generalizable, or even necessarily *valid* data set. As Polkinghorne (2007) pointed out, the point of narrative inquiry is not about the accuracy of events but rather to understand the meanings attached to those events by the narrators. As we worked with contributors, we emphasized the importance of their impressions and experiences while navigating the quandaries Polkinghorne (2007) observed in narration: that words alone are not always enough to adequately convey meaning, that narrators can be selective in their meanings, and that rhetorical situations shape how and what meanings are expressed. Our aim in providing editorial feedback, then, was to help our participants render their meanings for a broader audience interested in learning about the conditions of writing center labor. We also hoped that in writing and revising these stories, the contributors found new meaning in their experiences and, perhaps, new modes of action.

The Writing Collective: The Challenges of Storying Work

Even as we collected stories, though, there were challenges. At the virtual writing collective, we had to clarify expectations, help narrators articulate their stories, workshop narrative drafts, and commiserate. We worked to establish a community, encouraging participants to introduce themselves and share a bit about their work. We then broke into small groups. In one group, Dan provided feedback to writers who brought drafts. In another, Genie workshopped story and structure ideas. Other groups consisted of participants sharing their stories with one another and providing suggestions for writing them. This event—which had over 40 people in attendance—made us realize how hungry people in our field are to tell their stories and to connect and commiserate. Writing center work can be lonely, especially for administrators, as there is usually only one of us at an institution. But even among those who identify as tutors, professional staff, assistant directors, etc., there is also a desire to connect. As stories started to be shared, resources were given, comments were made, and people engaged with each other.

Afterward, we looked at the narratives people produced based on feedback and resources from the writing collective, and other early submissions we received, noticing that many contributors tended to "academize" their stories by including lengthy citations, sharing research findings, offering report-style accounts of their center's successes, and otherwise over-explaining many of the elements around their story rather than focusing on the story itself. We realized that it can be difficult for people to tell their stories without centering other voices, other scholars, additional data, center reports, and such. Because we are trained—and perhaps socialized into—believing that research and certain kinds of data are the main ways in which to communicate about the writing center when it comes to our individual and personal life experiences with work, we found contributors struggling to find the plot, so to speak, of their story. Rather than extracting testimony, we saw the writing collective—and the resources on storying work that grew out of it, as well as the multiple feedback rounds that took place before and after that event—as a chance to help contributors assert narrative agency and move away from the kinds of capitalistic accounting so common in annual reports, presentations, and even academic scholarship in our field.

Perhaps because we are both steeped in non-fiction—as readers, scholars, and writers—many of the things that we advised contributors to do come from the field of creative writing and, specifically, writing non-fiction, as the heuristic we shared with contributors via email (below) demonstrates. We recognize, however, that it might be difficult for practitioners to toggle back and forth between different ways of knowing, interpreting, and describing their work. To address this rupture and to support contributors in engaging in the storying process, we offered a heuristic for storying labor here and a more detailed resource below (Appendix A) that guides writers to "narrativize" their work experiences and engage in the storying process. We hope this will be useful for pedagogical settings where different forms of storying (e.g., counterstory, narrative, oral history, etc.) are taught or in spaces where individuals want to engage in the creative writing process about their work but feel unprepared or uncertain about how to get started.

Guidance for Storying Your Labor: A Heuristic

- Try to move outside of an academic/scholarly narrative voice.
- Reduce citations and use APA to avoid over-reliance on direct citation.
- Find the narrative thread—sometimes, this is visual, sometimes it is aural, sometimes it is conceptual, sometimes it is mnemonic—and work backwards from there.
- Set a specific setting (sitting under a desk with a drill; standing in an examination room in a repurposed children's hospital turned office complex) for your readers.
- Composite similar experiences into one arc to avoid confusing, repetitive, or circular details.

- Be creative with dialogue: draw from journals, emails, memos, and other records.
- Work towards interiority: what were you feeling (then and now)? Why might others behave as they did? Get into the minds (and identities) of your character.
- Think of a takeaway—stories don't always need to moralize but a lesson learned can help others to connect with your story and leave with a purpose or point.

We want to note here, however, the tension in presenting narratives as authentic while also mediating them for a larger audience or because of concerns about professional/personal retaliation. Personal narratives are mediated but they can also help us to reveal a kind of truth through engaging in the reflective and cognitive processes of writing personal non-fiction. Throughout the book—most especially in the Interchapters in Act II—we engage in the sorts of reflexivity required of narrative inquiry but we also want the stories to stand on their own as testimony about the experience of a variety of writing center workers in 2022.

Chapter 3. Key Concepts in the Book

Below, we share and define several key concepts (in order of appearance) that help to guide our discussion in this book. We bold the font of the concepts here and bullet point them for ease of reading, but they emerge more organically in the discussion of the book's exigency in Act I, in the stories and interchapters of Act II, and in how to take action in Act III. We also hope, however, that other concepts will surface for readers who bring their own identities and experiences of work to these narratives. Thematics—and Genie's and Dan's work on this—can only take the reader so far. Thus, we offer discussion prompts alongside brief interchapters that attempt to situate the stories while leaving a lot of room for interpretation. We have arranged the concepts below by their order of appearance in the project.

- **Neoliberalism:** A philosophy positing that governments and institutions work best by serving private interests and by privatizing its functions. It is "devoted to enforcing economic competition, protecting the power of businesses, and celebrating the 'free market'—that is, the capitalist market—as the wisest and best judge of people, institutions, and ideas" (Leary, 2023).
- **Anti-Capitalism:** Philosophy, political ideology, and set of social movements (e.g., Civil Rights, Black Liberation, Black Feminism, Global Feminism, Labor Movements, Occupy Wall Street, etc.) that oppose free market, capitalist economic approaches. Can involve replacing capitalism with other economic systems like socialism, but not necessarily so (See Wright, 2019).
- **The Managed University:** The result of neoliberalism's incursion into academia. This has led to "the emergence of a new kind of 'academic capitalism' . . . that shifts resources away from a wide range of traditional, but economically marginal, university activities, and redirects them to activities that generate revenues and enhance the competitive position of U.S. corporations in the global economy" (Mahala, 2007).
- **Metalabor:** Work for and about work. Metalabor is a form of invisible work most specifically engaged in the work of validating writing center labor so that the "actual" labor can occur and thus be compensated.
- **Labor Organizing:** The many and varied activities that include union drives, signing union cards, taking work action through strikes and walk-outs, collective bargaining, contract negotiation, union recognition by management, and other actions and processes related to the establishment and continuance of organized labor through unions.
- **Pleasure Activism:** Anti-capitalist activism or "the work we do to reclaim our whole, happy, and satisfiable selves from the impacts, delusions, and limitations of oppression and/or supremacy" (maree brown, p.

11, 2019). brown discusses pleasurable activities separate from intellectual (or paid) work, such as food, fashion, humor, the erotic, the arts, and "passion work," even as she also recognizes that there are "policies and power dynamics inside of everything that makes us feel good" (p. 11). Pleasure—and who feels it and who does not—in a capitalist society is bound by precarity, oppression, and scarcity. Engaging in pleasure activism—particularly focusing on "those most impacted by oppression"—we can tap "into the potential goodness in each of us [even as] we can generate justice and liberation, growing a healing abundance where we have been socialized to believe only scarcity exists" (p. 11).

Where Are We Going? Story Trends

While we discuss this more specifically in the interchapters of Act II, it is important for us to trace the labor trends of the field reflected in the stories that were submitted and that will be featured here in this book. We received a great deal of interest when we circulated our call for contributions in spring 2022. This, again, likely speaks to the current moment perhaps more than our specific call, insofar as there is a renewed interest in work and stories about labor.

The stories in this book are highly personal, weaving together personal life experiences and moments with ideas and experiences about writing center labor. Directors talk about students who have affected their work. Peer tutors talk about navigating the vagaries of their work—especially when they feel underprepared to do their jobs. Many talk about the gendered dynamics of writing center work and the precarity of marginalized workers. Some talk about class and how this impacts their work ethos and workplace interpersonal dynamics. Several stories talk about the transition from tutor to administrator—from job-to-job, including leaving the profession—which reminds us that this work, and our expectations of it, can change over a career. All kinds of events—first jobs, births, deaths, new positions—help to shape these stories. What this tells us is that we not only bring to the writing center the full weight of our life experiences; we also experience a lot of life (often divorced from writing) in our writing centers!

At the same time, material conditions can and do lead to workplace tensions. Contributors detail taking on more responsibilities with fewer resources provided to them: doing "more with less." Some talk about feelings of survivor's guilt and imposter syndrome as they received relatively stable (even tenure track) positions while their colleagues did not. Yet, others talk about their desires to grow beyond their current positions at the same time that they feel worn down by constant self-advocacy for their professional growth. Writing center work is described as a "side hustle," as a "dream job," as "unsustainable," and as "weird" (but in a good way!). In many of these stories, the contributors detail having to stretch themselves in ways they previously had not considered before they became writing center workers and they talk about some of the struggles with doing this work unsupported.

However, many of these accounts also present joy. Many contributors talk about the special something—sauce? spice?—that comes with doing writing center work: the gratitude towards mentors and feeling love and pride in empowering student writers; the experience of feeling like this work was *meant* for them—a calling, not just a job; the gratitude towards others; the community (and meaning) we find in our professional lives outside of our institution; the "weird" serendipity and pleasure of encounters between writers and tutors in the writing center as an under-explored mainstay of the work. Many also talk about the pain and guilt of having to leave untenable positions or having to take a step back from doing unsustainable levels of work for little to no compensation. The writing center work, however, never seems to be the mitigating factor in these stories. Rather, the material circumstances—the administrative callousness, the lack of professional advancement, the tensions between unions and management—often drive the decision to leave.

Despite these issues, several stories detail their protagonists (and they are heroes) refusing to give up. They continue to advocate for the importance of writing center work and the value of writing center workers even as they are sometimes devalued in this work themselves. They volunteer their time, they push to make more ethical and inclusive spaces, they do supportive work even when they are no longer affiliated with the writing center, they engage in collective bargaining, they advocate for tutors to HR for better wages and more accurate job descriptions, they question current administrative practices, they demand better of their workspaces and workplace practices. And while even just a fraction of this advocacy work is a lot, it is often far above and beyond their job duties. The invisible work of writing centers is so often hidden and under-explored, yet understanding it can make the difference between a sustainable position or wage and an unsustainable one.

These observations led us to articulate one of the core concepts of the book, explained earlier and further explicated in Act III: metalabor. Nearly all the stories featured in the project describe some form of metalabor. In writing center studies, the term first appeared in reference to one of Caswell, Grutsch McKinney, and Jackson's (2016) case studies. The pseudonymous Anthony was a second-year director struggling to balance his assorted identities/affiliations in the field: scholar, teacher, administrator, and all of the sorts of work associated with those roles. Caswell et al. (2016) explained:

> Anthony's internal struggles strike us as a kind of labor about labor: a metalabor, if you will. It is different from emotional labor, which we see as highly relational work. And yet this worrying about identification has the same drag on his everyday and disciplinary labor that emotional labor (sometimes) has for other participants. (p. 61)

And though the stories in Act II show the "same drag . . . on everyday and disciplinary labor," we would distinguish our conception of metalabor in this project from Caswell et al.'s (2016) use by broadening it: we argue that it comprises the various sorts of writing center labor that are not explicitly involved in the production of sessions. More specifically, *metalabor is the work done in order to make working possible, feasible, and/or sustainable.* It is the often-Sisyphean task of addressing (mis-)perceptions about what the writing center does in an institution; the constant negotiation over rank, salary, positioning in the university; the bargaining for wages, budgeting dollars, and other resources that make the actual act of hosting sessions possible; the advocating for legitimacy; the work found in community organization; and still more. If you have ever done this sort of para-work for the privilege of simply doing "the" work of writing centers, you have engaged in metalabor.

Beyond passing reference, writing center studies provide little formal conceptualization of how this vital and time-consuming work that writing center workers perform outside of their formal duties impacts the field. Our contributors talk about sudden changes to their material circumstances (loss of staff, reduced budgets, cut positions, etc.) that required a lot of metalabor (advocating, report writing, coalition building, meetings, etc.) in response. But under the surface of these accounts is how blindsided we seem to be by metalabor, despite how often it arises in our profession. We are not prepared for metalabor, which is perhaps why we tend to overwork and take a reactive stance to our labor rather than a proactive one. We are always on the backfoot. We need to reveal the metalabor we and our colleagues perform, we need to deconstruct it, and our professional organizations and publications need to analyze it; we should not do such labor individually and privately.

We hope that these stories help you navigate your own writing center labor. We hope that the contributors' experiences prepare you for new writing center positions while also recognizing how often our expectations may not be met with the resources or support that we expect (and perhaps were provided in the writing centers where we cut our teeth). We hope you are inspired by stories that reimagine writing center labor as more sustainable, mutual, and compassionate. We hope you turn to these stories if you are giving birth, mourning the death of a tutor (or family member), or are considering ways to disrupt your center. In short, we hope these stories inspire you and teach you and that they show you a world outside of your own work that is collective, connected, just, and fair.

Engaging with the Book

Because of the unique structure of this book, we envision many ways to engage with its contents. We see this book as having three interrelated but distinct "Acts." These Acts are temporal stages in our book project. We see Act I as looking back at our histories and examining our exigences. Act II looks at the lived experiences of our current moment. Act III looks ahead. We hope to create a kind of continuity that "parts" or "sections" do not fully capture. These Acts are not meant to invoke a play, though we do see drama unfolding in and through the stories collected here. The main throughline in each Act is work, but the first and third acts of the book are co-written by Genie and Dan and they provide a roadmap for readers, whereas Act II largely consists of the stories of 34 writing center workers along with inter-chapters that provide questions for discussion and some engagement with themes. We also hope readers bring their own analytical lenses to bear on these stories.

- Act I asks Where Have We Been? It provides context for the past and recent state of writing center work; it examines how neoliberal capitalism which gives rise to austerity impacts that work; it connects much of our labor to the concept of metalabor; and it argues for why storying this work is critical to collective action and a clear-eyed sense of the profession (especially for new practitioners).
- Act II considers Where We Are. It is a repository of stories that others can learn from, study through discourse and corpus analysis, and commiserate with. This is the "gossip" Robillard (2021) and Micciche (2018) allude to as being a means of circulating vital information to protect laborers and let them know they are not alone.
- Act III asks Where Are We Going? It further interrogates the concept of metalabor in connection with the stories in Act II; it provides a guide to unlearning internalized capitalism; and it further details how to take collective action in the workplace, reimagining writing center labor using an anti-capitalist framework.

After a lot of discussion, we *reluctantly* placed the stories in Act II in grouped themes (see below) that speak to commonalities in the stories as well as throughlines about labor, such as care work, advocacy, trauma, etc. Coding and organizing stories, as we anticipated, was challenging because even when a story examined precarity or workplace trauma, for example, it also talked about advocacy, joy, or other positive aspects of writing center labor. This is the double-edged nature of the work we do—the thorns and roses, so to speak. Some of these stories admittedly could just as easily have been grouped into one category over another. So, while we gave these stories themes for ease of reading and as a way to structure crosstalk between contributors, we encourage readers to make their own meaning (perhaps in courses or in book clubs) out of these stories as they move through the book. As we've asserted elsewhere, the structure we provide to these stories is mediated and incomplete. We recognize that the complexity of these stories might not be fully reflected nor contained in the themes we developed. Nor do we offer the final say on what these stories are accomplishing. In fact, we have kept the interchapters brief—and included discussion questions—because we hope readers will bring their own analysis and interpretations to each story. We also hope to create community around storying and its interpretative work.

For readers at different places in their professional journeys, we provide some prompts to consider based on subjectivity and career status. We can imagine early-stage practitioners taking away very different things about the current state of the profession and writing center work from these stories than those who are mid-career or senior practitioners. For those with more stability in their positions, we hope that you find these stories drive you to action on behalf of those with less stable positions; perhaps you can advocate for wage increases or you can recommend hiring tenure lines for this work at your institution and elsewhere (i.e., through external reviews, accreditation reviews, etc.). For those with less stable positions, we hope that these stories help you to create a career plan, and to advocate for yourself and others who are in similar positions at your institutions. We also hope that our organizations do more work to understand our changing field and become advocates. In many ways, we hope that this book radicalizes its readers and helps them to shape a burgeoning class consciousness but also labor-centered politics. This radicalization will help individuals navigate the managed university and hopefully encourage collective action. We would also argue that our approach is *not necessarily all that radical* in that it extends several vital strands of current scholarship around race, labor, intersectionality, social justice, and more. As a field, we are so adept at sharing trainings, budgets, reports, data, etc. Imagine if we applied that collective ethos to unionization, worker rights, and field-wide standards.

The thematics we decided upon are as follows:

- Theme 1, Career Trajectories and Labor: Narratives tracing the development of careers and stories of leaving the field.
- Theme 2, Precarity & Failed Advocacy: Narratives detailing the precariousness of writing center working conditions, focusing particularly on contingency and examples of metalabor that didn't succeed
- Theme 3, Advocacy Successes: Narratives where laborers successfully worked toward more just, sustainable, or meaningful labor conditions
- Theme 4, Identity and Labor: Narratives grappling with intersectionality and labor, including Queer labor, labor done by BIPOC workers, and with class consciousness
- Theme 5, Trauma and the New Workplace Normal: Narratives examining the role of trauma and how we adjust to it in our work whether derived from the pandemic era or from trauma external to the center, such as deaths and campus emergencies.
- Theme 6, Care Work and Sustainability: Narratives examining how mutual support, care work, solidarity, weirdness, and joy in communal practices can give rise to enjoyable and positive work experiences.

Chapter 4. The Untold Stories, The Hard Truths

As we close Act I, we need to address the proverbial elephant in the room; we believe it is critical that we be honest about our working conditions. Writing center professionals generally persist for five to seven years on average in the field, which means that there are a lot of people cycling into and out of jobs and our field at any given moment (unpublished data, Giaimo et al.). At the same time, unpublished data about the job market shows that jobs in the field are becoming more professionalized into staff roles and moving off the tenure track under "big tent" academic centers or learning commons models (Driscoll et al., 2017). If data—albeit unpublished data, in part—are showing the challenges in our field that we are currently facing, how are we going to prepare people for this field without acknowledging the deep hard truths about many of the lived experiences of people who take up writing center positions today? The current landscape we are preparing new professionals for is completely unlike anything that higher education has seen, even considering the 2008 financial collapse. Therefore, it would be unethical for us not to address this directly.

We thus share some questions here, offering some ways forward in Act III: How do practitioners in more stable positions leverage their privilege to make people in less stable positions have more equitable and flourishing work? How do we work towards addressing the gaps between the haves and the have-nots in our profession? How do we create organizations that represent the material realities of our profession? In what follows, particularly in Act III, we answer these and other questions. But the stories in Act II also grapple with these and related questions. They speak of the very real ways in which precarity, multiple reportage lines, retrenchment, and the loss of budgetary/supervisory oversight create all kinds of personal and professional trauma (e.g., anonymous narratives such as "From Dream Job to Unsustainable," "Writing Center as Life Raft," and "Counter Story: Ignored Labor"). At the same time, contributors also speak of the ways in which they can advocate from positions of less precarity to create more stable and fair workplaces for student and professional tutors (Anonymous's "Into and out of the Tutoring Center," Whiddon's "'. . . at least for now': A Story About Undergraduate Writing Centers and Labor Compensation in Five Parts," Tirabassi's "Advocating for Equitable Tutor Pay with Campus Partners," and Anthony's "Benefits and Drawbacks of Hiring Professional Academic Tutors").

Some of the themes we see emerging in these stories—from those who are most senior in our field and who are reflecting back on illustrious careers that span decades to those who are just entering this field trying to navigate their first jobs, or those who are in the "sandwiched generation" that came of age with less austerity and precarity but have seen major shifts in their work with the rise of the managed university. There are very real differences in the working lives of those who entered the field decades ago and those who are coming into the field now. As the data shared above notes, we ought to prepare those entering the profession for how the managed university has reshaped the structure, reportage, and even lines associated with writing centers. While there are often many jobs (we write this in late fall 2023 where only *two* assistant-professor level tenure line writing center director positions have been posted), many of these jobs are less stable, less prestigious, and pay less. As readers explore the stories in Act II, we ask them to consider the material realities that are constructed through these narratives. Most will not address the managed university, austerity, or neoliberalism directly, but these themes are throughlines that appear in many of the stories in this book. Stories of good-hearted and dedicated people doing more at their work with less. Stories of excited and well-trained people struggling when their expertise is not recognized. Stories of individuals who have joy and pleasure in the work of training tutors, teaching writing, and supporting writers, but who struggle with the endless rotation of administrators who do not welcome them to the decision-making table. It is in these tensions between joy and grief, between dedication and frustration, between power and powerlessness that we most productively engage.

Looking to the Future (Conclusion)

We hope this project helps to shape labor studies as scholarly inquiry and praxis in our field in the years to come. There has not yet been as comprehensive a collection of stories about writing center labor, or a book that offers explicit guidance to labor organizing and anti-capitalist frameworks in our field. As the companion archive to this project develops, this collection of stories will hopefully grow. Perhaps, as part of your own research and/or teaching, you will contribute stories about writing center labor. At the same time, we recognize the need to move beyond researching and theorizing writing center labor, as important as these activities are. We need to create a set of actions and heuristics that will help to guide new writing center workers as they embark on their professional careers and help those already in the field locate their own labor praxis and values. Implicit within all of this is the larger goal of engaging in labor advocacy and activism. Perhaps another goal is to raise consciousness. To share stories and swap experiences with the hope that information sharing shows that we are not alone in the work that we do. Act III, with its focus on advocacy, action, and praxis, and the interchapters in Act II, will help to guide these endeavors.

There is a fascination with work in our national consciousness. This is not a new trend. When Terkel (1974) published *Working*, it became a bestseller and later a musical featured on Broadway (one of our co-authors starred in *Working* the musical in high school!). But oral histories about how people work—from telephone operators to mechanics to flight attendants to one of the first Black police officers in Chicago—struck nerves and piqued interest. The sharing of stories impacting workplace conditions and worker sentiment did not just happen in the 1970s, it has happened as long as a labor movement has existed in the United States (and abroad), which has been for centuries. In the late 19th century, Eugene V. Debs created a railway workers union and in response to dangerous working conditions, low wages, and extractive company town prices, decided to strike. To do this, he brought Jennie Curtis, a seamstress, to tell her story of Pullman wage theft (she paid 9 or more of her 10-dollar wage for Pullman room and board) to the ARU, which began a history-changing ARU-led boycott of handling Pullman equipment (Mesle, 2021). Stories, in a very real sense, can sway the behavior of thousands of workers and create solidarity for worker movements. They can also, however, break apart along racial lines, as the ARU did when it voted to become a whites-only union. Therefore, the stories we hear are just as critical to labor consciousness as the ones we do not.

Perhaps it is because most of us work. Perhaps because of the complex feelings and positionalities that we have with respect to our work. Perhaps because hearing from workers who could be our relatives, friends, neighbors, and colleagues prompts us to empathize, commiserate, and join with others. In a very real sense, we believe stories can change working conditions and bargaining power. Stories—even difficult or sad ones—can inspire us to collective action, empathy, and change; these stories also show us that we are not alone as we ponder what is, for many of us, an existential but no less visceral search for "daily meaning and daily bread" in our work, as Terkel (1974) noted in the Foreword of *Working* (xi). We hope that this book can generate similar conversations, trace people's experiences, stand as a record, and also be a playbook that pushes back against extractive and exploitative workplaces and professional systems.

The current labor trends (and thus the contents of this project) can seem dire, yet we do not wish to discourage newcomers to the field and profession. This work *can* be enriching and even fun as this project's story "Keep Writing Centers Weird" demonstrates so well. Even for all its tumult, as Arlie Hochschild (2013) has pointed out, "One can enjoy emotional labor immensely . . . provided one has an affinity for it and a workplace that supports that affinity" (p. 25). We can take pride in our efforts in the deeply interpersonal work we do, in the sense of mastery that can come with learning to do a difficult job well, and in developing the empathy and resilience emotional labor requires of us. But emotional laborers, as Hoschild (2013) observed, can also face a paradox in that the job can also involve trying to protect clients, patients, students, and such from "the harm of life in a broken, globalized, over-bureaucratized, or profit-hungry system" (p. 30) leading to burnout or worse. Rather than accepting things as they are, then, she recommends *fixing the broken system* (p. 31). In such a world—demanding as it is—emotional labor could be fulfilling and fun. We would extend this by asserting that there can be joy (and fun) in the metalabor of fixing the system. We hope our readers find some clear-eyed optimism in that belief, as well.

Act II. Where We Are: Stories and Interchapters

Chapter 5. Genie and Dan's Origin Stories

This project began innocuously as conversations among Genie, Dan, and many of our peers in conference hotel hallways, meals between sessions, and phone calls to check in with each other. We shared stories.

What we present here is, at its core, a collection of stories: stories to challenge us, to upset us, to bring us joy, to excite us, to activate us, and most of all, we hope, to unite us. In the spirit of storying experience and of unity, Genie and Dan first share our own stories of labor and our burgeoning class consciousness as we entered the writing center profession. We offer them in hopes that others will consider what motivates them, what sustains them, and what they wish to change in their own experiences with work.

From there, we include stories from 34 contributors. We have broken the stories into themes, though, as we note in Act I, we hope readers find their own meaning and connections (of which there are many) among these stories. We also include thematic interchapters where we share some insights from reading and putting these stories into conversation.

But first, here are our origin stories.

Genie's Story

I have always been interested in people's stories. When I was dissertating, life narratives surrounded me. I heard people talking about their lives on the bus and the subway. I looked at advertisements from upscale supermarkets that promoted their organic food by telling its "story." I gobbled life narratives in comics, blogs, books, and documentaries. Stories also shaped my earliest memories. My grandmother, my great aunt, my mother, and her friends regularly swapped stories during social gatherings, large and small. These tellings were performative, they were instructional, they were aesthetic, they were effective, and they were visceral and deeply meaningful. Frequently, these stories were about work and its vicissitudes as much as they were about other things.

And though, as an undergrad, I studied stories under an advisor's research methodology (Bamberg & Georgakopoulou, 2008), once I became a writing center director, I moved away from this visceral, qualitative, creative, and powerful mode of knowledge sharing and data collection. I bought into what seemed like a very real (but misunderstood) argument that RAD research (Driscoll & Perdue, 2012; Haswell, 2005) was critical to expanding my field of study. Without empirical and countable research (which I glommed onto, though qualitative research wasn't excluded by RAD definitions) writing center studies would be *less than* other disciplines in the field of rhetoric and composition.

It happened over time and out of necessity. In looking for jobs and moving through this field as an outsider, with a Ph.D. in literature, I kept pace with current scholarly conversations about data, specifically, even separate from RAD. These arguments, however, are not value-neutral. So much of the research argued that without data our budgets would evaporate, our centers would shrivel on the vine, and our staff would languish in a kind of austerity hell. I bought into this thinking because, at my heart, I was a very good Capitalist (or a very bad one, by some definitions). I understood work as a meritocracy; I believed that with logic and data of a very specific kind I could convince others to support me. In short, I thought RAD research was the way out of financial precarity.

This story is about becoming an anti-capitalist writing administrator as much as it details my development as a researcher (these cannot be separated, either). What came with years of experience and time spent in different jobs was a hard-won set of lessons where all the data and logic in the world could not protect me from the creeping extractive fingers of neoliberalization (Giaimo, 2023). I traded narratives, stories, and personal life experiences for what I thought were generalizable scales. I added numbers to my reports: writers served, tutors trained, hours spent working, retention, and persistence outcomes. I wove magical proposals for further support, further resources, and stability. And, in the end, as I have written elsewhere (but not so honestly or personally), it was a zero-sum game played against administrators and unfeeling institutions (Giaimo, 2022). In short, data could not protect me from precarity, toxic bosses, laundry-list job responsibilities, my own workism, or any number of other work-related issues that arose. I needed to find another way.

Stories, I realized, are protective as much as they are kairotic and cathartic. Sharing detailed information about institutional culture, pay rates, toxic bosses and departments, state-level meddling in education can prepare us or position us for action. Stories give us information that is critical to navigating complex interpersonal relationships and institutional culture. Stories allowed me to share and mentor and be mentored in turn. They allowed me to be vulnerable, to connect with others, to advocate for change with specific detailed information, and, ultimately, to organize labor at my institutions. Stories, in short, were a way out of that zero-sum game where I provided ever more and complex data only to be told that there would be no raises this year or that my budget would be cut once again or there was no money to hire X (coordinator, graduate assistants, undergraduate tutors, etc.) which we so desperately needed. Stories are critical to understanding writing center labor.

I might be overcorrecting back towards a specific methodology/method—a verb and a noun as Aja Martinez notes (2020)—that I favor in what seems like an uncompromising way. Thing is, I still love quantitative research. I still conduct complex empirical work. These days, though, I don't think that this is the answer to our current labor-related predicament. I no longer buy into the hype.

And I am in good company. In this book, as well as in the larger field of writing center/writing studies, there is more research than ever before of a qualitative and story-centered approach, particularly on labor. As we detail below, much of this is in the necessary counterstorying work of our BIPOC and queer colleagues, but it is also in the testimony of wellness work, and in the ethnographic research that follows directors navigating their first jobs. Stories are critical to our field—to its origins, its development, and its future. Stories also guide us in our search for meaning, especially in making meaning about our work. Stories help us to realize that we are not alone—no matter how much it seems like it when we are often the sole writing center director or writing program administrator at our institution. Stories give us information which, in turn, gives us power. Below, we share resources for those who want to engage in storying about their labor, but we also share the stories of several dozens of practitioners in the field in the hope to bring a clear-eyed view of writing center labor in the 21st century, during a particularly charged moment for higher education, as well as for labor advocacy and worker rights (2022–2023).

I hope this book provides readers the solace I once felt sitting in my grandmother's apartment listening to her stories or the feeling of vindication that comes from a hurried explosion of truth in passing at a conference or the commiseration that comes from puzzling out day-to-day experiences "at the office" with colleagues. I also hope, however, that these stories help workers in our field to further examine their work and their relationship to it more fully. I hope this book can help workers to compare notes, and to advocate for change. In short, I hope that these stories—counterstories, testimony, testifying, and narrativizing—raise consciousness and lead us to develop more protective behaviors, even as we advocate for change. We are not our production. We are not our jobs. We are so much more. I hope this book and the stories of its contributors inspire others, as much as it has me, to figure out what "more" there is.

Dan's Story

My favorite way to explain the word "serendipity" is that it happens when you go digging for worms and you strike gold: when you go looking for one thing and you find something much, much more valuable. I have benefited from serendipity more than I probably deserve, and my hope is that the stories we've compiled will serve as such for others because serendipity and stories are what have enabled me to find and persist in writing center work.

Serendipity, for instance, led me to my first writing center experience. I was a military brat who changed schools once a year on average before settling in the rural upper peninsula of Michigan. I was also a first-generation community college student. As such, I was less than a model student my first semester. My grades early in the semester were middling in part due to never having learned how to really be a student—I had no experience with structuring study time, with annotation and marginalia, with what faculty office hours were even for, with peer review, and with even basic implicit knowledge like how to get student loans.

I was working part-time at a local McDonald's and part-time servicing air filtration units in local bars (this was back when people still smoked cigarettes in bars). So, in addition to my inexperience, I was also busy with work because I was paying out of pocket for my schooling and attempting to save for future semesters.

My saving grace was that I was an avid reader and writer. I wasn't great at school, *but I enjoyed it.*

My composition instructor that semester required conferences over our midterm papers, and though I figured my work was probably passable, I wasn't sure how she would receive it. I entered the meeting ready to plead for mercy and for the chance to revise. However, after playfully scolding me for not meeting my potential, she told me she was recommending me for the writing center. She felt my writing was good, but more importantly, she seemed to feel after meeting with me that I had an appropriate disposition for the work. I had only gone into the conference hoping to plead my case, and I came out with a potential new job: serendipity.

That experience was empowering for me and helped me to become a better student. Serendipity and the writing center continued to be themes for me even after my time in community college. After I transferred, my writing center experience helped me get a job as an embedded basic writing tutor, which later helped me land a job as a languages lab manager. In addition to supervising the assorted world language tutors, I worked with multilingual language writers. This, in turn, opened doors for me in graduate school, where I would return to the writing center. That return later secured precious summer funding for me and helped keep a roof over my new family's head. In each of these jobs, I had only looked for a way to make money, but the experiences kept landing me better opportunities.

That summer work was serendipitous as well. At the time, it was simply a means to pay the bills, but the experience later tipped the scales in my favor, securing my first job out of graduate school: a non-tenure line faculty position developing and directing a writing center. While it was in many ways a means to an end—I needed a job—it was also serendipitous. Now that I had to learn how to run one, I fell in love with writing center work. It was a *lot* of work, but like so many other writing center administrators (including those in this collection), I found joy and meaning in it.

That position also helped me transition to my current tenured position. However, after several years I fell prey to the same sorts of workism, lack of self-care, and shifting boundaries that readers will also find throughout the narratives shared in this book. I was ready to leave the profession—and academia—entirely. I started looking at jobs like those I had held while making my way through school: postal work, custodial work, and manual labor. Mercifully, serendipity intervened yet again.

One of these interventions was the timing of my sabbatical, which happened to be scheduled the semester after I had reached peak overwhelm. In addition to giving me a break, I was fortunate enough that the faculty member covering the center in my absence (himself an experienced tutor and administrator) was willing to "swap" positions the following year, extending his coverage of the center while I taught a full course load. The time away saved me—not because it was "better," but because it revealed a lot to me: the toxic work habits I had adopted, how I had been a much more effective advocate for the center than I had for myself, and how deeply my imposter syndrome ran. That imposter syndrome drove so much of my labor in and around the center. More than that, I learned a lot about the "survivors' guilt" that also informed so much of my labor. After all, in addition to having escaped my working-class roots, I was one of the lucky writing center practitioners in a tenure-line position.

Another serendipitous intervention was through the relationships I developed via conferences. I originally attended conferences to burnish my credentials, cultivate a professional network, and learn about new concepts and trends in my fields. However, I found something far more valuable there: friends and mentors. It was commiseration with these folks—particularly at a conference the semester before my sabbatical—that kept me going. Their stories and their familiarity with my circumstances helped me feel less alone, less like there was something wrong with me or like I was a poor fit for the work. I talked about my thoughts of leaving, and their encouragement helped me persist and reconnect with my original joy for the labor.

In discussing the conditions of our labor with each other and with others, Genie and I came to realize that many of the stories of labor in our field were being lost. There were others like me who considered—but actually went through with—leaving, and their stories left with them. Along with those lost stories were lost opportunities for solidarity, organization, and action. We originally began this project in hopes of capturing those stories and trying to render a clearer and more expansive sense of what it means to work in writing centers in the pandemic and post-pandemic eras. However, in yet another instance of serendipity, we have found allies, colleagues, friends, and fellow advocates. As readers will see throughout the narratives in this Act, writing center practitioners are often selfless advocates for writers and for writing centers. I believe it is well past time that we began advocating for ourselves.

Theme 1. Career Trajectories and Labor

Despite being primarily about labor, many of the submissions we received read as career retrospectives in many ways, so much so that they began to appear as a sort of microgenre among the selections. These career retrospectives vary greatly but what comes through most of them is either the excitement to create something new (such as Harris, this collection), or as in Lerner's piece in this collection, or what happens when possible work futures are denied because of the competitiveness of the labor market. Of course, movement is an important element in writing center work—people move into and out of jobs frequently in our profession. In "My Writing Center Side Hustle," the anonymous contributor talks about leaving the field for a tenure track position only to find themselves working for the writing center for free. Harris also describes the "volunteer" culture of early writing centers as both a unifying catalyst to produce change but also a behavior borne out of institutional necessity and, even then, austerity.

Most of us likely remember our first job—the excitement, the anxiety, the dreams, and goals for our work. In several submissions in this section, the contributors recall their experiences with new writing center jobs or leaving jobs for work both inside and outside of the field (Johnston, Cheatle, Anonymous's "From Dream Job to Unsustainable," this collection). Many of these stories, such as Cheatle's or Lerner's, speak to the impact of the market forces of neoliberalism on academic workers. These include hyper-mobility, regional competition, and limited tenure stream and promotion opportunities that are increasingly affecting what positions are available and showcase the competition to secure them. In this collection, Hallman Martini talks about searching for meaning (and better futures) in writing center work but from an academic and writing standpoint. She details the history of establishing a new peer-reviewed journal that combats hyperrevision and over-work in the peer review process.

We open this section with Harris' narrative about growing an academic field, because it encapsulates so well working conditions and labor at the beginning of a career and the professionalization of a field. It also speaks to many of the other themes in Act II, demonstrating how much of the field's progress is predicated on contingent labor and on the metalabor of advocacy. In turn, this section ends with one practitioner's story of leaving the field after realizing the labor of advocacy became too unsustainable. We ask, as in each thematic interchapter, readers to bring their own themes, questions, theoretical lenses, and more to the narratives in this theme. We also provide questions to help facilitate discussion and holistic consideration of the stories here and throughout Act II in the other subsections.

Discussion Questions

- What does Harris' narrative about starting a writing center offer us in terms of arguments of austerity and their influence on writing center culture? What echoes do we see in the current academic climate? What are some of the substantive differences?
- What sorts of testimony or storying do Lerner's rejection letters offer in terms of our narratives about work in the field? What is seemingly valued in these positions? In what ways do Lerner's experiences mirror, affirm, or challenge Wynn Perdue et al.'s (2017) observations reviewing 11 years' worth of job ads that "The most important trend is the inconsistency of expectations and rewards across different institutions" and that "key information about the nature of the job rarely was provided. In many cases, ads lacked enough information for a prospective applicant to understand the nature of the job" (p. 284)?
- "My Writing Center Side Hustle" explores aspects of professional identity alongside labor, compensation, and university configuration. In particular, many writing center practitioners may regard their center work as a form of social or institutional capital providing them academic work and institutional legitimacy—though perhaps not enough material compensation—in ways their schooling alone may not. What other counter-stories about writing center labor and legitimacy can be gleaned from narratives like this?
- In some ways, Hallman Martini's narrative reflects an aspect of her career in founding The Peer Review. In others, it speaks to the complicated relationship between writing centers, scholarship, and labor. What does Hallman Martini's narrative offer in terms of examples of invisible work and metalabor around the work of scholarship and writing for writing center professionals? What kinds of emotional labor go into reviewing and editing for publication? How does "hyper-revision" reflect or extend the already-existing complexities writing center administrators have in seeking legitimacy?
- Cheatle's narrative echoes larger stories and tropes around academic nomads—teachers and scholars who uproot several times in order to progress their careers (or escape stagnating careers), often relocating across the country or even internationally. In what ways does Cheatle's narrative reflect what is perhaps unique to writing center workers?
- What does Sockwell Johnston's experience going from peer tutor to faculty writing center director tell us about how we prepare aspiring tutors and graduate students for the work of administration? What relationships do you see between her leadership and her service?
- As mentioned earlier in the project, half of the subjects of *Working Lives of New Writing Center Directors* left the field. In what ways does

the anonymous "From Dream Job to Unsustainable" contextualize this trend? How does this narrative reflect some of the job creep, duty ambiguity, and institutional uncertainty that appears in some of the other narratives in this section?
- The theme of this section—that of the intersection between career trajectories and labor—is not expansive. As you read other thematic sections, what other connections do you see reflected in these narratives? What patterns or themes emerge from this section on its own that the contributors have not commented on?

Chapter 6. Laboring to Grow an Academic Field

Muriel Harris
PURDUE UNIVERSITY

My story about starting a writing center began in 1975 when I had only a vague sense of what a writing center should or could be. When administrators in the Purdue Department of English decided to offer funding for some kind of tutoring help for writers on a one-year trial basis, the academic world in the 1970s was coping with vocal charges of "Johnny can't write" (Palmquist, 2020). Solutions needed to be found. The call that went out to Purdue's English Department was answered by three grad students studying literature and me, a faculty wife and mother with a doctorate in English 16th-century literature, whom they occasionally hired as an adjunct to teach composition. The challenge the grad students and I faced was to plan a tutoring place where we could meet students to help them with their writing. Though we had all taught composition classes, we had only a vague sense of what that tutoring center should offer or how it should be set up. Since there was no internet yet, googling was impossible. But internet searching wouldn't have helped much because while there were a few writing centers in existence, there was no field of writing center studies, no organization through which writing center people could meet and share ideas, and no books or journals focusing on writing center scholarship. Thus, we lacked any basic knowledge of models to study, questions to ask, or ways to begin our journey, but we shared the belief that one-to-one interaction with student writers could be more effective than grading papers written by students with whom we had no personal contact.

Eager to start meeting writers one-to-one, the three graduate students and I began to collaborate before we even realized the value of collaboration. We asked ourselves huge, broad questions, such as "Where do we start?" and "What do we need?" as well as smaller questions, such as "How long should each session be?" and "Should we make up some handouts?" Giving students a handout to take away, we all agreed, would help students remember what we talked about and give them a sense of having gained something from the interaction. Only later did we realize how much we, as the tutors, needed those handouts ourselves because while we knew a comma was needed there or a paragraph went on too long, we didn't have the verbiage for ready explanations. The handouts were needed by both participants in those one-to-one meetings and helped to personalize a session as we marked important points on the handouts or added a few words of explanation. The collection of handouts grew and grew as we discussed at staff meetings which handouts needed to be revised and what other topics could become useful handouts. As the internet came into existence, those handouts became available through email, and later with the birth of web browsers, the handouts became the basis of the Purdue OWL (Online Writing Lab).

What emotional and physical labor was involved as we started a new learning environment without having a model, a plan, or even a well-defined concept of where we were headed? There was an eagerness that kept us working for dozens and dozens of hours through a hot Indiana summer as we labored to prepare for opening the door to our writing lab when the academic year started. What perplexes me now is why we never expected the English department to compensate us for our time and effort. I strongly suspect the mindset of volunteering still exists because people involved in the labor of writing center administration and practice continue to care deeply about their writing center, the tutors, and the students who seek help there. And for too many, there's also an awareness that institutional support for the writing center isn't the strongest. In my case, I became acutely aware of some other faculty members' unhappiness that our writing center was sucking up resources that could have been better spent elsewhere. Among the more overt indications of that happened a few years later, after I had joined the department as an assistant professor. At a faculty meeting, there was an oblique reference to me or the writing center (or, more probably, both) as "the camel that stuck its nose under the tent." The irony here was that I never managed to get the kinds of support we needed (more tutors, an asst. director, more funding for the OWL, etc.) because we managed to have a writing center on a minimal budget. As an administrator near the top of the university hierarchy once told me (when I sought information about how the writing center had fared in the most recent outside review), the institution valued our writing lab because it produced "more bang for the buck." Our problem was that we were receiving great ratings and results with our small budget. (I suspect readers reading that last sentence are nodding in recognition of having the same problem.)

There was and continues to be another form of labor that is somewhat unique to writing center work, and that is the multiple aspects of administering a writing center that instructors teaching in large group settings do not have to deal with. For a writing center director, there is data to collect; reports to write; tutors to hire, train, oversee, evaluate, and professionalize; instructors to talk to about using the center; the physical room to set up and maintain; clerical staff to hire; technology to purchase and run; a budget to keep within; perhaps social media presence to maintain; staff meetings to plan and lead; the need to be physically present for many hours in the writing center; publicity to keep the institution aware of the writing center; and planning for continuing improvement and perhaps an increase of services offered. And—of course—arguments and data to convince administrators higher up the food chain that, if the threat of cutbacks loomed, the center is successful and necessary. Whew! All that is in addition to the labor of other faculty and adjuncts which includes going to conferences, reading the current scholarship, writing for publication, taking on academic service responsibilities, and being reviewed by the department, though in fairness to classroom instructors, they go to conferences, read current scholarship and have research agendas, plus having to write syllabi, plan classes, grade papers, meet their classes, and hold conference hours—a form of labor that is not part of writing center work. Then again, many (most?) writing center administrators also teach in the classroom setting.

Not getting adequate support while continuing to offer services students appreciate and teachers ask for is a perennial aspect of the kinds of labor so many writing center administrators are involved in. So why do we continue to be so invested and experience so much satisfaction in our work, in spite of the overload, the complaints, the often total misunderstanding of our work, the minimal salaries, the constant need to defend what we do as educationally vital, and the effort needed to keep the doors open? One answer is the positive aspects of the work. We need to catalog those along with the negative emotions and effort as a way to stave off burnout. The joys, for me, included working with the tutors and their earnest commitment to being the best tutors they could be. And there were the tutors who found the professional world they wanted to work in, dozens of those whom I worked with who went on to work in writing center administration. Or the tutor who told us that he was hired for a position that was far more than he expected because the interviewer was impressed that he had been a writing tutor. Another tutor explained that most of all she loved her mailbox in the writing lab because she felt she had a home, a place she belonged to on our large campus. I suspect that in addition to having a mailbox, she also loved being part of the close-knit group of peer tutors who hung out in the Lab and bonded in the various ways undergrads spend time together (after-hours pizza was involved). For me, our long van rides to and from conferences were the highlights of the meetings. Equally rewarding were the reactions of students whom I met with in tutorials. I watched their reactions of relief, of satisfaction, of realizing they are writers, and their comments such as "I didn't know I knew that much" when I showed them notes I had taken as they talked about what they wanted to write. As classroom teachers, we often don't get the sincere and effusive thanks students offer when we've finished a session or finally worked through a last draft. There are also those gifts from appreciative students, especially the elegantly decorated bookmarks and silk scarves we all tended to collect.

While other newcomers confront similar emotional and physical labors, they too will confront the most all-encompassing question we all ask ourselves as we become part of a world we are not yet fully prepared for: "What don't I know that I should know?" The accompanying feeling is that of being enveloped in mists that don't clear, along with the perennial fear that our lack of knowledge will become public, the fear that hides behind the label of imposter syndrome. Perhaps we can seek some comfort in acknowledging along with that ill-defined unease should be an awareness that there will always be aspects of our work we do not know enough about. But that is also a very positive aspect of our work because it leads us to keep asking questions. And, as we all agree, asking questions is a foundational practice of our field.

Reference

Palmquist, M., Childers, P., Maimon, E., Mullin, J., Rice, R., Russell, A. & Russell, D. R. (2020). Fifty years of WAC: Where have we been? Where are we going? *Across the Disciplines, 17*(3/4). 5–45. https://doi.org/10.37514/ATD-J.2020.17.3.01.

Chapter 7. *Curriculum Vitae:* An Alternative History

Neal Lerner
NORTHEASTERN UNIVERSITY

Director of the Cooperative Learning Center's Writing and Reading Center, University of Massachusetts Dartmouth, 1992: I started my teaching career as a writing center tutor back in 1986 while pursuing my MA in creative writing and a high school English teaching credential. Some six years later, my wife and I would be moving to the Boston area so that she could start a tenure-stream job, and I would begin an education doctoral program. My application for this position was pitched on the basis of my experience as a writing center tutor and then another three years of adjunct teaching, largely developmental writing in community colleges in California and Maryland. I needed income, and directing a writing and reading center seemed like a reasonable goal. Why not give it a shot?

> Dear Mr. Lerner:
> I am writing to advise you that the committee determined other applicants had experience and qualifications more appropriate to the needs of the position.

Writing Faculty/Writing Center position, Merrimack College, 1995: Three years into my Ed.D. degree, I was getting anxious about my employment prospects post-graduation and was filled with dread of a career as a permanent adjunct/contingent faculty member after six years of such teaching gigs. I had committed myself to writing center work, pursuing dissertation research on a writing center on campus. And I was bound to the Boston area, given my wife's academic career.

> Dear Professor Lerner:
> I write to inform you that we recently filled the Writing Faculty/ Writing Center position for which you applied.

Director of Writing Programs, Wheelock College, 1995: Sure, this position was a bit of a reach, but my graduation was looming. I needed a full-time job.

> Dear Dr. Lerner:
> We have reviewed your application, and we regret to inform you that we have offered the position to a candidate whose qualifications more closely fits our present needs.

Director of the Bryant College Learning Center, 1996: When one finishes a degree program, particularly a doctoral degree, one looks for a job. And not just any job, but one that seemed relevant to my experience and aspirations. The Ed.D. I completed that year in literacy, language, and cultural studies seemed ill-suited (if not making me downright unemployable) for tenure-stream positions in an English department, particularly the ones in the Boston area that seemed like relatively closed shops, given my mixed success with finding adjunct positions in the four years I had lived in Boston up to that time. And faculty positions in teacher education also seemed out of reach with my lack of experience teaching K-12. Sure, it was a leap from being newly credentialed to running a college learning center, but applications did not take much physical energy, just the need to cushion the psychic blow of rejection.

> Dear Mr. Lerner:
>
> I regret that you were not among the applicants considered in the final pool of candidates. Although your credentials are excellent, there were a large number of highly qualified candidates.

Skills Instructor, University of Massachusetts Boston, 1996: Sure, the idea of a "skills" instructor did not exactly fit with the critical pedagogy vibe I inhabited (sorry, Professor Freire!), but I needed a full-time job. I wasn't going to be choosy about titles.

> Dear Mr. Lerner:
>
> I'm sorry to say that the Search Committee has selected another candidate for the position of Skills Instructor. Your qualifications are impressive; the decision was not an easy one.

Coordinator of Graduate ESL Tutorials, Bentley College, 1996: My days as a graduate student were nearly over, and I did teach 9th-grade English as a second language as a student teacher in my first semester of my secondary ed credential program, as well as having had many multilingual students in the first-year writing classes I taught as an adjunct. Why not apply?

> Dear Dr. Lerner:
>
> Your qualifications are impressive, and the members of the ESL search committee appreciate your interest in Bentley. Other applicants, however, offered different combinations of strengths more suited to our needs.

Associate Director of the College Writing Program, Boston University, 2001: At this point, I am five years post-doctoral degree, far enough into my first full-time faculty role as Writing Programs Coordinator/Writing Center Director at a college of pharmacy and health sciences, that I wondered what else was possible.

It wasn't so much that I was unhappy with my job—it's just that I could see that new opportunities were limited, that my conflicts with administration over the student newspaper (to which I was faculty advisor), a classic struggle between student autonomy and free speech versus administrative imperative to keep tight control of its brand, all of which led me to explore alternatives. Plus, I was familiar with this program, having taught for it as an adjunct in my last semester of grad school. That would give me a leg up, right?

> Dear Dr. Lerner:
>
> After careful review of the many excellent applications we received for this job, we are sorry to inform you that we are unable to pursue your candidacy.

Director of Writing, Brandeis University, 2002: Another year into my position at the pharmacy college, I wondered even more strongly about other possibilities, particularly ones that, in the job ad at least, seemed more straightforward than my involvement with anything having to do with writing at the pharmacy college (Run the writing center? Check. Coordinate first-year writing? Check. Attend to writing in the disciplines? Check. Administer a writing proficiency exam? Check. Advise the student newspaper? Check.). And six years post-completion of my doctoral degree, I hopefully had developed skills and strengths that would seem attractive to other employers.

> Dear Dr. Lerner:
>
> We have narrowed our choice to a small number of candidates whose strengths are in areas we feel we most need at this time. I regret that we must now eliminate all other applications, including yours, from consideration.

Director of the Writing Program, Northeastern University, 2009: Well, I did leave the pharmacy college in 2002 for a position teaching in a writing across the curriculum program at a STEM-focused institution. I was a full-time, non-tenure stream lecturer, reasonably happy with the work but still curious about the world beyond. Could I scratch the itch of a position on the tenure track in an actual English department (which I had only experienced as an adjunct; at the pharmacy college, I was in a department or arts & sciences with just as much contact with my math colleagues as with my teaching writing colleagues)? Could I position myself as having full-time and tenure-stream faculty writing program director chops after a career up to that point that included eight years as an adjunct, 12 years in non-tenure-stream roles, and a doctorate in education?

> Dear Professor Lerner:
>
> We have concluded our search for the position of Director of the Writing Program in the English Department at

> Northeastern. . . . We thank you for your interest, and wish you luck in all of your endeavors.

~~~

My thick folder of rejection letters, such as the ones I excerpt from here, is likely not unusual for an academic who's been around for as long as I have (though now those letters likely come in electronic form). It's well known that contingency, relatively inexpensive labor, and the financial precarity of U.S. higher education are long-standing forces, particularly in the teaching of writing (one letter that I do not have is when funding for a writing program administrator position I had applied to was pulled the night before my on-campus interview). And for me and for writing faculty as a whole, the need to make a living, the mysterious "fit" between one's credentials and experiences and the vagaries of search committees, the wondering if the next job will be better (or at least different) than the current one, the limits of geographic and financial mobility—these more personal forces are powerfully in play.

That my employment endeavors would, two years after that last rejection letter, bring me back to Northeastern University as English department faculty member and writing center director was not something I anticipated in 2009. And that I have most recently occupied the position of English department chair and see retirement as the next phase of my career rather than another faculty or administrative job were also seemingly abstract at that point. Certainly, the story of my job history is one of success and of privilege. And while I recognize the latter in particular, I still wonder about those positions I applied to that garnered nothing more than boilerplate rejection letters. I'm not bitter about those, just curious as to how things would have turned out had I been able to pursue those alternative histories. That seemingly random quality to one's career trajectory is truly frightening, given persistent narratives of "get your Ph.D., get your tenure-stream position, publish your first book, secure tenure." How can I now, as a faculty mentor to MA and Ph.D. students, advise students that the outcome is often out of their control, subject to economic, political, social, and educational forces that might overwhelm their intentions?

We all have these alternative histories captured in letters or emails or multiple versions of our CVs and resumes. They disrupt dominant, comforting narratives of "success" in higher education, whether as a writing teacher or writing center/writing program director. They are the cautionary tales that the next generation of academics needs to hear. Perhaps that's an eyes-wide-open starting point to countering those larger forces or at least trying to. Higher education is changing rapidly, and what might be "traditional" is only true for an increasingly shrinking student and faculty population. How do we prepare ourselves and others for that precarity? Sure, "change is constant," as some high-paid consultant would likely say, but that does not make it easier to endure, less cruel, and more forgiving. Our alternative CVs are a testament to the presence and force of change, of realizing that stability is likely the exception, and that academic careers are never a single story neatly curated on a *curriculum vitae*.

Chapter 8. My Writing Center Side Hustle

Anonymous

Since moving from a full-time contingent writing center director job to a tenure-track WPA job several years ago, I've maintained what I like to think of as a writing center side hustle. I use this term ironically because my particular side hustle doesn't result in any compensation—at least not in the form of course releases or money. The job description for my current tenure-line WPA job says nothing about writing centers, and we don't even have a writing center at my institution. We have a learning commons model, and through our learning center, we offer tutoring in different disciplines. Writing is among them. It's just one of many. Moreover, since I've been here, our learning commons has been a one-woman show. As a result, because of my background in writing center administration and research, I've supported a few different women who have ventured to coordinate our learning commons. I've taught a three-credit writing center tutor education course in the semester that we opted to offer it. I've also conducted tutor education at a start-of-semester orientation for new consultants who were paid to attend. I've even developed plans for consultant meetings and have run or helped run them weekly or every other week. I do all of this in addition to my official job. I do all of this because I love it. And in a way, I do all of this for free.

If my own upper-level administrators at my institution wanted to, and I imagine they would, they could justify what's happening by saying that it makes sense for me to do this work because of my status as the WPA. Writing programs and writing centers are partners within many institutions, however complicated that partnership is. (I'm thinking here of the exploration of this partnership and of the exploration of writing center directors as WPAs of a certain kind in Melissa Ianetta et al.'s "Polylog: Are Writing Center Directors Writing Program Administrators?" (2006).) Besides, as our upper-level administrators would say, our learning center has a full-time coordinator, albeit one who might identify as a side hustler, too, because despite her dedication to her work, she readily admits that she lacks expertise in the specific subject areas that her tutors tutor in. That coordinator is responsible for scheduling consultants, being present in the center, and doing other work in and for the center. From an upper-level administrative standpoint, this center really isn't my responsibility. It's my choice to get involved with it, and my supervisors, of course, support my choice.

I, too, could justify my side hustle at this center. I could say that my writing center work gives me what Pierre Bourdieu (1986) calls cultural and social capital. It gives me compensation of a non-monetary variety. I publish extensively on writing centers, and to do so with any street cred, I need to keep one hand in writing centers, especially given that I got my MA and my Ph.D. in literary studies with some rhetorical theory in the mix. Because of this focus in my education, I realize that I've actually been side-hustling in writing centers for quite some time. As a Ph.D. student in literary studies, I got my first administrative writing center side hustle. I got a job as a graduate student assistant director of a writing center. I then got another side hustle at a writing center at a small college near my Research-I university as I took a final semester to complete my dissertation, which was on literature. I then got yet another side hustle. My first full-time job out of grad school involved directing a writing center, and in taking that job, I felt imposter syndrome doubly so: because I'm a woman and because I didn't fully feel like a writing center scholar. I was and am still living a professional life at the margins—a life in which I am an imposter everywhere, no matter what I do.

I wonder, though, whom my approach to my profession serves. I don't know that my writing center side hustle serves the coordinator of our learning commons, who desperately needs a more robust official structure within her center so that she can do her job well and so her center can realize its mission. I don't know that it serves students at our institution who might feel the reality of scarcity in our center or who might not even make their way through the door because of the very scarcity I'm mentioning. I don't know that it serves me, even though I feel equipped to continue publishing on writing center work because of the everyday writing-centered work I do. My current side hustle invigorates my imposter syndrome in that it reifies my sense of myself as a kind of outsider looking in. Finally, I don't know that it serves the discipline of writing center studies, which, in my view, needs to reckon with the variety of disciplinary backgrounds that writing center professionals bring with them to writing center and writing studies work instead of only celebrating the elite writing studies Ph.D.-bearers among us.

We side hustlers are here, and we have every right to be here, or at least that's what I'm now trying to tell myself. We're also quite good at the work we do in writing centers, and we're quite capable of producing excellent writing center research. Nonetheless, I fear that the effect of hustling will forever haunt me in my working life as it may haunt writing center studies as a relatively new field, a side hustler itself in the world of writing studies, which is a side hustler in that broad category that we used to just call English. Because I'm neither here nor there as a scholar and practitioner, because of my unpaid writing center labor, and probably also because I'm a woman, I know that regardless of how I look to the outside observer or come to look as a result of writing this piece, I will, in all likelihood, keep feeling like a hustler. I'll keep feeling like I'm at the periphery and not quite in the center, even though I've spent decades investing myself in writing center work.

References

Bourdieu, P. (1986). The forms of capital. In J. G. Richardson (Ed.), *Handbook of theory and research for the sociology of education* (pp. 241–58). Greenwood Press.

Ianetta, M., Bergmann, L., Fitzgerald, F., Haviland, C. P., Lebduska, L. & Wislocki, M. (2006). Polylog: Are writing center directors writing program administrators? *Composition Studies, 34*(2), 11–42.

Chapter 9. Why Write?: Writing Center Publishing as Labor

Rebecca Hallman Martini
UNIVERSITY OF GEORGIA

> You seem to assume greater familiarity—with both your own arguments and those of others—than you actually have.
>
> — *Professor feedback on my first seminar paper*

I still remember the first piece of feedback I received as an MA student in rhetoric and composition. I clung close to what was at the time familiar ground, writing center scholarship, but my ability to bridge texts in second language writing and global English ultimately failed. When I received a B in the course, I remember wondering if this was a sign that maybe I shouldn't be in graduate school.

Although I was naïve and inexperienced, I was working as hard as I knew how to. I had no idea what to do with observation-like comments, like the one above, without clarification. I quickly realized direct writing instruction in graduate school was rare, but that learning how to write was essential. I did not know how to read sources together as part of a field's conversation, or how to identify a gap and make an argument that filled it. I was lucky to eventually work with Joanna Wolfe, who taught academic genres (like the literature review) explicitly and shared models of unfamiliar writing (like empirical theses and dissertations). With her help and more experience, I got better at writing.

Early in my Ph.D. program, I learned that publishing is critical to scholarly success. At the time, I was the graduate student representative on the International Writing Center Association (IWCA) board and an attendee at the IWCA Summer Institute. My original idea was to create a blog for emerging scholars that would facilitate the exchange of good ideas rather than being a space where people "signal" their intelligence in ways deemed acceptable by those with power in the field. When I mentioned the idea to then-president Kevin Dvorak, he listened to my pitch and said, "why don't you just start a new journal?"

This idea had never occurred to me, as I continued to feel unqualified to do academic writing work. My only experience with academic publishing up to this point was with rejection. And yet, I wanted to learn more. I became intimately familiar with what was obscured in the writing/publishing/feedback process, and how difficult it was to try and learn about it without a direct connection to someone currently publishing in your target journals. I began to wonder if there was a way to do so, if there was a way to open up the publication process to make it more transparent for new writing center researchers who had important contributions to make but had little prior experience with the process and thus faced uncertainty about how and where they fit. If you are likely to face cold rejection, why write?

With these ideas in mind, IWCA's most recent venue, *The Peer Review* (TPR), began. From the beginning, we centered mentorship by bringing in graduate students as reviewers and offering support to writers as they navigated peer review feedback and contemplated revision. The journal was open access so that all writing center practitioners could engage with the content, which I believe is one of the first steps to seeing yourself as a capable contributor. And the journal was more egalitarian than others as it was edited by both graduate students and professionals in the field on a rotating basis. In theory, this all sounded quite good and was supported almost immediately by the IWCA board. The funding and enthusiasm were there. Yet, in practice, we struggled hard for the first couple years with respect to the flexibility of the publishing platform, a lack of publication mentorship happening, and incompatibility of editorial leadership styles. It turned out all these central elements—open access, mentorship, shared editorship across roles—were not easy to work out in practice. Our field wasn't used to doing things this way.

I didn't know whether TPR was going to make it until my colleague, Travis Webster, and I opened a call for a special issue on *Writing Centers as Brave(r) Spaces*. We carefully crafted a call and then let the proposals that came in shape the direction of the issue. The writers brought in ways of writing that we hadn't considered before, and rather than being confined by the space of a typical print-based publication, we accepted whatever we wanted and had the space to enable writers to creatively compose and contextualize their pieces. In that issue, we had a wealth of thoughtful pieces, from both well-known and new voices, on diverse topics. For example, we had a dialogue between a director and a tutor as the tutor went through gender affirmation surgery while working in the center and living in a conservative state. I hadn't seen anything like this kind of piece in our scholarship before, and we hadn't anticipated it. We positioned ourselves as thoughtful readers with something to learn. When writers pushed against our suggestions or feedback and explained why, we tried to understand and ultimately support their writerly agency. This meant recognizing that sometimes (often), the writer knows best, not the reviewer nor the editor—a radical idea about publishing in academia.

> . . . there is an assumption that more revisions is always better, when, actually, the article reaches a point where more revisions simply make it incoherent and it begins to disintegrate. (Zebroski, 2020, personal email)

This concept, which Jim Zebroski would eventually term "hyper-revision" (Zebroski 2020), is a relatively new way of reviewing/editing in rhetoric and composition studies, and one that does not make for better scholarship. It's not something that was happening 25 years ago, but it's all too common now: gatekeeping at its worst, working from the assumption that the editors and reviewers know best, including when it comes to the minutiae of a piece. It makes the process of publication more about meeting the (often tedious) expectations of one or two editors or reviewers, not about the story or the message or the findings, and certainly not about the writer. If this is the case, why write?

My work with Travis on the Brave/r Spaces Special Issue helped me learn that writing belongs first and foremost to the writers themselves, and we can trust them. This means that revision and feedback should not be about fitting pieces into what we think they should be, but about trying to understand writers on their own terms and helping them revise in ways that make the piece a stronger version of what they want it to be. With this approach, TPR could be about something other than meeting the expectations of the editors and appeasing all reviewers. Since then, and during my editorship from 2015–2020, we had some tricky situations that required some risk taking on our part to move forward. For instance, we had writers who were incredibly resistant to editorial feedback and who were publishing work that was critical of experienced writing centers at their local sites, thus risking possible retaliation. We also had writers questioning long-standing scholarship and accepted practices in our field. It's a small writing center world, we worried, so might these pieces too directly call out programs and people in our field?

I began to ask: if not here, where? I began to think about the fact that these writers had chosen TPR as a venue to submit their intellectual labor; it was their chosen audience. As editors, here and elsewhere, we are given a valuable opportunity to help decide what stories are heard and told. It is our responsibility to respond with respect, and to recognize that, in some cases, rejection of scholarship is a rejection of an experience, a story, an argument, a voice. Pieces that challenge us, that make us uncomfortable, that require hard conversations, that offend us should signal greater attention and listening, not less. We should not let our ability to gatekeep kill projects of value. This does not mean that every piece submitted should be accepted, but it does mean that we don't have to like, agree with, or fully understand everything that gets published.

> . . . our continued establishment of a discipline, our very livelihood and sustainability, rests upon positioning ourselves as a research-based, dynamic discipline led by intersectionally diverse stakeholders. Our queer and of color practitioners are telling us to listen and to act through recruitment, retention, and research. What queer and raced research projects may lie dormant due to an imbalance of labor experienced by queer practitioners? (110–111, Webster, 2021).

In his seminal work, *Queerly Centered: LGBTQA Writing Center Directors Navigate the Workplace*, Travis Webster (2021) raises questions about the connection between labor, research, and how we will continue as a discipline. There is a lot at stake here. Publication is political, classed, raced, able-bodied, and gendered. Who gets to publish, the authority they are given once they publish, and all the possible voices that are left out of the scholarly conversation are critical to how our field makes knowledge, retains members, and ultimately works with writers. This intersectional approach to publication is one that we need to attend to more in our field and TPR led and continues to lead that charge in a very real way. As editors and reviewers, we should honor people's intellectual labor, hear their stories on their own terms, and provide mentorship through our feedback that helps instead of leadership that hurts and silences. Our entire field, not just the writers, lose when we further marginalize voices different from our own through our publication practices. Our journals should welcome new writers, unpopular opinions, weird ways of writing, and stories we haven't yet heard. Otherwise, why write?

References

Webster, Travis (2021). *Queerly centered: LGBTQA writing center directors navigate the workplace.* Utah State University Press.

Zebroski, James T. (2020). Hyper-revision in composition: Neoliberalism and the business of professional publishing. *Quarterly Journal of Composition, 1*(1), 18–37.

Chapter 10. Moving On to Move Up

Joseph Cheatle
OXFORD COLLEGE OF EMORY UNIVERSITY

In our field, and in our individual institutions, we frequently discuss the lack of resources for writing centers, whether that is a lack of full-time employees, student employees, funding, or institutional support. At my previous writing center (a large public institution featuring three full-time administrators, 9 graduate assistants, 30 undergraduate consultants, and 10 administrative assistants), we experienced budget cuts for two out of the three years that I was there. This resulted in one full-time employee's position being "reimagined" (administrative speak for downsizing) into a smaller role in order to save money, as well as the loss of a graduate student assistantship. At the same time these cuts were happening, we also went through the turmoil of COVID-19, which required us to go online for six months and then institute a hybrid model for delivering services. It would have been easy, in the face of budget cuts and COVID-19, to have smaller ambitions for the center.

However, at the same time as these issues were happening, we were able to expand our services, engage with more students, and positively shape perceptions of the writing center on- and off-campus. Using the same (or even sometimes fewer) resources than we previously had, we were able to expand our tutoring hours and writing retreat offerings. We were also able to build new services, including a multimedia communication center, a speaker series focused on linguistic justice, workshops by request, and embedded tutoring. And, we were able to provide leadership and professional development opportunities through the creation of student positions like a media coordinator, retreats coordinator, outreach coordinator, and pedagogy coordinator. But why, and at what cost?

I had many reasons for wanting to push against the tides buffeting our center rather than succumb to them. The first was personal pride and a desire to be a leader and innovator in our field. I wanted the center to be recognized as one of the best in the nation and as an example for other centers to follow. The second was a need to escape what can be the monotony of the position. One-on-one and group tutoring are excellent services, but they also follow a similar and well-worn pattern for those of us who have been in the field for a long time. The third was to demonstrate our value for stakeholders on campus, particularly administrators, that control our budget and resources. We wanted to ensure a larger footprint for the center that increased our visibility and impact on campus, thereby positioning the center to ask for additional funding while protecting it from budget cuts. The fourth, and last, reason was to position myself for the next position. Many writing center positions lack the salary, institutional support, and funding that would make them long-term homes to administrators. That helps explain the transitory nature of many writing center positions as well as the many job opportunities available on job posting sites like *The Chronicle of Higher Education*, *HigherEdJobs*, and *Inside Higher Ed*. It also might explain, in part, why we work so very hard.

It is the fourth reason, positioning myself for the next position, that I want to focus on. I have worked as a professional in four writing centers (including my current position). I left each of the first three positions to progress in my career. After serving as a writing center tutor during graduate school, I served as a professional consultant as part of my first position. I then transitioned into administration as an associate director and then as a staff director. My current position is a faculty director on the tenure track. Until my current position, I was always concerned with maximizing my performance, and the performance of the center, to progress to the next position. In some ways this was positive because it led to a productive and prospering center; however, it was negative because I was always doing more work than I was compensated for and often beyond the initial scope of the position.

My time in writing centers reflects two aspects of the labor practices of the field. The first is that we constantly optimize our own work and that of our employees. This optimization can be beneficial, but it can also be detrimental. We can reach new stakeholders through the creation of new programs and initiatives; we can also increase our footprint by elevating employees into positions of leadership; in short, we do good and meaningful work that impacts the lives of thousands of writers and hundreds of tutors over our professional lifetimes. At my previous center, we were able to create student positions for a media coordinator, pedagogy coordinator, and outreach coordinator. By doing so, we diversified our offerings while engaging new stakeholders. But this optimization can also be detrimental to both employees and administrators. For employees, they may be put into positions that they are unprepared, undersupported or under-compensated to perform. For administrators, they may take on new duties which are outside the scope of their job and make the lives of future administrators more complicated. As our services expanded and students were elevated into leadership positions, I became more of a people manager. My job was, increasingly, meeting with other institutional administrators and with my own employees. While I have been trained and had the experience to develop programs and initiatives, it was more difficult moving into the role of supervisor. I gave up, in some ways, a sense of control of initiatives and programs as I was no longer involved in the day-to-day success of them. It also meant "coaching," advising, and high-level supervision of projects. I was further and further removed from the day-to-day operations of tutoring, initiative development, and program execution; rather, I supervised the people who did these things.

The second is the transitory nature of writing center work. Because of the lean nature of writing centers—whether it is from budget cuts or understaffing—there is usually not an opportunity to move up in the center. And the best jobs are entrenched with administrators that have no intention of leaving their position. Therefore, the only way to advance is to move to another writing center. For me, that meant uprooting my life—and that of my family—three different times in the space of eight years to move from Cleveland to Michigan to Iowa to Mississippi. And the moves were basically the luck of the draw. Good writing center positions (whatever that might mean to an individual) often have people who work there for a long time. That means the best jobs in the field only become available once every 10 to 20 years. Even if good positions are available, they are highly competitive because everyone wants those positions. And those jobs may be in far flung places, geographically, or politically inhospitable, or far away from family.

Now that I am in a new position at an institution where I am a tenure-track faculty member who also happens to be the writing center director, I am not interested in optimization in order to get to the next position. That is a relief and a burden lifted from my shoulders. And, I will be careful and strategic about optimization for other reasons, including being a leader in the field, bringing variety to our work, and demonstrating our value to stakeholders. I will be mindful about what that optimization does for (and to) me, my staff, my employees, and our stakeholders.

Chapter 11. The First Year: A New Director's Experience

Allie Sockwell Johnston
AUSTIN PEAY STATE UNIVERSITY IN TENNESSEE

I started my first position out of graduate school as the first faculty member serving as writing center director. I graduated from my Ph.D. program in May, moved in July, and started my new role in August, all during the COVID-19 pandemic.

I aspired to be a writing center director from the time I was a college sophomore. I discovered the writing center in my own transition to college-level writing. I came from a rural public high school where I would receive A's on all my work. As I entered a private university, I struggled to meet the new expectations. The writing center is the place that reminded me I belonged. I remember leaving my first tutoring session in awe, knowing I wanted to be a part of that type of work, of ensuring student's agency in their writing and reminding them of their own abilities in new contexts.

Now I'm entering my second year in my role as assistant professor and writing center director at a regional state university. Our student body of roughly 11,000 serves a large percentage of non-traditional students, including many first-generation and military-affiliated students. My biggest challenge is making students aware of our services and trying to meet them where they are.

I entered this position eager to help. The Notes App in my phone was flooded with brainstorming ideas—what events we'd host, the writing workshops we'd offer, social media posts. I couldn't believe that I had secured this dream job of mine—all during a pandemic! And while I still feel the same passion I did as a student using the writing center and during my eight years working as a tutor, I've come to understand the almost impossible labor expectations of this role. During my graduate programs at R1s, I worked in an administrative role as an assistant director for the writing center. I was part of a team of five to six people, all serving the writing center. We had solid funding, staffing, and resources to draw from.

I quickly realized the shift as I started my own position. Being the first faculty-based position, expectations for my role were still being solidified. The team of administrators became one person: me. I realized my lofty goals of serving the students through writing workshops, campus events, and more would have to be scaled down. I started with eight students to staff 50 hours a week. Between my teaching load and administrative work, I stepped in and tutored numerous times when we simply didn't have the staff to do so. Our tutor hourly wage ($9.50) was lower than most campus jobs. It seemed like an impossible task. I first turned to blame myself: I was a good tutor. But maybe I wasn't a good administrator. However, I started understanding that the problem was less about my own abilities and more about the need for support. Now, looking back, I realize the immense systematic challenges I faced as a wide-eyed, recent graduate student-turned-director.

Our writing center staff has grown to 23 tutors and 8 front desk workers. With this growth, I have discovered new challenges. While last year we could not meet student demand because of our low staff numbers, this year I'm fearful we won't have enough students to utilize our larger team that I grew so quickly. I advocated for an increased hourly wage for our tutors to $13. This created more challenges: will we burn through our budget in one semester? How do I ensure our tutors have the amount of hours they want and need? Furthermore, how do I ensure the quality of tutoring, not just the quantity of tutors?

Our tutors come from a variety of disciplines, from Biology to Communications to English and Radiology. We have students ranging from first-year to graduate-level. Part of my job expectation is to host recurring tutor training. The training is not a course credit. I learned through trial and error my first year that there would never be a time all staff members could meet on Zoom. We're trying asynchronous training this year, with weekly readings and written reflections. This creates a different workload—one that I enjoy, but is still labor, nonetheless. I want to give each tutor the support they need at the stage they are in by reading their reflections, responding thoughtfully, checking in with them, and observing their sessions. I'm learning how to delegate now that I have a small administrative team around me with two dedicated graduate student assistant directors.

I've also learned how to advocate for our center. To me, that's the easy part. What is more challenging is advocating for myself. That's the part I'm continually working on. I'm making appointments across campus with administrators to advocate for increased funding. I'm learning to be loud. I'm learning to say no.

There have been numerous times over the last year in this role that I've doubted myself. I'm realizing now that doubt comes from the overwhelming feeling of taking on a role meant for multiple people and a larger budget.

I always tell my tutors, "You are never expected to know all the answers. We work together as a team to discover answers together." As a new director, I'm trying to take this advice myself. I am learning to ask questions, to learn from those around me, and to advocate for the creation of more of a team to assist in running our writing center.

In this last year, I have grown and learned from my tutors and students alike. My goal for my first year was relational-based. I wanted to learn about the students we serve and the tutors we employ. I wanted to see what needs our campus has and how we, as a center, can fulfill those needs. I'm striving to discover and maintain healthy labor boundaries. I wish I could have connected with more first-year or early-career writing center directors. Through the challenges, I continue to remind myself why I'm doing this work. I come back to that passion I've held since my first writing center experience when I felt self-doubt and overwhelm creep in. I'm learning to find and connect frequently with a mentor while also learning where to go to advocate for my center and myself. Perhaps the most important lesson I've learned as a first-year writing center director is to keep a record of what our center accomplishes. I'm constantly reminding myself of my value when I need to advocate for more resources.

Chapter 12. From Dream Job to Unsustainable

Anonymous

My undergraduate university had the kind of writing center that would make any writing center practitioner (and probably Stephen North) cringe: a "writing lab" relegated to the corner of an upper floor of the library that was never advertised or mentioned in any of my courses. It wasn't until I entered graduate school at a different university and began volunteering as a consultant in their writing center (while simultaneously enrolled in a rhetoric & composition course) that I learned what the space represented, in theory and practice, and felt a strong connection to its purpose and procedures. As a graduate assistant the following year, I served as the assistant director of the writing center; in addition to tutoring, I helped the director with training, attended workshops, and observed in more detail exactly what the center represented for the university and its students. This illuminated connections between tutoring and teaching, and I knew right away that composition studies were for me.

Toward the end of my last semester in graduate school, the director abruptly resigned and left the university. The writing program administrator and I collaborated to finish the semester (co-teaching the tutor training course and overseeing the consultants' daily work), and the English department faculty offered me a one-year interim director position (which later became permanent). I remember feeling shocked and honored, thinking to myself, *"I never thought I would get my dream job right out of graduate school!"*

My 11 years as writing center director were incredibly rewarding, and I credit my colleagues in the English department for embracing me (especially since I had been a student in many of their classes). They included me in department meetings, email discussions, and job interviews; listened to and considered my ideas; and even asked me for help with their own students, or with teaching writing or designing assignments. I had room to innovate in my position and developed a credit-bearing course sequence to help graduate assistants become more effective teachers. My visibility across the university increased when my colleagues introduced me to other faculty members or invited me to workshops. I received funding to attend conferences every year (and presented at many), and returned with ideas for the writing center, my own classrooms, and writing course curricula. I was never micromanaged and felt like everyone trusted me to make good decisions, report data, and request only what I really needed for the center.

Although I was happy and felt supported and successful, my job (like many in higher ed) was demanding, despite the fact that it was dynamic and multi-faceted. As time went on, my workload increased and expanded, yet remained compressed under "other duties as assigned." As an NTT staff member, I already felt pressure to say "yes" to anything I was asked to do—even when the "ask" involved becoming a program coordinator in an unfamiliar discipline. I worried that the one time I said "no" would somehow show up on my performance evaluation, or would give administrators the impression that I "didn't *really* want this job." That is how my singular position evolved into three: the writing center director (the job I was hired for), the coordinator of teaching for graduate assistants (a role I created and proposed), and the coordinator for a subset of writing courses transferred into the English department (a role I was asked to take on). Yet, in the eyes of the university, I was only the writing center director.

Complicating my work further was the fact that I felt like my position was situated "in the middle." Although I was classified as "staff," my work was "faculty-like": teaching, academic committee service, research, and presentations (by my own choice, not because I was required to). My reporting line was very confusing; the English department chair completed my yearly performance review, but I was technically aligned under the College of Arts & Sciences. My "staff" classification generated a "staff" performance evaluation from Human Resources, which did not provide room for me to report everything that my job entailed. I often felt like I was out on my own island, and that no one other than my department chair and closest colleagues *really* understood.

I felt fulfilled and valuable to many people (my undergraduate students, particularly in first-year writing; my writing center consultants; the graduate assistants; and numerous colleagues) but realized around my ninth year that at my university, I was at the top of my career. There was no room for me to advance, even if I got a Ph.D. (which I did not want to do). Even though I liked my work, I didn't like feeling "maxed out" (in position title and salary) at a young age. I tried proposing a more comprehensive position title after I added "program coordinator" to my workload; while administrators supported it, Human Resources denied the request and said that my new responsibilities only warranted another bullet point in my job description.

Faced with these realities, I began to do research into the labor of writing center professionals (particularly for NTT staff, faculty, and administrators). I connected with wonderful co-researchers, presented workshops and roundtables on the topic, and discovered that—even *before* the pandemic—many others had written editorials, articles, and books highlighting the same precarity, isolation, and edge-of-overwork feelings I was experiencing. While it was comforting to know that I was not alone, nor was I being overdramatic, the community of people and the existing research that surfaced were concerning. The question I kept coming back to was, *"Are all writing center professionals eventually susceptible to this experience?"*

The pandemic answered that question in many ways. Fortunately, I was able to retain my staff and my budget, and no one questioned me or told me what I could and couldn't do. Many others (who I met through virtual conversations in the *Directors of Writing Centers* Facebook group and "WCD Coffee and Chat" sessions) faced cuts to personnel, budgets, and spaces, or were forced to return in-person while COVID-19 spread and risks were still high. At a time when we all missed the in-person, "normal" environments of our classrooms and writing centers, and when our actual and emotional labor had increased exponentially, those virtual conversations were a respite. Here was a community of people who *understood* each other, in ways that many of us felt our colleagues outside of the writing center did not. Those conversations were therapeutic, productive, and emotional; for every question or problem someone posed, someone else had already experienced it and provided a suggestion. For every emotion expressed, at least one other person (if not more) felt the same.

What became evident, both through the virtual spaces for the field and in my own life, was that the pandemic represented a significant shift. Through the remainder of 2020 and into 2021, I saw posts from people who left their writing centers—and higher education altogether, in some cases—to pursue new paths. Others reinvented their centers and positions with energy and enthusiasm. While I tried to remain positive, I lost my enthusiasm during summer 2020, when my employment was up in the air for months, and I finally concluded, *"this is unsustainable."* Doing everything online in fall 2020 was tiresome *on top of* already-existing burnout, and I knew it was time for me to move on and listen to the quiet wondering that had been in the back of my mind for a while: *"I wonder what my skills would be worth in other industries."* I reworked my resume that winter and quietly began looking at positions elsewhere that focused on editing (the "side hustle" I had developed a few years prior). After a short search process, I was fortunate to be offered a position in healthcare; even in this new industry, I feel more valued, balanced, and focused than I ever had in higher education.

I have been out of academia for over a year now, and I do not regret my decision to leave. I miss my colleagues, and I miss having the opportunity to mentor others, but I have been able to remain connected to the writing center and higher education communities by outwardly offering support and a listening ear for anyone who is considering leaving. I also remain connected to some of the "long-distance writing center friends" I met online. It is still difficult for me to emotionally detach myself from the changes my former university announces, but I remind myself each time that it's no longer my concern. I am, however, grateful for all of the characteristics I developed during the first 11 years of my career (innovation, altruism, and a desire to help others improve), and if there is one thing I learned during my job search, it is that those characteristics—the ones that *make* a writing center director—are invaluable across all industries.

Theme 2. Precarity and Failed Advocacy

Here, we move into the subterranean elements of writing center work; the seedy, stressful, less-often discussed elements. This entire section is anonymous by the contributors' decision. This section serves as a sort of dark reflection on the previous section and the section that follows it: many of the narratives here encapsulate extended periods and even careers in writing center work, and all of them share instances where the metalabor of advocating for their centers and their work has failed them. Writing center labor is often precarious—especially for the many who are contingent workers. Although we shared an overview of the scholarship on labor in writing centers in Act I, here we pause to note the great deal of work emerging in recent years dealing specifically with contingent labor. Lerner (2009) found the birth of writing centers in 1894 to be tied directly to contingent labor. Isaacs and Knight (2017) found that contingent labor in writing centers had only grown since then, finding that 71 percent of writing center directors held non-tenure-track positions by 2017 (p. 48). Fels (2017) drew on this statistic to examine the relationship between contingency and precarity among writing center directors, arguing that "71 percent of our colleagues walk a fine line between having a job and experiencing the hardships that come with unemployment. Once someone higher up the food chain decides to eliminate or drastically change a director's position, very little can be done to save it, and nothing we say matters will" (p. 128). Many of the stories in this section echo Fels' (2017) sentiment and the work of others (Naydan, 2017; Fels et al., 2021; Herb et al., 2023), making clear the stakes of our institutional precarity and the risks that come with the field's failure to organize.

In "I've Got a Secret," an anonymous, long-time writing center director discussed their precarity and the ways in which their line changes over the years have brought them little stability despite profound success in the national professional arena of writing center work. At the end of their career, the contributor reflects on how contingency has shaped their work and advocates for changes to our profession to protect contingent workers, most especially in labor organizing.

The anonymous "Into and Out of the Tutoring Center," describes how one administrative decision can upend a writing center director's job with deleterious effects. And, while the story starts off as a cautionary tale about ignorant colleagues, it has a surprisingly positive ending. Here, advocacy—but also a lot of distance on the part of the contributor/director—helps them to navigate the (temporary) loss of their writing center.

"Writing Center as a Life Raft" provides a different cautionary tale from another anonymous contributor, demonstrating that precarity is not limited to contingent faculty and staff members. It highlights the fact that even tenured and decorated members of the field are subject to similar pressures and austerity politics: no one in the neoliberal university, regardless of positioning, is immune to its whims. Both this and the prior story reveal the effects of the managed university wherein supposedly economically marginal (but crucial) areas are under-resourced and micromanaged in favor of shorter-term "returns on investment."

The last story—"Counterstory: Ignored Labor with a Writing Center"—details the ways in which a writing center worker can sometimes fail to make headway in their job. Here, we follow Lan Wang-Hiles as she navigates experiences of being disempowered but also exploited because she has writing center expertise but is only called upon in very limited situations to interact with tutors. Wang-Hiles tries again and again to teach her colleagues and administrators about writing center best practices, but to no avail.

So many of us have felt similarly silenced, sidelined, and unappreciated for our knowledge and our labor. These stories—from a wide array of writing center workers in contingent and tenure track positions—show us how precarity lurks in our profession. In offering unflinching and honest descriptions of the kind of loss one feels when confronted with losing one's writing center, or one's job, these stories demonstrate the importance of critical distance from our work and the need for more advocacy for writing center workers.

Discussion Questions

- It was tempting for us to put "I've Got a Secret" in the career trajectory section. That said, this narrative has a laser-like focus on precarity and contingent labor in a way that the narratives in Career Trajectories did not necessarily share. As you read this section, would you group it with those narratives? Is there something unique to contingent positions that definitionally differentiates them from more faculty-oriented positions? Despite having been contingent for over 30 years, the narrator has remained in their position; how is this different from the conditions described in "From Dream Job to Unsustainable"?
- "Into and Out of the Tutoring Center" demonstrates the often-mercurial whims of administrators when it comes to reporting lines for writing centers. Like "I've Got a Secret," this narrative also demonstrates how bound up in institutional politicking and relationships the positioning of a writing center can be. In what ways can aspiring WCDs be better prepared to answer and adapt to changing lines of reporting, department/area housing, or other drastic changes to the conditions of the position? What sorts of metalabor are demonstrated in this narrative and how are they unique from those described in, say, Sockwell Johnston's narrative in beginning a new center?
- While contingency is a major sub-theme in this section, "Writing Center as Life Raft" demonstrates that even tenured writing center administrators are subject to precarity in the managed university. This particular

story was shared a few years before the recent, shocking cuts to faculty lines and departments at WVU (among other colleges and universities) in 2023. It has become increasingly clear that traditional conceptions of stability no longer hold true in this context. What can be done to better prepare newcomers to the field for these vicissitudes? How do we reckon with the "grand narratives" of being rewarded for personal sacrifice and hard work being shattered as it was for this contributor? What new narratives emerge? What narratives should emerge?

- Lan Wang-Hiles's story is in many ways an interesting inversion of a typical writing center narrative: rather than a contingent director or staff member expected to also teach courses, Wang-Hiles is a tenured faculty member who has tried to advocate for her university's center despite it being moved away from her home department and purview. What are the implications of the often-messy results of cross-area reporting and responsibilities? For example, Wang-Hiles teaches the tutor training course but finds the conditions dictated by its positioning sometimes at odds with the field's best practices. In this case, Wang-Hiles's center was supervised by someone who wasn't an expert. How might the field advocate for expertise and credentialing without gatekeeping? What are the consequences if we do not?

Chapter 13. Writing Fellows; Fellow Students

Eva Dunsky
BARUCH COLLEGE

In the summer of 2016, as a rising college junior, I worked as a writing fellow for my campus' pre-college preparation intensive. The goal of the program was to help economically disadvantaged, often first-generation and BIPOC students gain access to higher education by guiding them throughout their college careers with extra tutoring and support. Having worked as a writing fellow during the school year, I was excited to get started with these students and thrilled about the readings they'd been assigned (*Hamlet* and Nella Larsen's *Passing*, to name a few). I absolutely loved writing center work—reading about pedagogy, chatting with classmates about their writing projects, finding a close-knit community of writers on campus—so taking this summer job had been a no-brainer. I spent many afternoons beneath the frigid library air conditioning reading student drafts and planning workshops, decking out their accompanying PowerPoints with the ubiquitous memes of the moment and goofy transition effects between slides.

Working with the students, as it so often is, was wonderful. They were smart, funny, and tenacious; they had some of the hottest *Hamlet* takes I've ever heard. That wasn't the hard part.

The hard part was this program's pedagogy. It was run by a different set of staff than the writing center, which meant that while I was doing the same kind of work I did during the school year, I was expected to follow this other program's rules. They took a hardline approach: students spent from sunup to sundown in college-level courses, and then, after a short break for dinner, they'd have enrichment and tutoring followed by homework time and a mandatory curfew and lights out. This was meant to prepare them for college, but I was struck by the dissonance between the program's portrayal of college life and what my life at college was actually like: I definitely worked hard, but I also spent a lot of time napping, exploring the city, spending too long at dorm parties and then waking up late to leisurely read *Middlemarch* on the lawn. I was in charge of my own schedule, for better and for worse, and at no point did that schedule involve fourteen-hour days of pure academics. Weren't we preparing these students to see college as a constant uphill battle, rather than a time for self-discovery and fun?

At the time, I didn't feel like I could take these concerns to program administrators. I had gotten accustomed to the consistent guidance and open-door policy of my boss, who encouraged stopping by to discuss new ideas or tricky moments that came up in work with students. It was thanks to her training that I recognized problems with the program's zero-tolerance approach to conflict, whether it was lateness, absence, or struggle with the material. If students didn't complete or understand the reading, they'd be forced into mandatory meetings with advisors. This made students reluctant to seek help and went against everything I'd been taught at the writing center, but as a tutor with little say in the curriculum, I felt like my hands were tied. It didn't help that I met with students between 9–10 p.m. each night because their schedules were so overloaded. We were all exhausted. I love Shakespeare, but at 10 p.m. I want to be tucked into bed with a book, not discussing him with students in the empty hallways of the English department because all the classrooms are locked.

I was twenty the summer I worked in this program. I remember one particularly demoralizing evening as I walked back to my dorm, getting caught in a flash flood as I broodily made my way across campus. I was still so young, still tapering off my teenage years (and their accompanying bent for drama). I didn't know how to articulate the apprehension I was feeling.

Instead of having a conversation with my bosses, I complained during staff meetings about their rules, checked out during mandatory workplace development, and made clear to students that I also thought these policies were unfair. It seemed like we were erroneously telling them that they were already behind and that keeping up in college would mean never letting their guard down. Instead of caring for them as people and ensuring they were in charge of their own learning, we were engaging them with a pedagogy that tended toward a *Scared Straight!* mentality. They deserved so much better.

It also became clear that other students who visited the writing center during the school year were treated to a completely different kind of pedagogy. I had been taught to lift students up, reaffirm their strength as scholars, and always leave the session goals up to them. But the moment students were deemed remedial or "behind," all that went out the window. It showed me first-hand how only some students are considered worthy of transgressive teaching and student-centered approaches, and how learning goals shift based on how instructors see their students, whether those perceptions are accurate or not. Only some are provided the space to be creative, to use digression as a means for creativity, and to work at their own pace.

My main takeaways from that summer: writing center work should always center what the student wants to tackle, and I shouldn't spend sessions trying to improve student writing based on my own metrics for success. I'd been taught that the point of our labor was to help writers define and achieve their own goals, whatever that meant to them, and I needed to hold fast to that conviction even when faced with inflexible administrators and worn-out students. It's hard to write without being told exactly what to do and when to do it, but we owe it to our students to be honest about what writing entails (lots of nuance and negative capability; any Keats fans in the house?) and create the conditions for them to figure out their projects on their own. This doesn't mean letting errors slide and treating students with kid gloves, as some people incorrectly assume—this approach is actually in keeping with a high level of rigor. Part of the magic of writing center work is the ability to tailor our approach to individual students' needs and goals, and this summer job was a crucial reminder that working with students on their writing means acknowledging them first as thinkers and people. If writing is thinking, and thinking involves a synthesis of our lived experience, then how can you separate the writing from the person holding the pencil?

You can't, but that summer, we tried. And failed. The best workshops and writing conferences happened when I went off script, letting students chat, debate, and generally deviate from the course material. The worst workshops and conferences took place when I felt stressed about covering the curriculum and insisted on following the program's strict and too-fast-paced learning goals. Had I been listening more closely, I would've understood that students weren't ready to focus on constructing an argument or making a debatable claim, that they were still understanding and drawing connections to the reading material. Had I been more adept at navigating tricky workplace situations, I would've shared my concerns with program staff and we might've had a productive conversation. And had I had my finger on the pulse of cultural trends, I would've known that PowerPoint transition effects are embarrassing and my students were just too nice to say anything.

I think about this summer often, especially when I'm frustrated with a student who seems to be slacking off. I have to frequently remind myself that most effort is invisible and that even if a student isn't putting in the effort, there are lots of reasons this might be the case. I know that college is hard, and as a writer, that writing might feel impossible. So I pause, and reorient: instead of measuring their work by a rigid set of standards, how can I plant the seeds for them to continue developing the high-level cognitive skills required to get words on the page?

Writing is inherently messy—as is working with students, as is learning to teach, as is figuring out how to position ourselves as writing center workers—but the process is as important as the product (for the novice writer, maybe even more so). As teachers and tutors, our main job isn't to correct mistakes or even improve the quality of student writing. It's to show students what a writing practice looks like. It's to be the liaison between student and page, student and professor, student and administration. It's to create the conditions they need to develop a process that works for them, then insist on those conditions, external pressures aside.

Chapter 14. I've Got a Secret: I'm Contingent. (Wait, You're Contingent Too?)

Anonymous

I've worked in writing centers for over 30 years, first as a graduate student tutor and then as the person responsible for a center's operations. I realize that description is a convoluted way of describing "director," but up until very recently, I wasn't allowed to use the title of director. To be a director, I would need to report to a second-level supervisor rather than a third-level supervisor. I'm not going to even hint at my institution type or give those supervisor levels titles, since I don't wish to be identified. Why don't I want to be identified? Above all, my position has always been contingent, and I am employed at the pleasure of the president of my institution—with precious few protections afforded me by my "right to work" state. I'm not going to talk about scandalous things here, but I've witnessed contingent employees being punished for insubordination because they talked about their institutions in a negative light. I'm not necessarily worried about being punished as much as I am about damaging relationships at my institution that are new, as well as those that are decades old.

Back to the point: all my job titles have been far beneath the level of director, as has my pay. I've been both part-time and full-time. Even though I teach classes regularly, publish research, mentor tutors, and generally consider the writing center a learning space—a classroom, as it were—I have never held a tenure-track faculty position. Ironically, now that I report directly to a second-level supervisor, I have no disciplinary home other than the writing center. I was removed from the department/discipline in which I've taught for decades. I no longer attend department meetings or have any voice in curricular development in the discipline that houses the class that all tutors in my center take to become peer tutors.

When talk of making me a director started, the intention was that I would be a so-called faculty director who would teach as well as run the center—as I always had—and I would stay within my home department. Promises of instant tenure were made, but not at a full professor rank, even though the institution had just hired a person with less experience as a full professor. Promises of a substantial pay raise were also made, but complications of summer contracts (or lack thereof) and a teaching load untenable for running a writing center were thrown into the mix. As the mysterious negotiations dragged on for months, my supervisor told me that while there was support for the shift to faculty, it became clear that it would be better for me, my workload, and for the center to take the staff director option. And then, within a short month, it happened. My job was reclassified, and I was moved out of my home department and became director classified as staff. Just like that.

Why do I stick it out? Quite simply, this is my career, and writing center jobs are not easy to come by—particularly in my region of the country, with my educational level, and at my institution type. My work is in writing centers. My work is in educating peer tutors, studying the impact of that education, and implementing programs to enhance student literacy. Likewise, I've pursued leadership opportunities in the field's professional organizations, presented at conferences, and published with regularity. I receive no formal recognition from my institution for this commitment to the field. It is not a part of my workload or my requirements to advance. The only opportunities for advancement that I've had, in fact, are from instances like the one I described above, where I or my colleagues push for change in my position. Advancing isn't typically in the scheme of things for writing center administrators, after all.

My professional work outside my institution has helped me understand that most of us in writing centers are in contingent positions and writing centers themselves are often contingent spaces that are subject to elimination or restructuring within the institution on a whim.

According to the Writing Centers Research Project, which has run sporadically since 2001, about 60 percent of those who work as administrators in writing centers hold contingent positions (Ervin, 2002; Denny, 2015). We've also all heard the stories of tenured writing center directors who've had their writing centers ripped out from under them or have had them moved into an institutional configuration that doesn't best fit the needs of their students, their staff, or frankly, themselves. I know of three tenured faculty writing center director colleagues who have undergone these demoralizing experiences. Two chose to retire because of them. One stuck it out but was under continual duress from a new supervisor who knew nothing of writing center work but thought it their place to force their uninformed ideas about writing center work on them.

Those are tenured faculty colleagues in contingent writing center spaces. No one is safe, despite titling or, even, tenure, from these disruptive and life-changing administrative decisions. Imagine what it is like for the 60 percent of us who hold contingent positions. We've all heard those stories too.

"Why do we put up with it?" I hear you ask. I can only answer for myself, but this is the work that I want to do and love to do. This work does change lives. This work makes better people. I have always believed that writing centers are a keen solution to one of the problems of academia and managed higher education neo-liberal spaces: the tendency to conglomerate students in some sort of misguided industrial model and "stack 'em deep" to "educate 'em cheap." Writing centers, writ large, provide students with an essential, one-to-one relationship with a tutor that the ideal composition class of even 15–20 students cannot, and the more typical composition class size of 25 plus—certainly cannot, though it pales in comparison to lecture hall classes of 300 or more students. Writing centers also provide students with the opportunity to work as peer tutors; the very same opportunity I was afforded in graduate school. The growth that I have witnessed in peer tutors over the length of my career is tangible and I document it. The same goes for the work that student writers do in our centers with those peer tutors.

As I'm entering the last decade of my career, I am still energized by the thought of coming to work every morning and working with students, tutors, staff, and faculty. I look forward to doing program reviews to understand where the center can grow, adapt, and change to meet the changing needs of students. I look forward to teaching new sets of peer tutors, and learning from them since, as Freire said, "There is, in fact, no teaching without learning" (p. 31). I also honestly am looking forward to my new/old director status having a positive impact on how the center functions at my institution. My new supervisor has already been working with me to get an assistant director in place and to increase tutors' hourly wages. I will, though, remain contingent. I will never have tenure nor faculty status.

I was going to leave you hanging with that last line, like I've been left hanging there in my career, but in the interests of the possibility of change, I'll ask the question: what can we do? First, I say we need to organize for collective action. Yes, I do mean organize as in unionize. In states like mine, where such organizing is nearly impossible—and in some states, it has been made illegal for public higher ed workers to unionize—it doesn't mean that we cannot be in touch with our colleagues working at our institutions in different departments to collectively redress problems. I'm currently working on building these across my institution. It is not necessarily easy, but I've made a few close colleagues who are willing to speak out against inequities that we see and take public action. We can also use these intra-institutional collaborations to address conditions that may block our collective advancement. Speaking out against unfair evaluation practices, for example, did catch the attention of our accreditation body, and featured highly in their report.

Next, I think our professional writing center organizations can do far more to address labor and the issues of contingency. Our writing center organizations should have clear guidance on fair labor practices for writing center workers of all types: from peer tutors to writing center professionals. Our organizations need to focus on the people who do this work, not just on how they do this work. Furthermore, scholars (and there is a growing number of them) need to explore our working conditions and provide insight. We also need to be open and willing to share our employment status with each other across the profession. For years I kept that status hidden—and I'm still doing that here in this article—but over the last ten years, I've been openly sharing my story, and some of you might even recognize me from it. That's fine. I've explained why I am not sharing my identity in print, but I still hope that this story can help us come together.

Finally, we as individual writing center workers are the ones who are going to have to do this work. I know we're overloaded already, and would rather focus on our students, staff, our centers, but we also have to focus on ourselves and our working conditions. We need to be the ones who strive for change. We do that best together.

References

Denny, H. (2015). WCRP survey all years raw data. [Paper 1]. *Purdue Writing Lab/Purdue OWL Datasets and Research Projects.* https://docs.lib.purdue.edu/writinglabsdrp/1.

Ervin, C. (2002). The writing centers research project survey results, AY 2000–2001. *Writing Lab Newsletter, 27*(1), 1–4.

Freire, P. (1998). *Pedagogy of freedom: Ethics, democracy, and civic courage* (P. Clarke, Trans). Rowman & Littlefield.

Chapter 15. Into and Out of the Tutoring Center

Anonymous

"The writing center is being moved from English to tutoring. A decision has already been made. The change will happen quickly." Hearing these words is not hard to imagine for anyone who has directed a writing center for very long. I was familiar with similar narratives playing out in the lives of my colleagues, and I was never naïve enough to assume it couldn't happen to me. We are all one key change of administration, one reorganization, one person's "vision" away from it pretty much at any time. After over twenty years of serving as my writing center's founding and sole leader, I heard these words from my own provost.

My story has a satisfying conclusion, but it is an unfortunate narrative in which too few people with too much power made uninformed decisions. It is also a story where others with power emerged to save the writing center. As I lived through the next three years of upheaval, I endured a kind of stress I had never known. Through the course of it, I proved to myself that I possessed patience, restraint, resilience, and a passion for writing centers that extended beyond any desire for self-protection.

"It's all tutoring. It goes together," was the only response I received when I asked the provost why the move was happening. There was no discussion, no reliance on my expertise, not even a request for the years of data I had collected. In the months that followed, many important decisions about how to make the writing center "fit" in the tutoring center were made without my input. The staffing structure was quickly dismantled, and the writing center was physically relocated to a low-visibility and dysfunctional space within the tutoring center. At least weekly, I tried to defend writing center pedagogy after having been told by a tutoring center administrator, "We don't do things that way."

There were two silver linings. Most of the writing center staff, due to the restructuring, got better positions with higher pay. The other was that the full-time tutor who would co-lead the area with me where the writing center was positioned became an ally and trusted confidant. When that person left, and a new person was hired, my relationship with him was equally valuable. He and I spoke the same language and understood each other's frustration with the lack of interest in understanding our pedagogy and lack of trust in allowing us to forward our vision for a successful writing center within a tutoring center.

And then the ultimate staffing change happened. I was told by the tutoring center director that my position had been eliminated. I was thanked for teaching the tutoring center staff all about writing centers and told I was no longer needed. A newly hired provost had apparently already approved my dismissal.

Even though I shouldn't have been, I was surprised. I also began to feel an odd sense of relief. I had told my English department supervisor I was going to leave the writing center more than once already. He and various others had successfully talked me out of it: "You have so much invested in this." "Please give it time." "What will become of the writing center?" And so, I held on. This time I had no choice. I had been dismissed. I still had a full-time faculty position, just without reassignment time for the writing center. "Not such a bad deal," I consoled myself.

I shared the news with the faculty union president, and she was stunned. When I said the new provost had been the one to decide, she became uneasy. This new provost, she said, would not make a rash decision without being influenced by someone who used her lack of knowledge to craft a narrative in which I became disposable. The union president made me promise that I would ask for a meeting with the provost, simply because I deserved an explanation. Though I dreaded such a meeting, I couldn't disagree.

I could not have been calmer in explaining to the provost that I respected her decision but wished to know what prompted it. In my mind, the writing center was no longer mine to lead, I had nothing to lose, and I was ready to let go. The provost listened, took notes, asked questions, and, at some point in the conversation, asked me to back up and tell her the story of the writing center from its inception through the events that had just unfolded. When I finished, she sat in silence and then said, "I have made a decision based on limited information." She apologized and asked for my patience as she rethought things. I had never experienced such humility on the part of an executive-level administrator.

A week later, we met again. The provost said I was not obligated to accept her offer but wanted me to retain my position in the writing center with the promise that she would work closely with me and the tutoring center director. She went on to say so much more than that. In fact, I took notes in that meeting that I still have on a digital sticky note. She assured me that I would have control over all kinds of changes in the writing center going forward. The digital note serves as a reminder of both the sincere good intentions of a savvy leader trying to make things right and of the spectacular fashion in which they unraveled despite her efforts.

The provost kept her word and spent hours working closely with the tutoring center director and me. It felt like we were making progress. But after the meetings, with the provost no longer present, things fell apart. I was in no way allowed to have control over the methodology or delivery of writing support. Yet, at the same time, a new power dynamic had emerged. I now had the ear of the provost to whom the director of tutoring reported. I did not hesitate to reach out time and time again when I was not able to accomplish any of the things I had written on my digital sticky note. The provost coached me, guided my efforts to communicate with the tutoring center director, and offered to meet again. But the cycle would repeat itself. In our meetings, it appeared understanding had been reached, but when I operated on that understanding, I was stopped cold by various people in the tutoring center.

I found myself quagmired and had no choice but to tread water and wait. I knew by that point that if it were to remain in the tutoring center, the writing center would ultimately be absorbed as merely an area in which tutoring for English classes took place. I also knew the provost, even with all the time she had invested, wasn't at the same point in her thinking yet. I waited, watched, did what I could, and kept talking to the provost. The library building was being renovated, and the tutoring center, along with the writing center, would be moving into it soon. A large, open room had already been carved out for the writing center in a highly visible area.

The provost invited me to tour the new space. The tutoring center director narrated as we paraded through it, ending our tour in the room that had been earmarked for the writing center. Except that suddenly, it was no longer the writing center but a multidisciplinary tutoring center, a new vision the director had just arrived at days ago. This was news to the provost, too, and not good news. It felt like another confirmation of my longstanding fear that the writing center would simply become tutoring for students in English classes, indistinguishable from tutoring in any other subject area. The provost was silent as we walked out of the meeting together, and I mirrored her silence, understanding that she needed time to think and plan her next move. Just a few days later, she made the decision to move the writing center back to the English department. A three-year ordeal had ended.

A year has passed, and we are rebuilding while enjoying a kind of recognition and support we have not had before. The three-year sacrifice, the waiting, and the labor against misunderstanding and dismissal was no small feat. The toll of exhaustion it took on me will not be forgotten, and neither will my amazement at the provost's bold decision. Though this story is not uncommon, the specifics are as unique as the institutional context in which it unfolded. In the end, I am not sure what the concrete take-away is for a reader who might face a similar ordeal. The only guidance I can offer is that the limits of your patience must be carefully considered, and so, too, the risks you are willing and able to take. My tenure at the college, along with my good reputation undergirded many of the bold moves I made. If you are not able to hang on as I did, if the strain on your health is too much to sacrifice, forgive yourself, let go, and don't look behind you.

Chapter 16. Writing Center as Life Raft: The Fracturing of the Grand Narratives of Working in Higher Education

Anonymous

There's a grand narrative to working in higher education. The narrative goes like this: finish your undergraduate degree in four years with great grades, get into a great MA and then Ph.D. program with a good TAship. Complete your MA in two years and your Ph.D. in four years. Publish articles, engage in the field, go to conferences, network. Land your dream job as an assistant professor and writing center director. Jump through the hoops of tenure and promotion, sacrificing your life to publish enough and do enough to gain tenure and be promoted. Continue to publish and do good work, and get promoted to full professor. And when you get full professor, you can really settle into your career, do interesting work, and feel completely secure.

Grand narratives have a tremendous amount of power. They shape our behavior and mindsets, and when they are shattered, they leave us shattered with them. Narratives have more power for people who are working class, who come from nothing and have nothing, and who have had to carefully learn the "rules" and how to navigate the system.

My own story looks just like that opening grand narrative. I was a model student, model academic, and a lot of it was driven by my working-class background. I felt like I had to be the best because I grew up poor and in an extremely challenged area of the country that is known to be uneducated, racist, and religious fundamentalist. I felt like I had to rise above these roots, above my own marked dialect, and above my poor country girl status by working as hard as I could to be the best. Because of this grand narrative, I believed that if I jumped through all of the hoops and invested all the work, I would be in a good position, and I could have a stable and great career. This narrative continued to hold truth for me right up until 2020. I was the faculty director of a very well-respected, endowed writing center. I was a tenured full professor and a world-famous scholar, being invited to deliver writing center conference keynote addresses, workshops, and do consultations all over the globe. As director of the writing center, I had done everything to the best of my ability: crafting annual reports leveraging institutional mission and priorities, creating data-driven and effective assessment and research, expanding our services in strategic ways, and offering effective university leadership. I was also a model faculty member, publishing multiple articles per year, having high teaching evaluations, winning teaching and research awards, landing grants, and engaging in substantial service to my university, discipline, and community.

I had given up a great deal to have that career. I had given up getting married and having children. I had given up a lot of other possibilities for travel, freedom, and to have new experiences. I felt that from the time I entered graduate school at 22 to the time I became a tenured full professor at age 38—I had put my life on hold, and my career was the only thing that had mattered. I had been satisfied with my earlier life sacrifices because the payoff should have been outstanding—a stable career and good pay, reaping the rewards of being a well-published scholar, and having a kind of financial resources and stability that, for a working-class person, is generally unheard of. I achieved tenure at my second institution and was promoted to full professor in fall 2018, about a year before the pandemic and chaos began.

And then there's the moment when everything shatters. When you realize that grand narrative is nothing but smoke and mirrors. And the foundation upon which you have built your life, made decisions, and invested your energy for almost two decades is a lie.

~~~

Like many universities, my university was already having financial difficulty and enrollment declines before the pandemic began. The pandemic put this financial emergency into overdrive and created a great deal of upheaval, made much worse by cruel and inept university leadership. This mess included restructuring the entire institution in terms of academic units and refocusing our mission. This mess also included firing about 30 percent of the university employees while our upper administration (some of the highest paid salaries in the entire state) took multiple pay raises.

It all began in April 2020. We had moved online, gotten through the beginning of the shutdown, and were proud of the hard work we had accomplished. Soon, faculty began hearing about the university's financial emergency. In May 2020, our union announced the planned 28 percent faculty cuts, with cuts happening to those who had the least seniority—that is, years employed at our university—with tenure or rank being of no consideration. Every month, the news would grow more dire. That summer was excruciating, with everyone on edge and in a constant state of fear, reading the contract carefully, attending the meetings, and trying to figure out where the cuts would happen, who was safe, and who was not. I could hardly sleep. I had to start taking medication for anxiety and depression for the first time in my life, literally drugging myself through each day to remain functional. In early October, we learned how many faculty would be cut from each department but not names, adding to the torture. Somehow, we were supposed to continue to be productive, continue to teach, and continue to administer the writing center. Finally, on November 30th, I received a letter saying that my job—as a full professor with tenure—would be terminated by May 15th, 2021. If they had given us notice and then sent termination letters in a timely fashion, it would have been one thing. But to have these termination letters span such a terribly long period of time, almost a year from start to finish, and in the middle of a global pandemic, there are really no words to describe the anguish of this experience.

As someone who has survived sexual assault and rape, I recognize that this whole experience was for me almost identical in terms of emotions and suffering: feeling violated, worthless, and numb, having my entire foundation of life in upheaval, and feeling like my world was ending. Instead of my body being violated, I had my life and career violated. And since I had given up so much for this career—including having children and a family—the experience was so much more visceral. The idea that a career could do that to you, that upper administration could do that to you, is inconceivable to me, even now as I write this almost two years removed from the experience.

During all of this, I somehow continued to be the model writing center director. In order to save money, the university was restructuring, and the college that housed both my department and the writing center was being eliminated. This meant that where the writing center would be housed, who would fund it, or even if the writing center would continue was unclear. And so, I did what needed to be done. Despite my termination letter on the table and the anguish I was facing, I crafted a careful proposal that showed how our writing center aligned with the new institutional priorities and would meet them. I learned much later that I was the only unit on campus who did so and who showed positive support for the new strategic plan, and that gained me a tremendous amount of goodwill from upper administration, which bore fruit. I reached out to a college that I thought would be an excellent long-term fit for the writing center, and the dean of that unit and I crafted a proposal to move the writing center there permanently. I did what any good writing center director would do—I engaged in strategic thinking and action and found my way through the chaos.

In the months that followed my termination letter, a colleague stepped up to retire early and save my position. I was filled with gratitude and relief. The writing center, through my strategic work, was placed in the best possible circumstances in a new unit that would help us meet our many objectives with the financial and moral support to do so. In the time since then, the writing center has moved into the forefront of our new strategic plan as a model, and has gained a new space, new funding, and new stability. Crisis averted.

But everything is not fine. I still have the trauma of this violation embedded deeply within me. Trauma that makes me wonder if I can stay in this career or ever be happy in it again. Trauma that makes me question how I will heal from this experience and who I will be when I do. Trauma that makes me internally shudder every time a student says to me that they want to go into higher education and become a writing center director. Trauma that brings me to tears almost every time I drive to campus.

As I write this, my university continues to be in upheaval, and my department is faced with a tremendous amount of pressure surrounding our inability to deliver courses without adequate faculty, raising course caps on writing courses to some of the highest in the nation, and considerable bullying by upper administration. After the trauma of the termination letters, I feel numb in the face of this new upheaval. What more can be done to us that hasn't already been done?

And yet, I find myself retreating and focusing on the place I can control and which is positive—the writing center. As we have endured the pandemic together, I have created a haven of safety. I have worked to show every bit of compassion for my tutors and staff and the struggles they are going through. I have worked to create a kind of life raft amidst this ongoing chaos at our institution, a life raft filled with community, good food, feeling valued, and making a difference. I have worked to treat my staff in ways I wish I could be treated. And perhaps that will get all of us through.

What is a writing center? Who is a writing center director? What is the work that we do? If you had asked me these questions in the "before times," I would have given you a very different answer, rooted in the grand narrative of higher education and in my own success in the field. I recognize that I am no longer that perfect scholar; I don't even know who I am any longer. I don't have an easy end to this narrative. I don't have any grand lessons or advice to give. All I can say is that higher education is changing, and for those of us who choose to endure, we all need to find some life rafts to hold onto. May the writing center be yours.

Chapter 17. Counterstory: Ignored Labor with a Writing Center

Lan Wang-Hiles
WEST VIRGINIA STATE UNIVERSITY

This is a writing center (WC) labor story. I am neither a writing center director nor a peer tutor at my university; rather, I am an English faculty member who joined this institution in 2015 and is currently an associate professor, but I have an intersectional relationship with the writing center, as I serve as the liaison between our university writing center and the English department. I also teach the writing tutor training course. As a WC practitioner, I have published some studies about writing centers. At the university where I previously taught, I volunteered as a faculty writing tutor. During my doctoral program study, I was a writing tutor, and my dissertation focused on the topic of writing center ideology. Because of my multifaceted experiences and because I do not have direct administrative or tutoring responsibilities, I see myself as both an insider and an outsider to the WC. Different from other WC stories (e.g., Caswell at al., 2016; Giaimo, 2021), my story is a counterstory about how my labor is ignored by my university's WC administrators.

In 2017, the writing center was taken from the English department and subordinated to the Office of Retention and Student Success (ORSS); its official name became Writing Support Center (WSC), and it was supervised by a non-expert staff member. Its location also moved from inside the library to a classroom building with reduced space. Sadly, there was no official campus announcement about these changes. Students and faculty only heard about them later through word of mouth. As a new faculty member, I did not know about the changes either until one day, in early 2018, I received a phone call from a former retention specialist, asking if I would be able to conduct tutor training workshops. Recommended by my dean, I was considered an expert because of my writing center background, so I complied.

I understood the changes to the writing center because some universities locate them in student life departments, etc. Based on its utilization, a smaller space for the WC could also work. However, I believed changing the name to WSC was imprudent as *support* carried a negative connotation that reinforces the long-term stigma of a WC as a "fix-it" shop. It may mislead students and faculty. This name change, to some degree, might encourage those faculty members who do not understand the work of the WC to direct their students to visit this facility to fix writing problems. Students might be reluctant to utilize it as nobody wants to be labeled "weak" or in need of "support." What surprised me further was that it was only then that I learned that those tutors had not received any formal or informal training before they started working as tutors. They were merely recommended as strong writers by their composition instructors or even self-recommended as they needed an on-campus job.

Firmly believing that tutor training is essential for tutors and benefits writers, I immediately accepted this invitation with compensation neither offered nor requested. I carefully prepared a series of workshops, covering various topics throughout the whole semester. The workshops were well received. Because of tutors' positive feedback, I was appointed by the dean to be the liaison between the English department and the WSC. Tutors' questions regarding different issues during the workshops made me realize that there was an urgent need for a writing tutor training course. I then proposed this idea to my department. With the approval of the chair, the curriculum committee, and the Office of Academic Affairs, I planned to offer a tutor training course in the 2020 spring semester. I was excited and thinking of how to assist the WSC to better serve students through their collaboration. But events did not go in the direction I expected.

When designing the course, I shared my course syllabus with the WSC administrator for her input. I did not receive any response, which was frustrating, but not unexpected. As the liaison, I expected to work collaboratively with the administrator. For example, I suggested having a conversation about renaming the WSC. Again, I did not hear anything back. Knowing the WSC had neither a mission statement nor a webpage to communicate its purpose and service, and suffered from a declining staff and client base, I proposed two remedial plans: (1) creating a WSC webpage and posting flyers, including its mission statement, service, location, and hours, (2) allowing tutors to visit classes, especially writing classes, at the beginning of each semester to introduce the WSC. For my proposed ideas to be heard, not ignored, I purposefully shared them during the 2021 fall semester's faculty meeting. Unfortunately, my first idea was ignored, and the second was rejected immediately. The reason was "we don't want to interrupt any classes, we cannot do so!" even though I explained that a tutor's classroom visit would be brief, simply promoting the WSC's existence and allowing its service to be known. This short-sighted thinking demoralized me. But I told myself that laymen need persistent enlightenment, so I continued to persevere.

During the pandemic, many university writing centers quickly switched to online tutoring, synchronous and/or asynchronous. The WSC, however, failed to make such adjustments. Its reaction to the abruptness of COVID-imposed restrictions was to limit the number of sessions and only allow scheduled sessions, excluding walk-ins. Believing that my suggestions might be ignored as usual, I altered my approach in communicating with the WSC about the importance of online tutoring. This time, I shared my tutor training course students' research projects with my students' permission. In order to protect my students and be discreet, I purposefully removed students' names and deleted sensitive statements that pinpointed the WSC's deficiencies. In my email to the WSC and

ORSS, I applied an inquiring tone and admitted that some ideas were merely a starting point. I also expressed my hope for an open discussion to address these concerns about the WSC. Not surprisingly, I experienced the same results as before—I never heard back from anyone, not even an acknowledgement reply.

Occasionally, I received emails from the WSC administrator, addressing issues such as the arrangements of the WCS practicum for my students. The WSC administrator's emails to me, however, focused on matters pertinent to what the administrator wanted to address, such as recruiting tutors, but ignored discussing my concerns and requests. During the 2022 spring semester, when I brought my students to the WSC for their practicum, I invited the WSC administrator to meet my students. The administrator's first question was asking students' major. When finding out one student was majoring in computer science, the administrator immediately said to him "I need you, I will hire you to tutor math!" Later, I even received a follow-up email from the administrator, requesting more information about that student. This was not the only occasion where my well-trained students were redirected into other "more important" areas. I understood that the administrator supervised several centers, but I felt these interactions should focus on introducing the WSC to the prospective writing tutors.

For years, none of my initiatives were discussed, let alone accepted. I kept consoling myself that the WSC administrator's priority was to ensure that all the centers run each and every day. Yet, I felt frustrated with my wasted efforts and recognized that a positive, collegial, respectful relationship was definitely missing between us. Honestly, I lamented the fact that such an indispensable learning facility was not fully developed or even recognized, and my expertise was neither valued nor utilized. I sometimes even thought about reporting my observations to my dean so that the dean would use his power to push reforms, but I also worried that such an attempt would be viewd as further interference.

Reflecting on these administrators' behaviors toward me, I thought it might be a result of their protection of their academic fiefdoms. I even joked about myself that I am just a liaison that can be seen as an outsider in these administrators' eyes, as someone who does not understand their practices but keeps bothering them. Although my ultimate goal was to assist in improving the WSC for students, I felt alienated from any meaningful engagement with it.

My counterstory displays a writing center practitioner's labor and frustration. I want to identify the crux of such a situation and hope to seek solutions to overcome the constraints I face. Meanwhile, my alternatives are limited: I could bypass the current political structure to make independent announcements about the WSC to the student body, but this would be seen as insubordinate to my department and make me an enemy of the WSC administrator. Going to my chair, dean, or provost would risk my reputation as being pushy, and I might still have no guarantee of a response. However, not performing the little work I am allowed to do could harm students. I feel trapped by my situation with no ethical way out.

References

Caswell, N., McKinney, J. G. & Jackson, R. (2016). *The working lives of new writing center directors*. Utah State University Press.

Giaimo, G. N. (Ed.) (2021). *Wellness and care in writing center work*. Digital Edited Collections: An Imprint of WLN. https://ship.pressbooks.pub/writingcentersandwellness/.

Theme 3. Advocacy Successes

Although the prior section examined precarity, there are many ways in which writing center administrators and writing center professional staff advocate successfully for better working conditions. Advocacy—often not in the job description but absolutely necessary for a functional writing center—is perhaps the most visible and identifiable form of metalabor. One of the most important points that demands advocacy centers on tutor pay. In this section, several pieces talk about the importance of shoring up tutor pay (Whiddon's "'. . . at least for now"; Tirabassi's "Advocating for Equitable Pay"; and Anonymous' "From the Archive"). Writing center administrators are often tasked with a difficult moral calculus: every increase in tutor wages can often mean fewer tutor hours, which, in turn, results in fewer students able to access writing center resources. For Whiddon and Tirabassi, better tutor pay is critical because they both staff their centers with student labor and struggle with profound staff retention issues because of low on-campus pay for student workers. Both share ways they have advocated through collecting data on pay across the region and across the country. Tirabassi also details a collaborative campus-wide effort to organize different student learning offices to increase pay for workers. These examples of advocacy and tutor/worker-centered approaches anticipate and provide useful examples of the forms of anti-capitalism we describe at length in Act III. There is astonishingly little published research on the topic of tutor pay. These stories invite further conversation and advocacy on this topic.

In "From the Archive of a Tutor Representative's Email Correspondences (Summer 2022)," Anonymous provides a different take on advocacy related to union representation, professional tutor pay, hazard pay, and additional support for workers during the pandemic. Through everyday documents like email, Anonymous shows us how critical it is to both aggregate and share information about working conditions and union benefits and regulations. Without this kind of advocacy, workers can be adrift in the changing landscape of higher education. Even with this kind of advocacy work, however, upheaval tends to dominate the workplace. The emails not only share important information about pandemic pay; they tell the story of a director leaving their position and the writing center being moved. In this way, the union representative becomes a point of continuity in an otherwise chaotic moment in the workplace, highlighting the importance of labor organizing. Here we affirm and extend compositionist James R. Daniel's (2022) assertion that "Unions are the most effective means of securing stable faculty positions, improving salaries, defending intellectual labor, and combatting the university's privatization in ways that offer to provide contingent faculty the foothold they need in the academy" (p. 174). We feel Daniel's (2022) claim is applicable to writing center staff due to stories in this collection, such as Anthony's, which details the issues of retention of professional staff because of low pay and lack of benefits. While some workers might prefer a part-time job, as Anthony notes, this particular and perennial issue of writing center work (low pay, low stability, high turnover) deeply impacts writing center administrators, workplace morale, and continuity of service. Echoing the previous section on precarity, it is one of our greatest challenges and has few easy answers.

Training and support are also a subject of advocacy among several of the contributions to this project, echoing some of Wang-Hiles's narrative in the prior section. Imirie ("' I Have No Idea,'" this collection) and Dunsky ("Writing Fellows; Writing Students," this collection) each discuss the ethics surrounding tutor training. Whereas Imirie points out the problematic nature of assuming that a "good" writer will be a good tutor, Dunsky shows how organizations and the managed university can co-opt models that appear on the surface to be similar to writing center pedagogy but can often serve gatekeeping functions at odds with our field's best practices. Both narratives show the harm that can come to both tutors and writers through a lack of deliberation around tutor training and the kinds of work involved in taking an ethical approach to tutor training.

Finally, Keaton's "Overloaded" (this collection) examines how WCDs balance their own duties with professionalizing student tutors, with meeting the demand for sessions, and with outreach at the writing center. This labor, like so many other tasks around center work, is often fraught with implications both moral and practical.

Discussion Questions

- What are some of the challenges of hiring and retaining student workers in the writing center (especially during times when jobs are plentiful and wages are increasing)? What might we do to more fairly compensate writing center workers? Whiddon and Tirabassi share some of the actions they took in their narratives below.
- As highlighted in the previous sections, writing center administrators often face tension in balancing their writing center duties against their teaching, service, and research. Advocacy and other forms of metalabor associated with writing center administration obviously add more to this tension. Still, Whiddon's narrative demonstrates the viability of using research to fuel advocacy, and advocacy to serve as an exigence to identify gaps around labor and material conditions in the field. What other opportunities for advocacy do you see that are in need of more research?
- How do we build coalitions and organize on campus between various student support centers or spaces where student workers make up the majority of the staff? While Tirabassi shares some of her strategies in her story, try to develop additional strategies and actions that are specific to institutional context.

- An under-explored group of writing center workers—writing specialists—bring a lot to the positions they occupy in writing centers. At the same time, there are challenges in retention and hiring writing specialists. How can we create more sustainable and ethical writing specialist positions? What opportunities are there for bringing writing specialists into the writing center in ways that professionally develop them?
- Trace the different kinds of labor that Anonymous's "From the Archive of A Tutor Representative's Email Correspondences (Summer 2022)" undertakes to advocate for members of their union and, also, to push back against extractive workplace policies. What parts of the anti-capitalism framework (as we describe in Act III) are most applicable here and why?
- How do we prepare the next generation of writing center administrators for their work as on-the-ground administrators and as worker and workplace advocates? What lessons might we learn from Imirie and others who detail their on-the-job development?
- How do we frame writing center work as anti-capitalist? Is there value in doing so? And, if yes, what is the value?

Chapter 18. "... at least for now": A Story About Undergraduate Writing Centers and Labor Compensation in Five Parts

Scott Whiddon
TRANSYLVANIA UNIVERSITY

One/Context: Despite decades of evidence showcasing positive campus impact, undergraduate writing center labor is often institutionally undervalued.

Here's a story. In April 2022, I got an email from one of my tutors noting that they wouldn't be returning to their position in the fall.

Let's call this tutor Chris. Chris is an incredible young writer in multiple genres, a thoughtful listener, a campus leader, and an enthusiastic ambassador for the things that writing centers do well.

Much of our program's recent impact—especially given the challenges of the pandemic—was due to Chris' excellent and central participation: one-on-one sessions with a wide range of students, leadership in full-class workshops, programming for specific majors (almost entirely on Zoom, of course), success in a targeted writing fellows initiative, and service to students and faculty who were all in various states of exhaustion.

At the start of the pandemic, our program was busier than ever: over 1000 sessions in fall 2021, over 90 percent of patrons noting they'd recommend our services to peers, an award from our regional WC organization in early 2022, four undergraduate publications in writing center journals, and five online undergraduate presentations at conferences. In short, a lot of *labor* that serves student writers, institutional missions, and nearly everything in between at a time of worldwide crisis.

Chris sent me a kind breakup note. In the end, it was the pay: ... *given the time-to-pay ratio, I don't think it's practical for me to come back, at least for now.*

Two/Origin Story: Our writing center began in the early 1980s in an unused basement room with hand-me-down furniture and stale-smelling carpet. A place where young writers were often "sent," often with the best of faculty intentions. Our founder was a former nun and dedicated poet who thought that students needed peer-centered spaces for collaborative/creative inquiry. It's a story that's common to that generation of writing center professionals: *someone sees a need, someone finds a way to cobble together basic materials and a space, someone goes from class to class, professor to professor, talking about the value of peer mentoring and collaboration.*

One might argue that tutors such as Chris receive compensation via lifetime learning skills or career development (as shown in Hughes et al.'s 2010 survey of writing center alums). They'd likely not be aware of the complicated and politicized ecologies of writing instruction; they'd likely say—and they'd be right—that their faculty have been incredibly supportive, that their time as a tutor has been fulfilling, that their work has made them an even better thinker and communicator.

But Chris might also likely say that their labor as a tutor is more challenging than can easily be expressed to our campus community—even with visible commitments to writing culture, almost weekly accolades noted on campus websites, reports of strong student numbers and assessments for deans and vice presidents, etc. In short, praise and accomplishments don't pay for tuition.

. . . given the time-to-pay ratio, I don't think it's practical for me to come back, at least for now.

Three/Research: A few months ago, I reached out to other writing center professionals via a short, IRB-approved survey. Currently, my institution pays writing center tutors $8.20 per hour, and only for hours in which students book sessions or when we host events. Kentucky's minimum wage is $7.25.

I received 125 completed surveys.

I began with two subsets: writing centers who align with our regional affiliate, Southeastern Writing Center Association (39); and writing centers at institutions that identify as Small Liberal Arts colleges (50). If multiple pay grades were noted, I used the lowest as a baseline. I chose these two groups because they were the closest in defining my own institution. As of the time of this informal survey, there are 126 schools that are affiliated with SWCA; this includes high schools and programs outside of traditional colleges. It is more difficult to gain a specific number of colleges that identify as SLACs

Here's some of what I've learned so far concerning how institutions have not fully recognized the impactful roles that peer tutors play in sustaining college writing cultures via reasonable pay.

SWCA respondents:
- 3 percent paid less than state minimum wage/offered other incentives
- 15 percent paid their respective minimum wage
- 13 percent paid up to $1 more . . .
- 15 percent paid between $1 and $2 more . . .
- 53 percent paid more than $2 above their respective minimum wage.
- 46 percent offered increased pay based on time served, leadership roles, etc.

SLAC respondents:
- 6 percent paid less than state minimum wage/offered other incentives
- 34 percent paid their respective minimum wage

- 22 percent paid up to $1 more . . .
- 14 percent paid between $1 and $2 more . . .
- 24 percent paid more than $2 above their respective minimum wage
- 44 percent offered increased pay based on time served, leadership roles, etc.

One way to tell this story would be to highlight the differences between the upper tiers and minimum wage rates as a move toward progress, and, to be sure, colleges who offer more than a minimum hourly wage deserve commending. But this story isn't entirely fair. The SWCA sample skews high due to low state minimum wages, or lack of state minimum wage laws (defaulting to the national rate of $7.25). The most common hourly pay among SWCA-aligned respondents is $9.60/hour.

Another part of the story: the average pay among SLAC-aligned respondents is $21.00/hour. But this obfuscates things as well, due to wage differences between centers in Northeast and Southern states. The most common hourly rate for SLAC-aligned respondents is $7.25/hour.

Another way to tell this story: just under ½ of SWCA and SLAC-aligned respondents offer any sort of pay raise for time served as tutors, skills developed, certifications, etc.

If this story was for a different audience, I'd start rattling off all the ways that *tutors like Chris support peers, faculty, their college, etc.* I'd note mentoring roles that *enhance liberal arts aims* and that play into *retention efforts*.

But these are stories that we've told for *decades* as a field.

Four/Research Redux: Respondents in both groups frequently noted their attempts to tell their own stories to other stakeholders:

> I have tried to increase the undergraduate peer tutor hourly pay for years.

> No one seems willing to address the inequities in student pay.

> Administration said I can pay higher wages, but the consultants will get the same total amount.

Other respondents included frustrations concerning their inability to employ tutors working remotely/out-of-state at the beginning of the pandemic; how increased usage and/or moves toward pay equity led to overextended budgets. About ½ of each group of respondents noted that there were on-campus jobs that paid *more* than their respective writing support programming.

> . . . *the pay rate has drastically affected our ability to recruit and train tutors. We would, in a typical year, receive 50–70 applications for 20 slots. This year we received 26 (pay, of course, is not the only factor at work, but it certainly has affected recruitment across the board).*

> *We've had tutors request fewer hours to avoid burnout.*

The stories shared by these and other respondents get even further complicated if they are only allowed to recruit from certain groups of students (such as those eligible for federal work-study), or when a campus requires the same rate for all student labor, regardless of skills required.

Which leads us back to Chris: . . . *given the time-to-pay ratio, I don't think it's practical for me to come back, at least for now.*

Five/Coda: In reflecting on Chris' story and on the work that peer tutors do, I'm reminded that campus labor conditions are shaped by a complicated web of institutional forces. I hope that as a field, we can consider the question of what such work is actually worth—and how the worth of such work might be made more visible, even if such efforts seem somewhat futile at times.

But to dig a bit further, it seems that some of the most common stories I find myself telling—of deep educational experiences, of resume lines, of the sincere joy that often occurs in peer tutoring spaces—might somehow impede conversations concerning equitable pay for nuanced, skilled labor. In other words, there seems to be an underlying implication that community involvement and personal development are reasonable forms of compensation.

Such compensation is significant, absolutely. But that's hardly the whole story.

I hope our field can craft different stories—ones that avoid implying that *we only want folks who can afford such wages* to apply for positions, that show Chris' *time-to-pay ratio* as institutionally meaningful, that highlight how *almost every aspect of my university's mission can be connected back to skilled peer collaboration.* Such stories might more fully recognize our students' significant economic concerns, as well as the value of collaborative learning in the liberal arts.

Postscript: All data concerning pay scales—at my own institution, and at others—might have changed significantly since this initial study. However, given conversations with writing center professionals since this study began, and given my time in this field for over two decades, I argue that conversations about labor and pay scale for undergraduate peer writing consultants are still incredibly important as part of the larger conversation concerning student support.

References

Hughes, B., Gillespie, P. & Kail, H. (2010). What they take with them: Findings from the Peer Writing Tutor Alumni Research Project. *The Writing Center Journal,* 30(2), 12–46. http://www.jstor.org/stable/43442343.

Chapter 19. Advocating for Equitable Tutor Pay with Campus Partners

Katherine E. Tirabassi
KEENE STATE COLLEGE

When I started as the Center for Research & Writing director at Keene State College (KSC)—a small public liberal arts college in Southwestern NH—most of my tutoring staff had a second job off-campus "to pay the bills." The tutors, all undergraduates, often said that if they could pick one job, they would choose the center because they loved tutoring, and because the center offered the most opportunities for professional development. Tutoring is the primary focus of the center, but because professional development is an ongoing part of our work together as a staff, the center's administrative team included it in the job description students read during the training course they take before becoming a tutor. We emphasize to our tutors that time they spend engaging in professional development is always compensated time; we also make this case to college administrators, noting that to remain a relevant, dynamic, and responsive center, we need to build in time (and money) for our tutors to learn together, to come to common understandings about the mission, purpose, and nature of the work that we do, and to develop a vision (and become equipped) for what we hope to do in the future.

In talking with college administrators about the center, I often highlight the importance of investing in tutors' professional development *long-term*, noting that the depth of knowledge that tutors develop over time is not easily replaced and should be acknowledged through equitable and fair compensation. Rebecca Brittenham (2017) states that "in the current language of academic success—'retention,' 'time to degree,' and (most ironically) 'workplace readiness'—the multidimensional realities of students' actual work experiences are often rendered invisible or obscured through a narrative of interference" (p. 527). This narrative of interference, she says, implies that work interferes with students' ability to concentrate fully on their academics. Yet, Brittenham cites studies illustrating that "students working significant hours per week achieve higher GPAs and have greater academic engagement than their nonworking counterparts" (2017, p. 527), something I've found to be true of tutors in my center. Of course, students are not more successful in their academics *because* they work many hours; it's more likely that students gain skills and strategies through their work experiences that they apply in their academic pursuits, a reciprocal relationship that the narrative of interference misses. Although it arises from a concern about students' welfare, the narrative of interference privileges academic study over working, rather than acknowledging that both pursuits can be valuable, and even mutually beneficial, for students.

While Brittenham (2017) focuses on off-campus jobs, the language used to describe on-campus jobs often reflects a narrative of interference. Although the KSC student employment policy limits on-campus jobs to 20 hours/week, most KSC students work more than that in off-campus jobs. The student employment website states that students who work on campus, whether through work-study or other funding sources, "are expected to budget these earnings for education expenses." This policy, however, does not account for the economic realities of our students (and is not typically enforced). As center director, I heard my tutors' concerns about the rising costs they lived with daily—college loans, textbooks, rent, utilities, or food. Tutors secured employment off-campus because on-campus hourly rates and the 20-hour work week were not sufficient to sustain them financially. Additionally, the 20-hour limit meant that tutors working on-campus elsewhere had to split the 20 hours across all campus jobs. Over time, more tutors reduced their hours or quit working at the center due to better pay options off-campus.

Alarmed by this growing trend, I contacted the directors of our math center and Aspire (TRIO) Programs, and they, too, had several tutors reducing their hours or leaving in search of a more livable wage. In 2018, KSC's student hourly rates were set to the federal minimum wage, $7.25/hour, and capped at $8/hour, far below rates that students could get off-campus. The directors agreed to research tutor pay rates at peer institutions and at the other University System of New Hampshire's (USNH) academic support programs; this research revealed that tutor pay rates at other schools ranged between $0.60 to $3.60/hour higher than KSC, and that peer institutions in other states were paying tutors between $3-$8/hour more than KSC. Given this information, we appealed to the provost, proposing an institutional investment in peer tutoring.

Our proposal included six components:

1. Comparative data from USNH and peer institutions
2. Evidence that academic support units are essential to institutional retention efforts, including fall 2019 combined usage data indicating that 1:5 students (1:3 first-year students) accessed 1 or more of our services.
3. Evidence that the tutor attrition trend was due to low pay rates.
4. Tutors' job descriptions, illustrating that peer tutors are highly qualified, and meet a range of requirements prior to being hired.
5. Evidence of significant investment in tutor recruitment and training each year (ex. 3 support services employed 102 tutors in spring/fall 2019).
6. A cost analysis and implementation strategy for tutor pay increases.

Our cost analysis incorporated a phased approach, with incremental pay rate increases between $9–11/hour over three years to allow the institution to plan for the increases. While $11/hour is lower than the average off-campus hourly rate, we hoped that this incremental approach would result in pay rate increases for tutors. To sustain pay increases and maintain our current level of staffing and services, we calculated gradual increases to our student labor budgets, which for the center meant an annual increase of $2000-$3000 per year across a three-year time span, and for all units, $20,000–30,000 across three years—a fairly minimal institutional investment with implications for increased student success and retention, and recognition of the importance of compensating tutor expertise. The good news is that our proposal was successful, not only for our tutors, but *for all KSC student workers*; in the 2020 summer semester, the Cabinet decided that all student workers should have a base pay of $8/hour, with potential increases up to $12/hour. However, this success comes with a cautionary tale.

The outgoing provost had agreed to pay increases, but institutional cuts meant that the center's student labor budget was cut for the first time since I had become director. In 2020–21, the center absorbed the cuts because our services were entirely online due to COVID-19 restrictions. But in 2021–2022, with the return to in-person *and* online tutoring, these cuts meant that we had to reduce our hours and services to students, faculty and staff, which, ultimately, ended up defeating the purpose of our original proposal. Although we could pay tutors more/hour, we had to offer fewer hours overall, erasing the benefits tutors might have otherwise received from the pay increase. As a result, tutors sought off-campus jobs once again. To address this issue, we considered reducing staff sizes in future hiring cycles, but we hoped to make the case to the new provost that the administration should support investing in our tutors' expertise and professional development. In our annual report, we explained that the budget reduction resulted in a reduction of hours/services and that, with a fairly new tutoring staff, we would need to prioritize essential tutor training, which would mean reducing "direct service hours to students and limiting in-class workshops and outreach activities."

Thankfully, this cautionary tale has a happy epilogue. The administration agreed with our concerns and increased the student labor budget, though not to the amounts we'd requested in the original proposal. We've still had to make choices about what we can and can't do, including limiting campus outreach, tutoring hours, and whole staff training meetings during the semester. For our training meetings, we've prioritized community building and professional development during the meetings that we do have. Professional development continues in other ways, through session debriefs, daily conversations, book club meetings, and event planning, and center-based research.

In making the case for equitable compensation for tutors, we've learned that, for our institution, coalition building was the best approach to achieve the result we were hoping for. The work we did together, to share usage data, research tutor pay among peer institutions and the university system provided a united and stronger voice than one writing center leadership team could offer. The college administration took note, not only for tutors, but for student workers at the college overall. Our collaboration reminded us to work together more to support students' academic pursuits, including co-hosting weekly events together and offering collaborative tutor training. With regard to tutor pay, more needs to be done, and I wonder how to make progress as our institution deals with pandemic costs, enrollment declines, and ongoing budget cuts. My hope is that continued coalition-building across campus will help us to envision a sustainable future for our tutors; collaboration may mean compromise and re-thinking our work in terms of new, possibly innovative structures. The center's administrative team will, I know, continue to advocate for tutors on our campus, and, hopefully, to create conversations among like-minded administrators more broadly in the future.

References

Brittenham, R. (2017). The interference narrative and the real value of student work. *College Composition and Communication, 68*(3), 526.

Chapter 20. Benefits and Drawbacks of Hiring Professional Academic Tutors

Libby Anthony
University of Cincinnati Blue Ash

I used to have some strong and misguided opinions about who should be hired as tutors in writing centers. I used to think peer tutors were the most relatable—and therefore most effective—types of tutors, and professional tutors would be too authoritarian or too "sage on the stage" to relate to students. And it turns out that I was right—there are challenges with professional tutors. They're just not the ones I thought.

Let me back up. I'm the faculty director of a writing center at an open-access, two-year college within a research university. Our center has four 80 percent FTE professional academic tutors and one manager who also tutors for 16–20 hours per week. We don't currently have any peer tutors. Before I started working at my college in the fall of 2014, the only experience I had with writing centers was those with undergraduate and graduate student peer tutors. I myself was a peer tutor. I knew that some writing centers used contingent and/or full-time faculty to tutor students, but I figured there weren't many professional tutors out there, and if there were, the writing centers they worked in probably lacked the collaborative spirit that peer tutors bring with them to their work.

Like I said: strong (misguided) opinions.

Once I started working at my college as a faculty member (not yet as director of the writing center), I quickly realized how wrong my snobbery was. After my composition students visited the center, they came back with thorough, in-depth, and engaged feedback from the tutors. The center's director went on sabbatical, and I filled in for him during the 2018–2019 academic year, so I spent the spring of 2018 shadowing him to prepare for the role. That's when I really began to understand some of the profound skills professional tutors bring with them to their work. When the previous director's term ended in the summer of 2020, I took over and I've been the faculty director since. That means I've had the opportunity to witness first-hand the benefits of having professional tutors. While these qualities are not necessarily exclusive to professional tutors—many peer tutors also have many of these attributes—I do find them especially striking in our professional tutors.

First there's the obvious: professional tutors are highly knowledgeable about and experienced with writing. We hire extremely qualified people who are passionate about writing and talking to students about writing. Of our four current tutors, three have master's degrees, one has a Ph.D., and our manager also has a Ph.D. (the educational requirement for the tutor position is a bachelor's degree in

English or a related field). All of them have prior teaching experience, and some have also tutored in other places. They've written books and articles and have presented at professional conferences. They are eager to engage in professional development—we've read and discussed many books and articles together—and they have an interest in engaging with the college and university. For example, they participate in the college's faculty and staff learning communities, they've collaborated on projects with staff units throughout the college like the Library and Accessibility Resources, they've served on search committees for other staff positions, and one even was elected the chair of the staff representative council at the college. And in addition to being highly qualified, tutoring over 30 hours per week means that the tutors become very, very good at their jobs. They are professional people who bring with them a variety of educational backgrounds and life experiences. They integrate those experiences into their tutoring, and they do it in a way that is collaborative, holistic, engaging and welcoming to students.

But having professional tutors does have some drawbacks. As I mentioned, we have high expectations and requirements for their qualifications, but the pay is low. The current approximate pay range we list in our job ads for our professional tutors is $16.00-$17.16 per hour. The pay scale is set by the university, and it applies to other professional tutors in other support labs as well. I should say that this isn't necessarily part of the typical "writing centers are underfunded" issue, but rather a labor issue related to staffing at universities writ large. Many staff don't get paid enough at institutions of higher education, so this is not a problem unique to our tutors. As a director, this means it can be challenging to hire and retain qualified individuals who are willing to take the low hourly wage. We've extended interviews and job offers to tutors in the past who have turned them down and cited the low pay as the reason, so we've started to list the pay range directly in our job ad. This has understandably limited our applicant pool. The pay range also means that I often find myself in the position of trying to advocate for pay raises for our tutors while coming up against institutional constraints.

The low pay also leads many professional tutors to be on the hunt for new jobs. While the position is a good fit for some people—for example, those who have partners or parents who can help support them, people who want to partake in the tuition remission program, or even retirees—it's not a financially sustainable job for most of the people who apply. We are currently fully staffed with four tutors and one manager. With such a small staff, when people quit, it's a big deal for two chief reasons: 1) a smaller staff means we can't accommodate as many appointments, and it also overburdens the remaining tutors, and 2) the staff hiring process is quite lengthy, usually taking multiple months. And this doesn't count the time spent by the manager, myself, and the tutors to help onboard the new hires to prepare them to begin tutoring. These unsustainable hiring practices make all of our work lives more complicated and frustrating and can take energy away that should be devoted to the core of our work: tutoring and teaching students.

And this problem doesn't just affect our professional lives; this type of turnover and overwork can result in physical and mental health repercussions as well. Here's an example of how this can play out: in fall 2018, when I was filling in for the faculty director, two tutors resigned before November. That meant, going into the busiest part of the semester, to serve a population of around 5,000 students, we had two tutors and one manager. The process to hire new tutors took around three months. Understandably, during this time, our two remaining tutors and our manager were exhausted and overworked over winter break. I got shingles, which my doctor attributed to stress. While I appreciate that many workplaces—mine included—have begun wellness programs for their employees to deal with the physical and mental health effects of these types of working conditions, it sometimes seems like treating the symptoms rather than dealing with the root cause of the problem.

So what is there to be done? Frankly, I'm not yet sure. In addition to the pay scale, the university also sets the position's required education (Bachelor's degree in English or related field) and required experience (at least one year of teaching or tutoring experience), so those can't be changed. But perhaps adjusting the job description—or even the job itself—to make it less demanding could start to bring some parity between the position and its pay. However, I worry that changing the job description could make it harder to find qualified people. And that would, in turn, put more pressure on the manager and me to train the new hires. Hiring peer tutors could also help, but again, that doesn't really solve the compensation problem with our current tutors. It's tough to hire people in good faith when I know that they might not be adequately compensated for their talents and hard work.

Despite these challenges—or maybe in part because of them—my time directing the writing center makes me want to bring attention to the excellent work professional tutors are doing in writing centers; working with professional tutors encourages me to be a better teacher and researcher. My experience has made me think a lot about how important it is to highlight how complex and varied writing center staffing and labor can be. It has also made me think a lot about expertise and the ways we reward it—or fail to. And I've thought a lot about the work and emotional labor directors and managers have to do to advocate for people whose livelihoods depend on it.

References

Peck, K. F., Tyson, L. N., Gomez, A. & Dambruch, S. (2021). Professional tutors, shifting identities: Narratives from the center. In M. S. Jewell & J. Cheatle (Eds.), *Redefining roles: The professional, faculty, and graduate consultant's guide to writing centers* (pp. 71–85). Utah State University Press.

Chapter 21. From the Archive of a Tutor Representative's Email Correspondences (Summer 2022)

Anonymous

For many years, the administration of a small, private liberal arts college in the Northeast fought to deny contingent workers' right to union representation. Fortunately, in 2010, the contingent workers won the right to establish ABC, a local union that includes adjunct professors and other instructional staff such as tutors. SR, who has worked as a professional writing tutor since fall 2007, has volunteered for the (unpaid) position of tutor representative (2010-present). She advocates for better wages and working conditions for professional math and writing tutors in the college's academic support and tutoring center. Since she cannot interact with most of her fellow tutors in person on a regular basis due to the working conditions of contingent labor (especially since the onset of the COVID-19 pandemic), she relies on email correspondences to communicate with them. Although there was no tutoring in the summer, she had to cope with the extraordinary challenges when the tutor coordinator abruptly announced leaving his position, and the center was relocated to a smaller space.

The following excerpts are from SR's email correspondences with tutors and the union president. Although these excerpts have been edited to protect the confidentiality of certain stakeholders, the integrity of the content remains intact. While *** represents content that was deleted, information in square brackets [ ] was added to provide the necessary context to facilitate readers' comprehension. Readers reviewing this information can gain an insider's glimpse of the complexity of her role.

***

June 13, 2022: Union Update: Medical Assistance Fund (MAF) Reimbursement, Additional 5 percent Compensation for Online Tutoring, and Adjunct Professional Development Fund

>CC: XYZ Secretary and ABC President
>
>Dear Tutors,
>
>I hope this email finds you well. Below are several important items for you to review:
>
>(1) Please review this very urgent message from the secretary of our sister union XYZ, which represents staff employees at the college. She helps facilitate the application for the Medical Assistance Fund (MAF), a vital, shared resource for both

unions. Her email is in the CC if you have questions regarding MAF reimbursement:

***

[MAF is a pool of money that the college had agreed to establish after collective bargaining with ABC and XYZ, which means that the amount allocated for MAF may be negotiated with each contract. Part-time employees who belong to ABC or XYZ that are not eligible for health insurance coverage from the college due to their limited hours of employment may apply to MAF annually to receive reimbursement for their out-of-pocket medical expenses.

Every year around April, Human Resources (HR) sends the XYZ Secretary the application, which she subsequently distributes through a mass email. Applicants must complete the forms, attach their receipts, and send the entire package to the external contractor that administers the fund on the behalf of the college by the stated deadline. Applicants are given about a three week period from when the application is made available to complete this process.

The external contractor must review all applications and calculate the amount of each eligible applicant's reimbursement. The percentage of an individual's reimbursement is dependent on the number of eligible applicants and their total qualifying expenses each year. This mechanism ensures that all eligible applicants receive at least some percentage of their requested reimbursement. Usually, around the middle or end of May the funds are distributed, but this year, for whatever reason, the funds had not been distributed yet.

The XYZ Secretary had been anxiously waiting to hear from HR to determine when the funds would be deposited in applicants' paychecks. She finally obtained the list from HR with the amount of each applicant's reimbursement. She is planning to email the individuals on the list along with "a final e-blast" to ensure that all applicants receive news from her. If an applicant does not receive an email from her, that individual should contact her immediately. She provides an estimated time frame of when applicants should expect to receive the reimbursements in their paychecks. She also notes that these benefits are tax deductible.]

If you are approved for MAF reimbursement, you should see "Medical Reimbursement Account" (MRA) noted in your pay stub along with the amount you are approved for.

(2) I reached out to HR about the additional 5 percent compensation for online tutoring. HR reassured me that Payroll has received the list of each tutor's cumulative online hours from the tutor coordinator. As a result, if you performed any online tutoring in spring 2022, you can expect to receive retroactive pay for that work in your paycheck. However, HR has not heard from payroll about the exact pay cycle yet. The next two pay dates are 06/23/2022 and 07/07/2022. You can check

on the college's electronic payroll system then to see if you have received it.

[In response to the drastic demand for online work due to the pandemic, ABC union negotiated the additional 5 percent payment for online work in the new contract to compensate members for using their own equipment at home. SR discovered through a tutor's complaint that a few tutors who did work online during the winter intersession when the center was closed did not receive their retroactive 3 percent raises. As a result, she contacted HR to ensure that tutors would be paid the new hourly rate along with the additional 5 percent for online work and then followed up with tutors].

> (3) If you are engaging in any professional development related activities such as attending conferences and/or conducting research, you can apply for reimbursement of your expenses through the adjunct professional development fund. The guidelines and form are in the attachment for you to review carefully. After you have completed the form, please email the form and supporting documents to the Coordinator for Academic Affairs for processing.

[The adjunct professional development fund is a much under-utilized resource, which ABC fought for its members to have. During the lockdown period when the college was closed due to the pandemic, members could apply to the fund to receive reimbursement for technology upgrades since all operations moved online. Since SR has applied and received reimbursement from the fund to attend conferences and purchase materials, she strongly urges tutors to take full advantage of it.]

Best,
SR

June 23, 2022: Retroactive Pay for Online Tutoring

CC: Tutor Coordinator

***

[SR informs tutors that they should have received the retroactive payment for online tutoring in their paychecks today. SR thanks the tutor coordinator responsible for accurately tracking each tutor's online hours and submitting the paperwork to HR.]

June 30, 2022 Email A: Updated COVID Protocol Effective July 1, 2022

***

[SR forwards Campus Safety's message to tutors.]

June 30, 2022 Email B: Tutor Coordinator's Departure

> CC: Tutor Coordinator and Associate Vice President of Academic Affairs

***

[SR forwards the coordinator's message to tutors regarding his departure. She graciously thanks him for his invaluable fifteen years of service to the center.]

July 4, 2022: Center Update: Tutor Coordinator's Departure and Moving into New Space

> Dear ABC President,
>
> I want to provide you with a brief update on important changes affecting the center's operations.
>
> The tutor coordinator has decided to leave his position, and he will begin working in his new position at the college tomorrow 07/05/2022. He called me on 06/30/2022 to let me know personally, and he did send an email to all the tutors informing us of his decision. As a result, the Associate Vice President of Academic Affairs will oversee the center's operations including contacting tutors in regards to their fall 2022 schedules.

[Two administrative assistants from another department contacted tutors to confirm their fall 2022 schedules.]

> The center is moving to a smaller space. The tutor coordinator should have everything set up in our new (unmarked) room located across from the cafe on the first floor of the D Building. Although the tutor coordinator informed us about the move, tutors have not seen the space yet. We shall see it for the first time when we start tutoring in fall 2022.

[During the 09/09/2022 orientation meeting on Zoom, tutors found out that the start of tutoring must be delayed a week until 09/19/2022 because the new room is too small to accommodate all of the furniture from the old center. Thus, the excess furniture had to be moved out first to make room for tutoring. The Associate Vice President of Academic Affairs noted other challenges with space, which may prompt the need for increased online tutoring in the future.

The Associate Vice President of Academic Affairs has appointed the former director of the center, who now occupies a different position in the college, to graciously step in to help manage the center. However, the former director admits that she can only devote half her time to managing the center since she has not left her primary position. She hopes tutors and student workers will contact her when they encounter any problems. Everyone expects a rocky start to fall 2022.]

> Best,
> SR

Chapter 22. "I Have No Idea What I'm Doing": Why Training Is An Essential Part of Labor Conversations in Writing Centers

Olivia Imirie
WOR-WIC COMMUNITY COLLEGE

When I started tutoring in a writing center as a well-intentioned undergraduate senior, I had no idea what I was doing. Although I received a few hours of "training," this training mostly involved individual conversations with my supervisor and filling out paperwork. I was recommended by a faculty member because I was a "good writer," and the writing center coordinator generously agreed to include me as part of the team. After asking me what hours I wanted to work, she put me on the schedule, and suddenly, I was responsible for supporting writers in one-to-one tutoring sessions! Unfortunately for my clients, prior to working with them, I received no training in how to actually give feedback or talk about writing, nor did I understand how to structure a session. Rather, I relied on "good writerly intuition," a bubbly attitude, and a true enjoyment of talking with peers.

One day, I was working with a student who wanted to work on her grammar. We reviewed her paper together with me pointing out different grammatical concerns for her to fix.

"This is a run-on sentence," I said, pointing to the sentence with my pen. "You need to break this up into smaller sentences or connect them with a comma and a conjunction like 'and,' 'but,' or 'or.' This will fix the problem."

The student stared at me with a smile on her face, though she clearly didn't understand what I was talking about. I felt a bit uncomfortable but kept moving. Again, I pointed to her paper. "You need a comma here, because . . . well I don't really know why. But you need a comma here."

At this point, I felt more uncomfortable and definitely embarrassed. Why couldn't I explain this grammar rule? Did I need to? Did the student want to know how grammar worked? Did I want to waste my time explaining to her? After all, if I just told her what needed to change, we could get through a lot more of her paper in the 30 minutes that we had together.

But maybe it didn't matter. The student asked for help with grammar, and she got it. I did my job, and the student left satisfied. I think.

As I have talked to other writing tutor friends, many of their stories are similar to my own; we became tutors as undergraduates because we were told we were "good writers." But a good writer does not automatically make a good writing tutor. Thus, the training of tutors must become an essential part of the conversation about labor in writing centers.

My own experience speaks to how the myth of good writers equaling good tutors simply does not create effective tutoring practices. As an undergraduate student hired to tutor for credit, I loved writing. In fact, I still do, and I even believe I'm good at it! But as my session about grammar shows, I didn't know why something worked. I just knew when something was wrong. While I had good intentions and probably helped some students, my lack of training and knowledge about good tutoring practices made me less effective as a tutor. There's only so far that a "can-do" attitude can get you, and I quickly learned that my intuition as a writer worked great for me but not for the writers I worked with.

As I tutored more (which often felt like fumbling in the dark for a light switch), I took it upon myself to try learning more grammar rules and just get better at my job. After I graduated, I got hired on as a part-time professional tutor, and then later interviewed for another part-time tutoring position at a community college, where I was also an alum. At this new institution, I was expected to participate in mandatory staff meetings and complete a training checklist, which included being observed during a session and working with a librarian to review research in the databases. I was excited by this, especially because I was more explicitly taught how to structure a session and set expectations for my role in a tutorial. Consequently, I felt more comfortable in my tutoring work.

However, I would continue to make mistakes as a tutor. At this community college, I worked with a student who was in an English 102 class. As a former English literature major, I was thrilled to work with her and talk about her project.

"So you're reading *The House on Mango Street*? I've never read it before. What did you think of the story?" I asked, twirling my pen excitedly.

"Um . . . it was okay, I guess. Now I need to write an argument about it," she said. She looked worried about the assignment and looked down at her prompt.

"Okay. Well, what do you think the story means? Why is it important? What do you think the author wanted to tell everyone?" I could feel myself getting more and more interested, leaning forward to show my enthusiasm about her project.

To my surprise, she leaned away from me with widening eyes: "I . . . I don't know."

Oh. Well, that's a little disappointing. Maybe she needs a little more prompting. I started asking her about metaphors and personification and noticed that instead of getting more enthusiastic about the project, she just looked more overwhelmed. I stopped.

"I don't understand what you're talking about. How do I make an argument about any of this?" Though she tried to disguise it, I could hear the catch in her voice that indicated she was getting overwhelmed to the point of tears.

Oh no. I paused and took a breath. Then I said, "I'm sorry. I got a little excited and got carried away." I paused again. "Let's back up and look at the prompt together . . ."

I had good intentions here, but looking back, I feel horrible about nearly making this student cry. I had never considered that too many questions could get frustrating, since I find questions super helpful in my own writing process. Once again, my lack of awareness and knowledge kept me from being an effective tutor. I learned a few things that day. One: once again, what works for me does not always work for other writers. Two: what works in one session does not always work in another session.

I have continued my training as a writing center tutor, and now I'm able to reflect on my experiences and recognize how helpful this training would have been from the start. My continued training, which included a class on writing centers and tutoring in graduate school, taught me the importance of valuing the voice of the writer whether we look at global or local concerns in their projects. I wish I had understood what it meant to give students agency over their own work from the beginning. In both of these stories that I've shared, I took these students' projects and made them into my own. Without training and understanding how to be a tutor, I didn't consider the writer's agency and ownership of their work. I know that there are other instances in which I copyedited papers to tell students exactly what to do. How many students did I unintentionally drive away from the writing center because of my ignorance? How much damage did I actually do? While training alone does not eliminate the potential for a poor interaction between tutor and student (as demonstrated by my overly enthusiastic approach to the literature paper), it certainly better prepares the tutor to support writers.

Lack of training also hurts tutors; I felt unequipped for my job for a long time. It took a while for me to finally feel like I was supporting students in the way that writing tutors should. When tutors don't understand what their role is, they are left to make something up based on what they know about themselves as individual writers. Unfortunately, without training, tutors' knowledge about the writing process is incomplete, and they will continue to fumble in the dark.

I know that providing training takes time, energy, expertise, and funding. Certainly, even as I advocate for ongoing tutor training as an important issue in writing center research and conversation, I also want to recognize the implications of the additional labor that this training requires. Yet, without such training, tutors go into sessions just as underprepared as their writers. Tutors must have training; without training, their sessions will continue to be ineffective, and tutors are placed in an unfair position of relying on their "good writer" reputations to support students.

The labor of training is worth it. If we market writing centers as effective resources for students, then the investment in the hired tutors should reflect this.

Chapter 23. Overloaded: Balancing the Ethics of WC Administration and Student Labor

Megan Keaton
PFEIFFER UNIVERSITY

Writing center administrators (WCA) often need to come up with creative means of accomplishing all of the duties of our positions. Sometimes, duties may be offloaded to other writing center (WC) workers, such as graduate students. If we choose to offload duties, we must weigh the ethics of the responsibilities we give to those we employ. In this story, I detail the successes and struggles I experienced in asking undergraduate students to take on administrative duties and question the ethics of this kind of labor.

I am the sole administrator of my institution's writing center and a faculty member. Though I was originally hired with a 2–2 teaching load, one of my course releases was taken away in fall 2021. I scrambled to meet all of the expectations of my job with less available time. One of the ways I tried to do this was by creating positions for my staff members—undergraduates who are paid through work-study—to carry some of the responsibilities. My biggest time fillers that could be passed to undergraduates are (1) promotion and outreach and (2) scheduling needs. So, in the 2021–2022 academic year, I created two new positions: promotion specialist and staffing coordinator.

Creating these positions did take labor off of me, particularly in terms of promotion and outreach. The promotion specialist and I met for 30 minutes at the beginning of the month to decide on the events, workshops, and campaigns for that month. Beyond this meeting and the occasional check-in, I was able to be hands-off with promotion. By creating this position and filling it with a qualified student, I was able to let go of most of the promotional requirements of my job.

As I reflected on this position, I realized that in offloading some responsibilities to tutors, WCAs need to be cautious that they do not put their tutors in the same position we are in: requiring them to do more work than they have time for. In my case, I struggled with making sure the load on the promotion specialist was not too great. Because promotion can be carried out in a number of ways, a person in charge of promotion could easily get overloaded. For example, because a tutor in the writing center had multiple ideas for events and workshops in the spring, the promotion specialist planned one event or workshop every week for a month. This was on top of sending emails to the campus and maintaining our social media. This particular student is a good advocate for himself, but what about the students who are not? Because I am an authority figure—often, I am the student's employer *and* professor—students may feel they cannot tell me no. I would, therefore, be putting a student in a position to be overworked.

The staffing coordinator position helped in some ways, but not as much as I hoped. While the student who worked as the staffing coordinator was responsible and organized, there were times I still needed to step in. Particularly around midterms and finals, students became less willing to volunteer for shifts. Though some would respond to the staffing coordinator asking them to fill in, occasionally the weight of the director needed to be applied before a student was willing to substitute. At other times, no one could substitute because they all had class. During these times, it was my responsibility to decide whether to close the center during that time or otherwise figure out how to proceed. In an ironic turn of events, hiring someone to take care of staffing substitutes sometimes created more work for me. I not only needed to find a substitute or handle scheduling in other ways, but I also had the extra step of going through the staffing coordinator to find out who needed their shift filled and who had already been contacted.

For this position, I needed to consider the extent to which I should be asking an undergraduate to take on the ethics of staffing. In the fall semester, only one student regularly volunteered to fulfill substituting needs. Prior to hiring a staffing coordinator, I would personally contact other available workers so the frequent volunteer did not become overworked. Once I created the new position, I needed to decide whether this issue would be put on them. The staffing coordinator could easily feel awkward coaxing their reluctant peers to fill in as substitutes; this could be especially difficult for a student who struggles with anxiety. Additionally, the tutors may feel no pressure to say yes when they are responding to a peer. In a similar situation, I needed to decide how much responsibility would be put on the staffing coordinator to find substitutes at the last minute. There is significant stress that can come with needing to find a substitute for someone whose shift is in, say, two hours. Even more so if the staffing coordinator happens to be in class. In my position as WCA, I can get away with stepping out of a class I am teaching to find a substitute. It is unlikely a student could do the same. In the end, I decided that it would be more ethical if I took on these responsibilities. For how little the staffing coordinator was paid ($7.25/hour) and for their, frankly more important, responsibilities as a student, I could not justify putting this amount of pressure and stress on my undergraduate student.

It can be very tempting to put students in potential positions like those above. There are certainly benefits for the student; they gain experience that they can put onto their resumes, which may set them apart from other graduating students. There is a more practical reason, though: WCAs have a myriad of duties that they often do not have time to complete. Like many other WCAs, I am both an administrator and faculty member. I struggle with finding time to balance not only my administrative duties, but also my faculty and advisor requirements. The main administrative duties that I can drop without harming the operations of the WC involve helping my staff conduct and disseminate research. However, this is where much of my advising experience comes from, experience that is required for me to go up for promotion. I also often conduct and disseminate research in collaboration with my WC staff, which helps fulfill the scholarship expectations of the faculty side of my job. Dropping these administrative responsibilities may help with my director role, but it would seriously harm the faculty parts of my job. As the number of course releases I have does not equate to the time I need to effectively run all parts of the WC, handing responsibilities off to other workers can allow me time to attend to both the operations of the WC and to my faculty requirements.

As can be seen in my story, WCAs handing off administrative duties to undergraduates need to consider emotional maturity as well as financial compensation. Generally, we assume that undergraduates have less maturity than graduate students. However, some students come into college with not only work experience, but also experience of taking care of family members or other responsibilities we often assume occur later in life. Also, like my Promotional Specialist, some students have already become good advocates for themselves. So, we could potentially hire undergraduates who could emotionally handle administrative responsibilities. We would need to do the work, though, of ensuring that the students we hire are truly emotionally ready for the labor. On the other hand, even if an undergraduate student is mature enough for the position, the financial compensation needs to be enough for the stress of the duties. Graduate students in administrative positions typically have financial compensation through stipends or tuition coverages. Yet, undergraduates are infrequently offered these kinds of opportunities. As many workers in the States seek fair wages, we must ask what a fair wage for WC administration is, particularly for workers who are also balancing their undergraduate school careers.

Thinking long term, WCAs must consider what happens in the center as students fill these kinds of positions. If the student is overworked and put in unethical situations, the overall work environment is likely to suffer. If the work environment is poor, the students who come for writing help will likely feel that and stop coming. On the flip side, if a position is created that is successful and ethical, what happens when students graduate? For instance, my current Promotional Specialist is wonderful, but I will need to be aware of my expectations for a new student in that role. Each student has different strengths and interests, so WCAs need to make sure they are willing to be flexible with the specifics of the position and the students' workflow, so they are not trying to force a new student into the exact mold of the previous worker.

Theme 4. Identity and Labor

The stories in this section show us all the ways in which identity and intersectionality impact our labor and our workplace politics. Although we have reviewed much of the literature around intersectionality and the hostility to non-white, cis-het voices in writing centers, we also want to emphasize that we do not wish to cordon off these voices from the others in the collection. Here we also include white working class consciousness as well, and each of us (Genie, Dan) would likely have placed our introductory narratives in this section. In particular, we wanted a space in which to de-naturalize the ways in which whiteness and heteronormativity dominate writing center spaces. For instance, in "Writing Center Exile: Third Gender as Third Class in a Third Space," the pseudonymous Silk Jade, an international writing center worker, identifies the ways in which she occupies a third class both in her current university and in her home country. Occupying a specific (and very limited) staff category—neither faculty nor staff—she struggles with institutional stigma because of her position in the university and with prior experiences with stigma because of their gender and education level in her home country. Here, we see the real pain that is caused by fuzzy job descriptions that withhold rewards and promotions to workers. These inequities are inextricably enmeshed in gender and racial categorization.

Queerness and class are other identity markers that impact how writing center workers approach their labor and how they are treated in the workplace. In this section, Anand identifies the importance of mentorship in his career trajectory, as a queer Indian man in "Thank You for Carrying Me Through," and Ryan creates the queer mentorship and learning spaces she was denied in her own education ("Coaching Queerly," this collection). Witt ("'Fucking Up' and Listening," this collection) shares a story of how one's class background can be harmful in white-collar workspaces. Unable to connect with his boss over a misunderstanding, Witt describes feeling chastened for doing the overt labor of writing tutoring instead of the implicit labor of research. As such, he struggles to find a place in his graduate writing center. Class is an important marker of how writing center workers situate themselves vis-à-vis their labor. Giaimo ("Boundless," this collection) details the ways in which their precarious upbringing caused them to internalize all kinds of harmful values about work, including overwork and "workism." We carry so much of ourselves into our professional lives and, in many cases, we are guided by our identities as Witt so eloquently describes. But sometimes, as he also notes, we are punished for them in workspaces.

Though we write about the lack of racially diverse voices in Act I, we continue to wonder about the barriers to sharing stories around labor for people of color in writing center spaces. We hope this section will serve as an exigence for still more voices around this subject.

Discussion Questions

- "Writing Center Exile: Third Gender as Third Class in a Third Space," details how liminality—in gender identity, nationality, academic titling, and reportage—leads to different kinds of "third space" experiences: part of the university, but also apart from it. What kinds of third spaces do you occupy at work? Would you consider the writing center a third space (as distinct from work or home but still communal) or not? How do you define the writing center in your workplace ecology?
- How might specific identity markers like race, class, sexuality, disability, or nationality, contribute to your relationship to work? How does your workplace imagine your identity or who (or how) you are "supposed" to be?
- Do you feel like your identity impacts your socialization at work? For example, Witt notes not really understanding the expectations or "rules" around work and prioritization because those rules were never taught or are different for working class folks.
- As Anand notes, mentorship is—for many of us—a critical part of our academic and professional development. Who are your work models and/or mentors? How have they shaped your attitudes toward work?
- In what ways do you bring your identity into your work? For example, Ryan details bringing queerness into the writing center to increase queer visibility and to create welcoming space for student writers. Do you think identity is important to the work we do in the writing center and, if so, in what ways? What kinds of metalabor do you do to make workspaces more inclusive?
- Think about your earliest experiences with work, perhaps watching family members work, and think about what values were instilled in you around work even before you started working.
- What are your current attitudes towards work? How have those developed throughout your career?
- In what ways might "workism"—overwork that borders on a kind of religious or otherwise powerful relationship—be a cultural construct? Have you felt this? If so, in what ways does work control your life? If not, how do you find work-life balance?
- Explore your institution's workplace culture (i.e., is email limited to working hours, or not; vacation and sick time packages; professional development opportunities; staffing levels, etc.) and identify policies or strategies that are working and those that are not. What changes might you make to your workplace culture, if you could?

Chapter 24. Writing Center Exile: Third Gender as Third Class in a Third Space

Silk Jade (Pseudonymous)

My story begins as an exile from my heritage culture, where I am called a third gender. In the culture I was born and grew up in, I should not be a doctorate or Ph.D. because of my gender. The culture, which practices binary categories of gender, has labeled female Ph.D.s as the third gender which has negative valences of being odd and abnormal. The connotation of this third gender is that female Ph.D.s are too knowledgeable and professionally powerful to deserve male partners. The stigma expects female Ph.D.s to live a forlorn life. Before the cultural stigma was somewhat lifted, I fled to the US, a land without this stigma and with support for me to become a female Ph.D.

But now here in a current U.S. institution, being put in the third-class category (i.e., neither tenure-track nor non-tenure-track line) in a third space (i.e., the writing center) brings me back to why I fled. Writing centers were generated with some impossible missions—fixing students' writing products and skills, catering to larger minority populations, and countering perceived declines in literacy skills (Boquet, 1999). But they are not classrooms. They are seen as an extended academic space between academic and non-academic spaces. It is a type of third space.

I chose to be a writing center administrator with the ambition to apply my background in teaching English to speakers of other languages to training pre-service and in-service peer tutors and helping multilingual student writers. Even though teaching is the only recognized form of academic labor in my contract, more is involved in reality and expected in my annual evaluations. I mentor pre-service and in-service peer tutors and encourage them to engage in scholarship. I cheerlead them to present in conferences and guide them to submit for publications. I advise them to use their experience and reflections as data to make their agency and voice in academia. As to the tangible outcomes of such mentorship during the last four years, there have been six academic publications from the collaborations with my mentees, four of which are replicable, aggregable, and data-supported (RAD) research as advocated by Driscoll and Perdue (2014); there have also been four creative publications solely from my mentees. Thanks to such extensive interactions with student tutors, I know them more and more deeply. We inspire each other academically, professionally, and at times personally. From my end, it is an ecosystem of academic, intellectual, affectionate, and emotional labor. Such a system helps support the writing center to be progressive, inclusive, and humane and inspires student tutors to infuse positivity in their tutoring sessions for their peer writers. Peer writers understand writing and publishing as a progressive process with multiple layers of labor.

Despite the academic achievements of my mentees and myself and excellent teaching evaluations, I am still in a third class in terms of my position classification. My faculty work, no matter how outstanding it is, is in limbo when it comes to potential recognition, like faculty awards, and tenure and promotion. There is no clear pathway for professional growth for people like me who occupy third spaces (Kim, 2020). According to the National Census of Writing (Gladstein, 2017), 28 percent of the 240 WCAs were tenured or on tenure track and 24 percent of the WCAs were on non-tenure track. These two categories, though, as majority, do not represent the whole story of WCAs because many in these two categories were hired as faculty first and as WCAs second. I, unfortunately, did not belong to either of the categories. I was hired as a WCA with the job category faculty administrator, below tenure-track and non-tenure-track faculty. The category was fully absent from the institution's tenure and promotion manual. After I learned the problematic category that I was in, I started to advocate for myself by reaching out to different levels of stakeholders at the institution and seeking category transition and promotional pathways. I talked to my direct supervisor and the college equity advisor, and nothing happened, even after two years of advocacy. I emailed the college supervisor and the email was a stone to the ocean. Some diversity, equity, and inclusion leaders intervened but nothing came out. Some of the institution's top leaders know the issue of the job category and decided not to solve it. At my institution, there are 49 individuals in the database in this category among thousands of employees. In the writing center, there are two faculty administrators out of four full-time employees. I have no clue why the job category hasn't been proposed with a solution because there are either so many or so few affected employees.

And the unsolved status might have something to do with the underrepresented minority (URM) identity that many people in this position also occupy, including me. Like other individuals in this category, I don't look like the mainstream university worker and I don't have a native accent. I don't know whether I was hired because I am an URM. In other words, I am contributing to the institutional diversity in some matrix but suffering from the institutional policy that makes this job a dead-end.

The complexities of my working environment—lovely students and student employees, supportive but powerless colleagues, and institutionalized microaggressions—perpetuate my inner fight. I have been proactively seeking changes about the third-class job category for years, but with slight progress. So, what leaves me now is one of the following:

- To leave the third space to find a clear pathway for my faculty advancement, which describes me as a WCA exile.
- To leave higher education for industry, which turns me into an academic exile.

I am aware that no matter what option I choose, I passively allow the existing systematic oppression that other individuals with terminal degrees may also experience. I feel dark many times in this fight and I believe I am not the only WCA with such feelings. Can WCAs form a union or some form of organization with a collective voice for field negotiation and bargaining? Editors, contributors, and audience, please advise.

References

Boquet, E. H. (1999). "Our little secret": A history of writing centers, pre-to post-open admissions. *College Composition and Communication, 50*(3), 463–482.

Driscoll, D. L. & Perdue, S. W. (2014). RAD research as a framework for writing center inquiry: Survey and interview data on writing center administrators' beliefs about research and research practices. *The Writing Center Journal, 34*(1), 105–133. https://www.jstor.org/stable/43444149.

Gladstein, J. M. (2017). *The national census of writing.* https://writingcensus.ucsd.edu/.

Kim, Y. K. (2020). Third space, new ethnic identities, and possible selves in the imagined communities: A case of Korean heritage language speakers. *Journal of Language, Identity & Education, 22*(1), 1–17. https://doi.org/10.1080/15348458.2020.1832493.

Chapter 25. Thank You for Carrying Me Through, Thank You for Your Labor

Saurabh Anand
University of Georgia

This piece is my thank-you letter to my mentor. It also mirrors bits and pieces of my early journey as a queer writer in the English language. With this piece, I intend to communicate that writing and the motivations behind it are often subjective, as is writing mentorship. Some learn to write because they are aware of its powers, and some aren't exposed. In the latter situation, people like my mentor are the real harbingers of positive changes for people like me.

Subject: Thank you for carrying me through, thank you for your labor.

परिये Ranjit जी,

My heart rejoices to share that in fall 2022, I will begin my rhetoric and composition studies Ph.D. at the oldest U.S. public university. This news still feels like a dream. I know I couldn't have achieved this without you carrying me through. Do you remember how frustrated I was when I expressed my desire to return to academia to you after years of surviving corporate burnout and accepting myself as a gay man in India? No words can quantify my gratitude to you for being my guru. Writing became a way to answer questions related to my sexual identity. You introduced me to that kind of writing. Through exchanging long WhatsApp messages after our day jobs, you guided me on how to analyze my actions and others' reactions by picking up specific instances I was going through at my workplace as examples. Such relatable situations prompted me to notice the society around me, empathetically yet constructively. You bridged my process of peeking inside my ideologies and anointing my voice, even though it was dissent at times.

You exposed me to writing as a powerful way to be an activist. I learned that commonsense is not universal but always contextualized. You reaffirmed my gut feeling that nothing was wrong with me, though until 2018, being a gay man was a felony according to Indian law. You introduced me to Indian Queer history and connected me with local Queer activists. I happily started embracing my "frivolous" (according to many) parallel beliefs, locating opportunities, and gathering support for people like me. I started recognizing writing as my source of seeking solace, poking holes in my anguish. Thanks to you, I could begin the journey of helping myself and people like me.

I am not sure if you know this, but before meeting you, I had almost given up the hope of beginning my graduate studies. Reasons were many, be it financial constraints or upheavals in my personal life. Solutions always seemed far-fetched.

Requesting help was anxiety-inducing, which often translated into frustration. Yet, you sensed what I was capable of if given opportunities and mentorship. I remember you guided me on my writing improvement, even canceling your plans to do so.

I sometimes wonder if I'd ever be able to put a number to the things I am indebted for by your existence in my life. Should I be more grateful to you for scaffolding me to develop a better awareness of myself or prompting me to be a harbinger of liberal change or other things? I know my writing journey under your apprenticeship hasn't been a cakewalk for you. I remember how often you would be in the middle of your work, research, and (even while) doing groceries, but still you attended to my panicked calls because I'd be so anxious to put my thoughts on paper. I didn't understand the exact efforts you put in, at least as much as I should have then. But now that I tutor in the writing center, researching writers' efficacy, I acknowledge those conscientious efforts were so invaluable.

Your selfless investment in my writing development helped me mediate my visions to read, mushroom my thoughts about societal issues, and provide the ability to translate my aspirations into practice through writing. Learning those critical thinking skills proved to be life skills for me. I give back to society by replicating your mentoring style. I feel I am a better and happier person now because I could help my tutees anoint the notions that are paramount to them via the act of writing, similar to how you did. I dedicate my tutoring to your trust in me. I apologize for those panicked calls I made, and I appreciate your dedication so that I stayed focused on the visions I had for myself. Maybe I hadn't said it enough earlier, but you became that straw in the ocean, which became my driving force to build a better future for myself.

I appreciate you trusting me when I didn't know my potential: tapping resources that interested me, leading to lesser anxiety. Learning to write was a solitary process for me for most of my educational trajectory in India. I had to figure out the areas for improvement in my writing without even knowing its nitty-gritty. I was all alone, except for some empathetic but overburdened teachers in high school who would also sit with students beyond their working hours. Because of a lack of resources, I could not flourish as a writer since I hardly had anyone to turn to. As a result, writing first became frustrating and then daunting. Writing was a practice where I only restated what I had read, often something I couldn't relate to in the real world, without adding my voice to the topic.

This is why I hope you know why I took longer to invite and put your mentorship into action, because what you would ask me to do would often contradict my previous writing literacies. Do you recall, during the early days of learning about academic writing, how I was a bit taken aback when you told me to read "Shitty First Drafts" and "The Importance of Writing Badly" and instructed me to summarize and compare them? I remember calling you just after reading the titles of those readings containing words such as 'Shitty,' 'Drafts' (with an 's'), and 'Writing Badly.' I, in fact, remember the brief conversation I had with you:

Saurabh: I think I downloaded something (readings) weird.

Ranjit: What do you mean by weird?

Saurabh: One has the word "shitty" in the title, and the other is about not writing well (shitty). I am a bit confused.

Ranjit: You have the correct readings. What the authors recommend in the article may sound a bit different than what you are used to, but I want you to trust me. Perhaps we can talk about things that are conflicting to you once you have read them, but for next week's assignment, please read and compare them (smiling).

Saurabh: Oh, okay. Are you sure?

Ranjit: Yes, trust me.

Obviously, I did what you suggested, then, but please know I called because it was something I had never seen celebrated before. It was almost awkward. From a young age, I felt pressure to score the highest through the summative assessment we received on our examination papers. Trusting you illustrated a new path of assurance, support, and calmness in my writing transformation. From the bottom of my heart, I want to extend my appreciation for all these conversations with you that provided me an outlet to express my writing-related inquietudes. The writing strategies you shared to engage with the text and unravel my thoughts on readings were previously unknown to me. Such guidance helped me overcome my enigmatic and convoluted ways of writing and notice things around me to analyze broader meanings.

For example, sensing my interest in movies, I remember you once asked me to watch *Aligarh*, a biographical movie based on the life of an Indian linguist, Ramchandra Siras, and had me write a reflective piece on it. At that time, I did not quite understand why you did that, but being an English composition instructor and writing mentor, I now do. I appreciate you incorporating multimodality and my interests. You helped me notice and explore societal conflicts. I learned ways to relate and empathize with others through my writing.

Though learning to write was mostly liberating and stimulating, I'd often have moments of fear of failure, nervousness, and inhibition of my writing not being on par with other students. In those instances, you took me out for a meal/coffee, wrote me encouraging letters, or said, "*Slowly cooked food tastes better*," an Indigenous metaphor, which often proved to be encouraging for me. I often use the same metaphor while teaching, too. Thank you again. प्रणाम.

आपका शिष्य,
सौरभ आनंद

Chapter 26. Coaching Queerly: Healing in Writing Center Work

Molly Ryan
Virginia Tech

There are few things more draining than the constant cycle of coming out.

My boat, compared to the sea of academia, is still small and made even smaller by my queerness. I'm a graduate student at the gateway of my career, existing in the liminal, blank-horizon tides where the boundaries of student and professional are blurred. So often I feel adrift, unsure of my course, relying on distant stars in a midnight sky to guide me to my next port.

As I try to navigate the waves and swells, I'm disrupted by the wake of larger vessels—the monstrous, leviathan ships that demand I yield to their course. Each time one of these rogue waves rocks my boat, I brace myself: shield my face from the spray, seize a rail to hold tight, and pray I'm not thrown from my craft.

This is how it feels each time I come out in academia. I don't know if I can ride out the wave, if I'm going to be safe, if I'm going to, once again, feel the sting of saltwater in my eyes from someone's telling silence. And though I've developed a feel for the fickle water, I remain pervasively seasick.

In my first two weeks of graduate school, I encountered more of these disruptive unmoored moments than I had in years. I sat paralyzed in my department orientation, uncertain of how my identity might be received. When my cohort was pushed to define our research interests immediately, I shied away from the word queerness, instead evasively mentioning "justice rhetorics" and "minoritized student belonging."

In that first tumultuous week of adjustment, I was confronted with another unexpected ship in my path. As part of my graduate assistantship, I would work in my university writing center, which required a biography using a woefully small number of characters.

Are you going to come out to your clients? The slithering voice murmured in my ear, almost mocking me, taunting me with images of no-faced students expressing horror, disgust, and storming away. I doubted, as I so often do in the workplace, whether my identity was something I "should" share. In a heteronormative world, I have internalized the risks and pitfalls of centering my sexuality at the forefront of who I am. In academia, I've grown accustomed to peers wrinkling their noses, faculty's eyes flickering in surprise, or worse still, the positing of microaggressive statements in class surrounding queerness that I then meekly and guiltily confront by mumbling about my wife—and the resulting awkward silence from all in the room. These uncomfortable situations are just a small corner of the possible consequences of coming out, many of which are far more damaging.

The cursor blinked at me as I pondered what to write in the text box. The biography genre is inherently threatening to queer people; its unsaid expectation of authenticity and quick summary is conducive mainly to the straight experience. I had to pause, to consider if I wanted to elide my sexuality or confront it. This moment felt like a crossroads for me, a definitional moment for my fledgling journey as an academic. Either I was going to face the waves head-on, or I was going to turn for quieter waters at the cost of my own ethos.

With shaking hands, I typed what I quietly hoped to study: LGBTQ+ rhetoric and writing, to try it on. *Send a light in the dark,* said the kinder voice in my head, despite the cruel smirk from my self-doubt.

I have worked at the same institution for nearly ten years: as an undergraduate, a student affairs professional, and then a graduate student.

As an undergraduate, I made just one appointment at the writing center in four years, and only at the request of a professor for extra credit. I brought a rhetorical analysis paper that had received, at least from my fragile perspective, a woefully poor grade. I was an "A" student, and the "C" on this paper cut me deeply. At the time, I did not know that rhetoric and composition would become my greatest passion.

When I searched for a coach, I didn't see any mention of queerness. I remember the slight sink of my heart, but I wasn't surprised.

I don't remember the specifics of the appointment with the graduate student I chose, other than the rush of blood in my ears and my sweaty palms. I remember the crushing fear of offering my writing, already critiqued by my professor, to a stranger. I recall the welling in my stomach that I might have to sidestep any conversation around my identity with a quasi-peer.

The appointment didn't go badly. Instead, it was just as all my other academic experiences had been thus far: expected, unsurprising, normative. And when I recalled this feeling, I realized that perhaps there was an unrealized potential. Maybe the writing center—with a staff willing to invest the labor needed to make it so—could become a safe space for students struggling to connect to their university.

As an undergraduate, aside from my partner, I had no queer companions. I had no mentor; I had no hands to grab in the dark. I never told a peer or a professor I was a lesbian. I was never encouraged to study queer theory. I didn't even know the field existed. There were no indicators that identity should be offered, let alone celebrated. To hide was the smart and safe step, even as I was surrounded by pervasive straight expression.

So, as I waivered over the keyboard, considering deleting the research interest I'd typed, I thought of the ghost of my previous experience in this same writing center and how she didn't come back again. Instead she haunted the space, reminding me how she didn't feel like it was a place she could be herself.

I thought of how she left with confirmation that sharing writing was difficult, and she felt isolated and alone in her university.

I thought of how desperate she was for someone to understand, and no one—from her perspective—bothered to try.

I saw her standing there, black and gray backpack over her shoulders, waiting for me to make a decision: to rewrite the story or not. To face the waves or turn for smoother, though inauthentic tides.

And for her, I left the line in my biography.

To my knowledge, I was one of very few, if not the only, coach to specifically mention queer topics as a research interest in their biography. At the time, I didn't understand what would evolve from this decision: not only a bold, if not slightly unstable, healing of my self-authorship, but the agency to approach my coaching style with "queering" at the forefront.

What I observed, over time, was that my declaration seemed to draw students who were experiencing a similar sense of disillusionment, whether that was with their writing, their identity, or their experience as a student.

A moment this was particularly clear for me was when I worked with a student on a piece that they quietly confessed they were very proud of, but their instructor had reprimanded them severely. "I love to write," they said softly, "but I don't feel like I should anymore."

I spent that session with the student, not only working through the instructor's comments, but assuring them that, regardless of the situation in this classroom, I didn't want them to lose their joy in the craft. This wasn't the only example: students brought me papers on topics of queerness, taking solace in my affirmation of their work. I worked with students from all kinds of minoritized identities: they were my most consistent clients. Writing is full of labors, and too often, the traumas students carry with them are dismissed. In some ways, particularly in the stressful ethos of college, methods of care and empathy are a facet of queerness themselves. "Getting over it" and "getting through it" are too often served up. My clients often expressed to me how a kind word from me made their day or boosted their confidence to head back to class. That was kindness I did not feel as a queer undergraduate.

Of course, this role was imperfect. There were moments where I found myself slipping into old habits: when I'd introduce myself, for example, I'd say I was studying rhetoric and composition generically. My healing was imperfect, and there were students who I suspected did not appreciate my signaling—I certainly got the occasional hard look and closed-off interaction.

But in general, as I worked with my students, as we faced their traumas and celebrated their successes, as I watched my clients beam with pride as they indicated their improving assessments, as I held back tears as they told me their applications to scholarships were accepted, as I quietly grinned to myself when they told me what a wonderful professor I'd be one day. I thought of my younger self, who'd sat just a table away from my station. She'd been so lost back then, so unsure. And throughout my tenure in the writing center, she haunted me less and less.

On that final day of work, when it was time to say goodbye, she smiled at me. And I smiled back.

Chapter 27. "Fucking Up" and Listening in the Writing Center

Ryan Witt
The College of Idaho

Some years ago, I was part of a team of grad student tutors and administrators studying the literacy histories of tutors within our writing center. We interviewed research participants and met once a week to analyze data, talk about emergent themes and concepts, and discuss the research process. Even though this work was unpaid, as a research nerd and someone learning the qualitative research ropes, I was excited about this work and looked forward to our meetings. Plus, I loved working with this group of colleagues. They were bright, funny, and asked interesting questions about the data and one another.

But a problem emerged. During the upcoming spring term, our meeting time was in the middle of one of my regular shifts at the center—the same writing center directed by one of our research team members. From the director's perspective, my problem was easily solved: rather than completely re-doing my schedule, I could use our existing shift-covering protocol to have a fellow tutor cover my shift during the meetings throughout the term. This is the same protocol I needed to use, for example, when I accepted a request to visit a class to talk about the writing center during my typical shifts.

Unbeknownst to me at the time, my director wanted me to get coverage for *both* these class visits *and* our research meetings. But I didn't do that, in part because I didn't know that was the expectation. I also didn't seek coverage because of complicated feelings about getting coverage I couldn't unpack at the time—about my role in the group and what my focus should be during my regularly scheduled tutoring shifts. So, I didn't seek coverage. For weeks, I worked my normal shift in the center, popping into and out of the research meeting as needed to take a tutoring session. And when I was booked, I wouldn't be in the meeting at all.

About halfway through that term, I had a meeting with my boss, the center director. Though cordial to start, she expressed some annoyance. Despite never being explicitly told before this moment that my performance wasn't meeting expectations, despite never being explicitly told that I needed to get coverage to perform these other functions, and despite being praised by one of my experienced and respected colleagues as "one of the best tutors we have," I was told that I was fucking up.

I expressed some regret, but at the time, I wasn't sure I made a mistake. Not one big enough to warrant this reaction, anyway. Besides, surely my director could have told me all of this earlier when I had a chance to change course.

The meeting must not have been going the way the director had hoped. At one point, she said, "Why won't you just say that you fucked up?" not exactly in exasperation—more a tone of surprise or confusion. We ALL fuck up, sometimes, of course. That was her point—that if I just say that I fucked up, that I acknowledge it, we can move on.

And I could see why the director thought so. I *should* have been more proactive about finding coverage and meeting those other important demands. Besides, maybe there were some things going on with my director that I didn't see and, because of my positionality as a white, straight, cis-man, can't understand. Maybe she felt the impact of gender—the fact that, in most of their relationships, even in positions of power, women in the US are expected to apologize, "make nice," and smooth over difficulty. Perhaps she was confused and hurt because I seemed defiant when really, I was clueless. I can empathize with her more now and feel bad for letting her down.

At the same time, I'm troubled by how my administrator didn't wonder what was going on with me and didn't seem to want to identify and solve the issue. I'm troubled, too, that I wasn't made aware of these problems before this extremely consequential meeting. I lost my full assistantship and was moved to half-time, a demotion that cost me tens of thousands of dollars in benefits and wages. And, as far as I know, nothing ever came of the project we were working on—the project that brought this tension to a head. I recognize now that earlier check-ins, warnings, or feedback may have been difficult for my boss to provide. She was busy and perhaps didn't want to create conflict. Yet, I realize that this lack of communication—followed by a conflict that was life-altering for me but perhaps not so much for her—had serious impacts that I feel to this day.

Looking back, I can explain myself and my actions a bit better. It's taken years of processing and some reading about how students like myself with working class backgrounds experience and respond to the norms in higher education to unpack what was going on. I write this to help explain what sometimes can't be connected in the moment: the murky soup of our past experiences, our miscommunications, and the mistakes that good, genuine, well-meaning people make. I believe my director was a genuine, well-meaning person, and I did my best to be a good-faith actor, too. But I was also never explicitly taught how to prioritize work duties for this center or for academic work more broadly, or how to seek guidance, useful feedback, and clarification from my boss. My class background and gender helped make me oblivious to these possibilities.

I write all of this to create space for grace and to offer a suggestion: maybe our judgments of employees and mentees—finding them either lacking or sufficient to the task—are raced, gendered, and classed. Maybe what we see when we judge our consultants, tutors, and colleagues is the extent to which they are privileged, particularly as that privilege relates to the norms, conventions, and power operant in academia. It's much easier to get along and get ahead when you arrive knowing, say, that constantly checking in with your bosses is expected and not "ass kissing" as I thought it was. My cluelessness to these norms probably played a significant role in what happened.

I struggled in this situation, too, because of my incomplete understanding about the purpose of my work at the center and the work of the center itself. *I thought that my main job was tutoring fellow students.* It turned out that outreach and connection-making were highly prized in this center. Indeed, these kinds of outward-facing events and activities—where less-visible academic support services like writing tutoring take center stage for a few minutes in a few classes every semester—were politically important enough to be worth the resources and hassle. This was unimaginable to me then. And because no one bothered to explain the high relative value of these events, I dismissed them, believing that by tutoring students, I was doing the *real*, most important work of the center—an understanding I see now was woefully incomplete.

Compounding this cluelessness was a persistent case of imposter syndrome. Because my boss knew the meeting was held during my shift and didn't change my schedule, I presumed this was a message: I wasn't needed or wanted in this meeting. This wasn't true, but without an avenue to talk with my director and process these negative feelings, my harmful presumptions festered. Unbeknownst to her, other parts of my grad student life were also sending me the message that I didn't belong: maliciously competitive classmates, other recurring meetings scheduled (in my anxiety-wrought mind) deliberately when I couldn't attend. And my working-class background prepared me poorly to advocate for myself. It was going above my station to tell bosses—in this case, the faculty and staff leaders of a committee on which I was the student representative—to accommodate my needs.

I recognize now there was plenty I could have done to smooth this out for everyone. I could have worked on my anxiety and checked in with my director more frequently, even if I thought everything was fine. I could have asked more questions about my full-time-tutor role and made sure I prioritized job duties correctly. And, now, as a writing center director myself, I know I'll need to be curious—to ask questions of those not performing as I believe they should and provide support. But I also worry about how I will make my *own* tacit rules and expectations clear to my first-generation, BIPOC, working class, and/or international-origin tutors. The cluelessness I describe above is a relatively small tip of what might be a much larger iceberg for so many of our tutors. I wonder, given the challenges I faced, how I can explain all of these powerful but quietly operant assumptions to them, better preparing them for academia than I was.

Chapter 28. Boundless

Genie Nicole Giaimo
Hofstra University

I was a young teenager when my father fell off a roof and broke several ribs. He was a construction worker who did not have insurance or paid time off. He worked "under the table" which, to a child only just entering adulthood felt mysterious and powerful. His money didn't go to "the man" or to taxes that never really covered things in our underserved part of the city. It went right into his pocket, and, as he told me, he wanted it this way since the day he left high school to start work.

What I didn't realize at the time was how precarious he was in his labor. Reliant on his body to do punishing construction work (like roofing), even a few days off the job could mean an emergency for our family. A few days after his fall, he was back at the job site, bandaged and medicated—but not through any effort or expense from our official healthcare system.

My parents didn't usually fight, but I remember vividly my mother's pleading and then insisting that he take more time off and go to the doctor. My father, ever suspicious of institutions, said he already knew what was wrong. And in his words, what were they going to do anyway? Money earned with his kind of sweat and blood wasn't easily parted with.

My father died at the age of 41 at the entrance of a construction supply store. His enlarged heart seized, and he was dead before an ambulance was even called.

While his fall off the roof had little to do with his death a few years later, I have always seen these two events as intertwined—perhaps because both times, the owner of the construction company called and offered "under the table" payment for his, and later our, silence. No official records. No worker's comp. No life insurance. No long-term support.

Even in a city with some of the most powerful unions in the world, my father managed to fly under the radar of so many official worker-related programs for his short adult life. And while he often talked about preferring it that way, I now think that perhaps he didn't see any other way forward. He dropped out of high school. He had financial difficulties most of his adult life. He was always one cash wad away from defaulting.

Under circumstances like that, it is hard not to think that he was mostly just focused on moving forward and making it to the next paycheck. When you have so little and work so hard, what else can you do?

The men (and even many of the women) in my family die young, often in their 40s and 50s. And, almost always, they die while working. Again, as a child, this seemed normal to me. But, as the first person in my family to go to college, I soon realized that there are many people out there who are blessed with long life and fewer health issues than my relatives.

I am sure here I can offer a platitude about how "work kills" blue-collar workers but, again, this all goes much deeper for me. I have not only seen how work kills but also how people live only to work. They miss track meets, parties, and weekends with family. They refrain from taking sick time (even if it is offered) or allowing their children to call in sick from school. They center everything around their jobs to the point where work subsumes both the joyous occasions and the emergencies.

Even when they are in mourning or violently ill, they work.

This is the lived reality of what I grew up with and this is likely why I have my own very toxic relationship with work. I am not sure if the factory model of writing center work is what initially appealed to my blue-collar roots—serving people, moving staff around, opening and closing sites, expanding services, cleaning, sorting, prepping, recording, doing more more more. In this sense, "counting beans" is a toxic analog to Fordist visions of labor: more cars assembled, more sprockets sorted, more burgers served than any other [enter institution here]. The neoliberal university thrives on such figurations of work because we are always expected to do more with less.

Unlike some colleagues who write with surprise at all the emotional (and often physical) labor they take on in writing centers, I never felt surprised when I was expected to expand the conception of my job outward. Crouched on the floor assembling desks felt as natural to me as comforting a student whose parent died unexpectedly. This is because the bounds of work in my family were limitless. We didn't have job descriptions to guide us. This is another intentional element of precarious work: no clear boundaries.

Unlearning these deep cognitive and behavioral structures is hard. I hesitate to compare it to anything else (how many false comparisons do we make between different kinds of suffering?) but I want to contextualize this because perhaps we all have these unhealthy relationships to our work but we've never thought of them in this way.

Work is an addiction.

Work is a compulsion.

Work is a cult.

Work is a companion.

Work is a kidnapper.

Without understanding and personifying (but not individualizing) work, we fail to understand how deep these structures reach inside us and impact how we behave. Work can make us do irrational things like sacrifice our bodies and our families. It can also give us a kind of meaning and emotional high found in a few other things (at least from what I have experienced).

Work, in other words, is complicated.

In trying to contextualize how I was socialized into work, I want to talk about how my family (and I) talked about work. Work was immutable. All other deadlines, priorities, and needs took a backseat to it. Life was centered on work because life was centered on money. This was not about greed but about survival.

I came into my first academic job with this mentality: work is survival. Growing up with such precarity (despite my family trying to shield it from me), I knew that we were a cash wad away from disaster. Everything, it seemed, centered on money: who had it, who didn't, if we had enough, and how to spend it. Every expense seemed a necessity and, at the same time, a luxury.

Academia didn't help me overcome such precarity or change my relationship with work because I circulated in precarious spaces. I worked in a community college where students like me were only one paycheck away from disaster. There, I worked on weekends, in the evenings, and whenever I was told I was needed. And I did this for a 50,000-dollar salary (before taxes) offered by one of the largest college systems in one of the most expensive States with one of the highest tax rates in the country. But, back then, the money felt like a windfall after living well below the poverty line in graduate school in one of the most expensive cities in the country.

So, for working class academics, graduate school feels less like a temporary setback than it does a dress rehearsal for what's to come because it signals what has already come to pass. We are already socialized into expecting less and living with less. When we leave graduate school, we accept less and continue to live with less even as we work more because we are dedicated to the "mission" of our work.

Not everyone I graduated with ended up in this situation but among those who grew up first gen., poorer, BIPOC, perhaps internationally, it seems we just fared worse in the academic job market. We don't own houses. We don't have children. We earn less and live with less because the constant state didn't really change from childhood to now. This isn't by happenstance.

Why and how does this relate to writing center work? It seems like writing centers are havens for the dispossessed. We are drawn to this special helping space because we want to work with writers who need and want support (whatever that looks like) and if we have lived with precarity ourselves it is likely we are willing to always go that extra mile. To always make our relationship to our work boundless.

Precarity—in more ways than one—compels us to work beyond our means for less which, in turn, causes us to live less.

It's been 20 years since my father died. In that time, I promised myself I would go to school, take a job that didn't break my body or refuse me access to basic necessities like healthcare and worker's comp. Since then, I have lived in five different states and had multiple academic jobs, some of which were better and some of which were worse for my well-being.

But the thing that I have only come to grapple with in the past few years is what structures of work ethos, attitude, and socialization I need to unlearn in order to live more.

Time is a precious commodity as the pandemic has shown us. And I am not so willing anymore to exploit myself for work. I mean, work structures are already yearning to exploit us so why give them a boost?

Theme 5. Trauma and the New Workplace Normal

This section explores what happens when awful things that are outside of our control happen in the writing center. Trauma has become an increasingly important topic in writing center and composition literature (Brentnell & Dixon, 2021; Clinnin, 2020; DeBacher & Harris-Moore, 2016; Giaimo, 2023; Owens, 2020; Perry, 2016), but here we focus especially on the labor associated with trauma—whether it is emotional, logistical, preparatory, or response-based. We see this especially in the metalabor that accompanied university responses to the pandemic. Although trauma clearly pervades (and is sometimes referenced directly) in many of the stories in Act II, in this section we focus less on the traumas inflicted by our positioning in the managed university and more on how our experiences in the managed university interact with traumas originating elsewhere.

Pseudonymous contributor Belkin ("Tragedy in the Writing Center," this collection) shares the sad story of a tutor who completed suicide. Detailing "William's" development as a tutor and his engagement in the writing center, Belkin shares how he honored his tutor's life but, also, the need for us to support tutors in their labor even as we acknowledge the labor of writing center workers who cope with and have to address these kinds of tragedies (likely without any training).

Lack of preparedness runs through this section whether it is the sudden loss of a tutor (Belkin), an active shooter situation on campus, or the effects of the pandemic on writing center workers and their responsibilities (Chadderdon et al., "A Story of Writing Center Labor," McMurtrey, "Boundaries and Labor During the COVID-19 Pandemic," Lundberg, "Bearing Witness"). We navigate these situations often with little training or support. But as we see in these stories, the contributors make meaning and support their workers. Through this kind of community work, they process trauma and make their workplaces more ethical and more sustainable. This post-emergency responsiveness does, however, come with personal burdens and challenges. Chadderdon et al., for example, structure their story as a dialogue that details the events leading up to and following an active shooter situation on campus. While there are no easy solutions when violence presses into the center, this story is evidence of restorative practice and offers ways to process traumatic events together.

The pandemic, of course, features in many of the stories in Act II. Although a wealth of material on writing center work during and after the pandemic has emerged (Giaimo, 2021; Guay, 2023; Jiang et al., 2022; Mayo & Dixon, 2021), we hope these stories provide readers a felt sense of this challenging time, especially long after the pandemic has finally receded. McMurtrey details the dissolution of work-life boundaries during the pandemic and the positive ways in which Zoom and online learning impacted their work. However, they also recognize the need to reestablish their work boundaries as writing center work is not really in crisis (even if tutors can't work their shifts). This urgency, which has driven many of us for the past three and a half years, is rightfully examined here. We need to find ways to break out of the "on-call" nature of our work that the pandemic (and our institutions) demanded of us. The managed university worked to ensure that labor continued to produce surplus even during this trying time, and the narratives we see in this section bear witness to this exploitation.

Lundberg frames her story as one of bearing witness during the pandemic. Moving online dissolved the boundaries between personal and professional lives, and it unearthed a lot of personal pain and trauma that writers brought into virtual sessions. While many contributors write about difficult topics, Lundberg believes that the remote environment and the pandemic gave rise to an acute vulnerability (and loneliness) in tutoring sessions that otherwise would have remained invisible. From these experiences, she advocates for trauma-informed ways of both tutoring and also talking about tutoring work. The story ends with hope for the future that is accompanied by a reduction in the emotional labor of the past few years.

Hochschild, the originator of the concept of emotional labor, has decried the concept creep that has come with the term (Beck, 2018). She observed that the term has become elastic, leading to a certain blurriness around it. She defines emotional labor narrowly as "the work, for which you're paid, which centrally involves trying to feel the right feeling for the job. This involves evoking and suppressing feelings." Many of these narratives demonstrate just that. While others may not always conform to a narrow definition of emotional labor, they do highlight the often-invisible work that comes with managing emotions and administering during traumatic times. This sort of labor, though not often in the job description, is crucial to writing center work. And we are neither prepared for this work nor recognized for this work. Still, this work is critical to our missions. Trauma finds its way into the writing center, after all.

Discussion Questions

- In "A Story of Writing Center Labor in a Violent Age," Chadderdon, Herb, and Hundley share their perspectives during an active shooter situation and its impact on them (as well as the writing center). What are some feelings that have arisen in an on-campus crisis in the writing center? How have tutors and administrators processed these feelings and experiences?
- How do we, as Belkin shares, respond to the death of a tutor in the writing center? How do we honor workers? Do we have plans in place for responding to the death of a community member?
- McMurtrey details how boundaries around work and availability dissolved during the COVID-19 pandemic, yet the ongoing crisis also

shifted how McMurtrey responds to day-to-day crises. How do we set boundaries in our jobs, particularly during periods of protracted stress or upheaval? What might these boundaries look like? What might we apply from Wright's (2019) strategy of "escaping capitalism," such as pleasure activism and "work to rule," to McMurtrey's discussion of work boundaries?

- Is your writing center "back to normal" or has the culture and the work shifted since spring 2020 and the start of the COVID-19 pandemic? How has your work-life balance been impacted by the COVID-19 pandemic?
- What positive lessons about writing centers and our work can we take away from the last four or so years, since the start of COVID-19?
- Do we feel like we need to perform certain emotions in our tutoring and administration work? If so, what are those emotions? And, what happens when our emotions about and around our work shift?
- What kinds of emotional labor do we perform in the writing center? Do you think this has shifted over the past several decades and, if so, in what ways and why?

Chapter 29. A Story of Writing Center Labor in a Violent Age

John Chadderdon, Maggie M. Herb, and Elijah Hundley
SUNY Buffalo State

> We will have to write it down. Write it down. Things are happening, and we cannot write them down fast enough or well enough.
>
> — *Michael Blitz and C. Mark Hurlbert,*
> from Letters for the Living: Teaching Writing in a Violent Age

The following depicts the feelings and experiences of three writing center colleagues—a peer tutor, a professional tutor, and a writing center director—as we reflect on doing our work in a violent world. In this narrative dialogue, we focus, in particular, on our memories of one specific evening during our spring semester of 2022, in which our writing center went into lockdown due to the threat of an active shooter on campus. While this threat turned out to be only that—a threat—the emotional toll of this evening lingered on for each of us. And then, several months later, our campus community and city were witness to devastating violence, when a white supremacist opened fire in a grocery store in a predominantly Black neighborhood just a few miles from our campus, murdering ten people and injuring three others. As the three of us reflect back on the semester and the specter of violence that surrounded our campus and our work, we find ourselves alternately numb, angry, and sad, with conflicting feelings about our work and its value. Here we attempt to make sense of these feelings and memories using the tools we know best.

Elijah, peer tutor: Upon reflecting on the traumatic events of this semester, all conventional means of expressing my ideas escape me. I'm frustrated, suffocated by a pair of hands strangling me, keeping any words from coming up, grasping at my neck with such strength that perhaps they hope to crush the words along with my throat.

How does one write about a traumatic experience?

John, professional tutor: The afternoon of the lockdown was the second shift of the spring semester for me and the second shift in which I was serving as a professional tutor. I had just graduated with my master's degree the previous semester, and my anxieties about the uncertainties of the future prompted me to return to work at the writing center. It was an easy decision to make. At the writing center, I was comfortable, having worked there for nearly the entirety of my five years as a student. At the writing center, I felt safe.

Maggie, writing center director: I had been working from home that Wednesday when I saw the emergency text from campus police. Someone thought to have a gun was spotted near campus, and everyone was ordered into lockdown. I texted Elijah and John, who were working the evening shift, asking them if they'd seen the alert. I heard back right away; yes, they'd seen it.

John: My immediate thoughts were those of survival. Shut off the lights. Close the door to the writing center that is protected by a keycard lock. I looked at the glass panels that made up the entire front of the center and thought—*that glass will not stop a bullet*. I suggested we relocate to the inside of the break room and lock that door as well. Once inside, Elijah and I worked together to haul a huge metal filing cabinet in front of the door. Out of breath, we sat and we waited, in utter uncertainty.

Maggie: When they told me what they'd done, I was impressed by how quick-thinking and calm they were. It wasn't until later that I thought about why: they were just kids, maybe not even born yet when Columbine happened. They'd probably been doing active shooter drills as long as they'd been in school, maybe since before they could read. Of course they knew what to do.

Elijah: Safety drills tell us how to react in a dangerous scenario, but they also condition us to simply expect violence without ever really understanding why the violence is happening in the first place.

John: I began to think in headlines, the kind written in a bold black font that we all have had the misfortune of reading far too many times. Lists of names and dates attached to accounts of harrowing violence. Notes on an obituary—an entire person reduced to a photo, a paragraph, an occupation, a vague synopsis of interests, and a heartfelt gesture towards a lost future.

Is this really happening?

I took to my phone to frantically update family and loved ones. Maggie messaged us with words of concern and sympathy. There was comfort in the responses, and they took my thoughts briefly out of the small break room. I did my best to reassure everyone that I was okay. I didn't know whether or not that was a lie.

Elijah: "How could this happen?" This was the sentiment that kept echoing as we waited. I wanted to find some kind of answer, but I couldn't, so I simply kept quiet and kept waiting.

John: After an hour or so, Elijah and I raised our heads sharply. The sound of a door opening and closing prompted both of us to turn one ear toward the room outside. After a moment of prolonged silence, I decided to move the cabinet just enough to open the door a crack and peek out. A group of students had just been herded into the writing center by a library staff member with a key card. I whispered from the crack in the door, asking if they wanted to join us in the break room where they wouldn't be seen from behind the glass. They agreed. This process repeated itself several times. Soon we had around a dozen students crammed into the tiny break room with us. The collective fear added weight to the air.

Maggie: I continued to check in by text with Elijah and John throughout the evening, trying to send encouraging words, though probably more for my own comfort than theirs. Because, all the while, I had an acute feeling of guilt. I had always thought of myself as someone who did my best to be cognizant of my tutors' working conditions, and who made the center a workplace that felt comfortable and safe for them. But on this evening, I was overwhelmed by the truth: their working conditions at that moment were profoundly physically, mentally, and emotionally unsafe, and my privilege as a faculty member, who has no set schedule, who can leave work early or come in late or choose to work at home for the day (as I had done that Wednesday), protected me while putting my employees—who do the real essential labor of our writing center—at risk. The sense of safety and comfort that I always told myself I created for my tutors was just an illusion, and probably always had been.

Elijah: Despite warm and worried sentiments from my friends and family, I felt an extreme level of futility as I could do nothing but wait. Later this futility would turn to anger. This anger was unparalleled, and my irritation almost turned toward my fellow companions in the room, especially as the same sentiment continued to be echoed: "how could this happen?" However, acting out in anger due to my own lack of understanding of the situation would have resolved nothing, and I'm glad I didn't lose myself in a moment of genuine frustration.

John: That heavy feeling persisted, magnified by the slowed pace of time and the awkward silence of a room full of strangers packed far too tight for comfort.

But then, something broke. We began to joke with one another. There was talk of HBO's *Euphoria*, upcoming travel, and plans for the future. Stories were passed back and forth between us. Hushed laughter lightened the air. Little had been learned from police updates, but in spite of that, there was hope. The threat of violence has become an implicit fact in our society, and yet, at that moment, we continued to believe in the necessity of our education, our work, and our shared humanity.

Maggie: After a few hours, we got the all-clear from campus police. I texted John and Elijah again, telling them to close up the center early and go home. I told them, too—recognizing the inadequacy of my words—how sorry I was that this had happened.

Elijah: Once at home, I felt a startling amount of apathy; after stressing out and having to reflect upon my own rage, sentiments of safety felt oddly superfluous. So, after hugging my mother and petting my dogs, I simply walked to my room, lay down, and slept. Or at least attempted to, only to stare at my ceiling and think, "oh boy, I have to go back tomorrow." While Maggie said I could take a break the next day, I didn't feel like I could. As much as I would like to think it came from a higher calling to selflessly assist students at the writing center, I'm not that selfless.

It's a job, and I felt I had to go purely because of that.

Maggie: Elijah sent me an email later that night, assuring me, "I'm okay. I'm told these things build character."

"I think character-building is overrated," I responded.

John: I have struggled with whether or not I would have anything profound to say about this experience—whether or not I would have any insight to share about what the night felt like. I am still not so sure I do. But something that has stuck with me since that night is the very real impact that events like these have on our collective psyche. How does anyone truly go on with daily routines knowing that at any moment the patterns of our work days could rupture into life-threatening violence? I assume most of us get by not thinking about that if we can help it.

Maggie: When the writing center reopened the next day, students were lined up outside as usual, and John, Elijah, and the rest of our tutoring staff went to work—brainstorming, reading drafts, and offering words of advice and encouragement. It felt normal. Except for when it didn't. Like when I overheard a student panicking about an annotated bibliography, and suddenly, all I could think was, *how dare we?* How dare faculty ask their students—how dare I ask my staff—to concern themselves with the minutiae of APA citation on a day like today, during a semester like this, in a world like this one?

Elijah: Perhaps the most traumatic part of the incident is that I never had time to process that it was a traumatic incident; once the moment had passed, it turned into any other event in my day-to-day life like it was no more than a small inconvenience. Perhaps humans are not built for this level of stress, and our minds simply cope by blocking out the unsavory stuff.

Maggie: In the days that followed, I felt lost on how best to proceed. Should I call in someone from the counseling center? Should I schedule a staff meeting to check in with everyone? Should I close the center for the day? Every option felt like an overreaction and an underreaction simultaneously, particularly on the heels of the prior year and a half in which all of us at the writing center had continued to perform our labor amidst a global pandemic; a summer of police brutality and the ongoing fight for racial justice; and an insurrection against the government, not to mention the personal struggles that many of us carried quietly. Which collective traumas deserve a post-mortem meeting, I wondered? And which do we just endure?

Ultimately, I talked with Elijah and John, offering them time off if needed. I reminded the entire staff of the mental health resources available to them and to our students, and I offered my feedback and suggestions to the building-wide committee that was formed to review and revise our library's emergency protocols. It felt inadequate, though, and I'm reminded of that inadequacy every time I walk into the writing center break room and see the deep gash in the floor, outlining the path of the filing cabinet that John and Elijah had pushed in front of the door as they hid.

Elijah: Looking back, I feel as if I understand myself and my emotions at the time a little more. Anger is a natural emotion; it is universal and can manifest in different forms, but the important thing to recognize is that it can be a powerful tool if used effectively, and it can be dangerous if used brashly.

While it can take away, it also can create and renew, and writing is one of the most powerful ways we can do that work.

John: Through writing center work, I have observed—many times over—how communication, sharing stories with one another, and finding mutual understanding brings us closer together. As we look toward the horizons of our contemporary moment, it is tempting to see only the gargantuan dark clouds that await us in the distance, gliding eerily closer each time we read the news. However, to also glimpse the potential of hope on the horizon is imperative in these times. And in the writing center break room that night, I was reminded that hope is not just a passive feeling but an active experience that we create together.

Maggie: As the semester drew to a close, I called a friend, a writing center director at another institution, to catch up. I recounted to her everything that happened in and around our center, campus, and city over the prior few months. She shared the story of her semester, too, and although she works at a different college, in a different city, in a different part of the country, we had many of the same concerns and fears—for our communities, for our students, and for the world we live in. We reflected on how overwhelmingly insignificant our work feels amidst the chaos of the moment, but also how the conversation, collaboration, and learning that takes place in the writing center space somehow feel more important than ever. We talked about the privilege inherent in our ability to even have this conversation—alive and safe.

"We're okay," I said.

"Are we, though?" she asked.

And the question hovered in the air like a fog.

Chapter 30. Tragedy in the Writing Center

Vincent Belkin (Pseudonymous)

Emotional labor is perhaps the most difficult and most ignored side of directing a writing center. Our evaluations rarely consider the emotional labor involved in looking out for the well-being of our tutors and helping them find stability. There is no quantifying the time we spend consoling our tutors, reassuring them of their skills, and talking to them about work/school/sleep balance, even though we may spend more time working with them on these issues than in training them in specific tutoring strategies. Given the nature of our job, we tend to know our students better than the average professor does. And, more often than not, that's a real perk of the job. But this IS emotional labor that often goes unaccounted for and rarely gets discussed.

As most of you have witnessed, the writing center is a crucible for all kinds of social dynamics. The most common seems to be camaraderie and care for each other, year after year. There are the occasional disputes, the spats, the complaints about dirty dishes left by the coffeemaker, the inequities of who opens and closes the space, etc. But far more often the tutors stand up for each other, back each other up, lift each other up, tutor each other, cover shifts for one another, and just bond. It can be a difficult job, but I have seen that the tutors truly support one another.

So what do you do when one of them dies? We're so accustomed to seeing students graduate, flourish, go on to grad school, go on to careers, and leverage their talent to make a difference in the world. But no one is prepared when one passes away. Suicide complicates the matter, as we are all left wondering what we could have done or said differently.

Five years ago, my dear tutor of three years, William, took his life. He had some medical conditions—more serious than he let me know about—that had apparently severely limited his future options. He came to my colleague's class the day before, more ebullient than usual, so it didn't make sense.

I met this young man in his first semester of freshman composition. He loved reading, which was reflected in his writing. I was in my second year as the writing center director, and I noticed his talent in the first few weeks of the semester. I normally seek out students who have both writing talent and excellent social skills. William, however, was weird and didn't feel compelled to connect to others. This weirdness is not rare for most of us, as writing centers tend to attract budding heretics and iconoclasts. Perhaps those sensitive enough to talk meaningfully about the written word tend to be more sensitive overall. I don't know. William wore those Vibram shoes, which were in style a decade ago, though they were made specifically for barefoot runners, with each toe showing. The mean girls in class mocked him, but I don't think he noticed. I certainly did. Pointing at his shoes, I asked William if he was a runner. And he responded, "Not at all—I just like how these look." He wrote daring essays. He read thick science fiction books before class started. And he seemed comfortable in his skin and in his weirdness.

So, I hired him to start tutoring his sophomore year. Training was a breeze for him, as he was sharp and got along wonderfully with all of the other tutors. He loved to laugh and he seemed to really love tutoring. I could see him growing as a tutor—asking his fellow tutors and me questions (a sign of growing confidence) and giving smart and abnormally thoughtful feedback to his tutees. He seemed to adjust to college life so well. The mean girls went away to other majors and parties, and he found a home both in the writing center and in the English department, where he would crack jokes and write wild and hilarious essays about living on Mars.

He didn't seem to stress out like many high-achieving students, but instead went about his way with a genuine smile and a sci-fi book. Others gravitated to him, reading his weirdness and confidence as audacity and authenticity. He always returned the warmth and kindness he received from others. He was a special person.

During one training session in the spring, I asked all the veteran tutors to write down advice to give to the newly hired tutors. I'll never forget William's. He wrote, "Don't let your self-worth be harmed by one bad tutorial." It jolted me, as it gave me the distinct impression that he had let a bad tutorial or two hurt his self-worth at some point. And in this time of heightened anxiety among students, it has since become the first piece of advice I tell new tutors.

When William completed suicide, I was at a conference in Germany. I was woken in the middle of the night by a cluster of texts from my tutors. The first one I read was "Oh god, Vincent's in another time zone and probably hasn't heard." A week after I returned, we opened the writing center to all of the tutors and William's friends. We shared stories about him, we read poems to help us deal with our grief, and we made it clear how much we meant to each other. I later spoke with his parents and learned of his medical ailments and his difficulty switching from one medicine to another. They assured me that William had only positive feelings about the writing center and found real meaning in the work we do. They were so kind and grateful that William had felt at home in our department and in the writing center that they left us money for an endowed scholarship that we award annually to brilliant students who don't walk the same path as everyone else.

I still have the notecard William wrote his advice on. We have a large framed picture of him up on our "wall of people who inspire us to write well" along with one of his writing center articles. Though his death was unrelated to his writing center work, these are both reminders to me and our current tutors that camaraderie is more important than tutoring perfectly. Support is more important than knowing all the comma rules and conventions. Kindness and humanity are more important than clear and concise topic sentences. The tutors tend to put enough pressure on themselves to tutor well that I don't need to add any more. What they really need is support and encouragement, even if they seem quite confident. Job ads for writing center directors do not ask for someone who can look out for the emotional well-being of our tutors, yet it's perhaps, in key ways, the most important part of our work. Our bosses do not assess emotional well-being, even though a healthy dynamic in the writing center is so dependent on it. Indeed, we need to train these tutors to be able to work well with their peers, to know where to find answers regarding mechanics and citations, to be able to identify what to help the tutees with first, to keep careful and accurate records. But first and foremost, we need to remember that these tutors tend to be high-achieving and sensitive people and to never lose sight of the sense of humanity and grace that should be at the core of every writing center culture. And perhaps we need to do better communicating to our colleagues and deans the unacknowledged labor we willingly perform for our tutors.

Chapter 31. Boundaries and Labor During the COVID-19 Pandemic

Anne McMurtrey
The University of Utah

I received a text last night from a tutor saying that she wasn't going to make it to her 9 a.m. shift. I looked over at my alarm clock. It was just past midnight. I sat up in bed, asked if she was okay, and waited for the *dot, dot, dot* on my screen to turn into words. Yes, she's okay, but she's having trouble keeping up with all of her classes on Zoom, and she can't bring herself to sit at her computer for her three-hour shift tomorrow. I replied, "I understand. Take care of yourself, and we can chat more tomorrow." Though my mind was exhausted, I stayed up for another hour thinking about how peculiar it was that I was texting tutors after midnight on a Tuesday night. This pandemic had altered my boundaries and upended my ideas about work-home balance.

In early March 2020, my university went on spring break. At the end of that week, we were informed that we wouldn't be returning to campus. "Stay home," they said. "Put your classes and services online." Some departments didn't have to change much, and they posted videos of their lectures to Canvas. The writing center, however, needed to change in drastic ways: while we would normally meet at an arm's distance in a small, windowless room in the library, we were now relegated to remain unknown miles apart, connected only by technology.

We needed to have synchronous Zoom tutorials, which we had never done before, and that required learning how to access the platform through our scheduling software and how to tutor writing over Zoom. We also needed to ramp up our asynchronous tutoring, which required intensive instruction, usually via telephone. Labor changed, and space between us increased.

In October 2020, my department chair urged me to reopen the physical writing center to support the limited number of students who returned to campus. But the writing center would not be the same as when I left it. I needed to safeguard our space, and my work responsibilities quickly included the work of a safety officer. While the majority of my department worked from the safety of their own homes, I donned a mask and, with some hesitancy, headed into work. My first task was determining what safety measures the ever-changing laws required, what other directors had purchased for their centers and in what quantities, what product brands were well-reviewed, and which companies might deliver promptly. I spent hundreds of dollars creating physical boundaries in my writing center, including Plexiglass desktop barriers, floor decals directing students to stand at least six feet from the reception desk, face shields, nitrile gloves, and boxes of disposable masks.

As soon as the equipment arrived and facility operations helped me to install the desktop barriers, a few tutors returned to our physical center. I was excited to see them again and return to some level of normalcy, but I worried for their health, my health, and my family's health. The isolation I experienced during those first six months of the pandemic was justified by its promises of safety, so leaving my home to return to work came with much trepidation. I'm sure my tutors felt something similar, and I'll be forever grateful to those who risked the return so early into the pandemic.

Perhaps the anxiety of returning—or even the prospect of communicating with people outside of one's social pod—explains why the feel of our writing center didn't return to normal that October. Whatever the reason, the distance I had been feeling for six months remained even as I sat just one cubicle over from my tutors. Across-the-room waves and friendly nods replaced handshakes and fist bumps, and silence replaced conversation as the tutors toiled away on their online coursework. The comradery and intimacy of our space was missing, and unwelcome sterility took over.

Though the number of in-person tutorials our center led stayed low, our online numbers increased. But instead of feeling impersonal and sterile like the physical writing center had become, Zoom tutorials somehow accomplished the opposite: they opened up our lives to strangers in ways beyond our control.

Pre-COVID-19, we were only judged by how we presented ourselves on campus. When working and learning over Zoom, however, people reveal so much more about themselves; the boundary between the personal and professional is blurred. I've spoken to K-12 teachers who have seen this in the extreme. Children resist the requirement to keep their cameras on during online school because they don't want to show their teachers and classmates that they live in their family car. They don't want to display their families' filthy or tiny apartments or reveal things about their parents (their language, substance abuse problems, appearances, etc.) that would typically remain private.

My tutors have reported similar problems, though with much lower stakes. One of them reported being embarrassed that she had to hold tutorials from her bed since her apartment was so small and no professional spaces were available. Another said with a smile, "Clients can see my bedroom. It's weird that I have to clean *my room* for *work* every day."

I, too, have been in a similar situation, with admittedly fewer consequences because of my privilege. Without a spare room in my townhouse, I have to use the kitchen table for my desk when I work from home. I drape a towel over the liquor cabinet and position the camera to avoid the painting of the Laphroaig Distillery that adorns my dining room. When my young son is with me during meetings with my department chair—or worse, a dean—I try to control my uneasiness when he approaches me mid-meeting because he misses me or because he needs assistance with his button. Doesn't he know I'm trying to project professionalism and not my maternity?

Not only has our work changed because of our switch to Zoom, but so have the many ways in which we see—and judge—one another. During a Zoom call, we judge each other by the contents of the closets we see in the background and the non-academic books on our bookshelves. We see each other with multifaceted identities—of mothers, roommates, caregivers, and pet owners—regardless of our desire to share those facets of who we are. Our boundaries are less defined now than perhaps they've ever been. The actual labor—the work we do and how we do it—is only part of the big picture about how mid-pandemic online tutoring differs from pre-pandemic in-person tutoring.

I know my boundaries have been compromised these past two years. I share more of myself than I want to over Zoom. I've given all of my employees my cell phone number, and, as I've already revealed, my tutors text me at all hours of the night. I used to check my email between eight and five Monday through Friday, and now I check my email in the evenings and on the weekends, as people's situations seem to change hourly. I check my text messages and new Slack channel countless times a day. Especially during a pandemic, some things can't wait until Monday morning.

However, as we approach the third year of this pandemic, I have to admit that most of my office's communications lack the urgency they held early on, and that has allowed me the space and time to reimagine how my boundaries—and those I create for my center—will look. This pandemic has taught me the importance of health and family, and so one boundary that I will instate will be the use of the Do Not Disturb feature in both Slack and iMessage so that I can reestablish some uninterrupted family time at home and give my tutors my full attention when I'm at work. I will also allow tutors to choose where they hold their Zoom tutorials so they do not have to reveal their private details online. And finally, I've recently removed the Plexiglass dividers in my center; students and tutors can decide the distance between them and navigate their proximity collaboratively, just as they work collaboratively on a piece of writing. Tutors are gifted in this regard.

These recent years have dissolved old boundaries and created new ones in our writing centers. But writing centers have proved to be resilient. Though I would be foolish to believe that we can fully return to a pre-COVID-19 workplace—one with the physical closeness we once enjoyed and where we could more easily control our professional images and means of communication—I am confident that our resiliency will continue into the years to come and that we can create healthy, reasonable, and sustainable boundaries that most benefit our centers.

Chapter 32. Bearing Witness: The Emotional Labor of (Pandemic) Tutoring

Margaret Lundberg
University of Washington Tacoma

It was a Friday. March 6, 2020. Reports of a "novel" coronavirus spreading like wildfire throughout our community had infected nearly every conversation on campus as we all contemplated the final two weeks of winter quarter. Then, at 2:34 pm on the last day of week nine, my director brought word that beginning Monday all instruction would move online, including our writing center.

"We'll be working from home for a few weeks," she said. "Administration is still working out the logistics, but you'll get information later today about how to connect with our students."

Turning in the doorway, she added, "Forward your phone, and take whatever you need. Head home whenever you're ready."

Locking my office door that day, I had no idea those last few weeks of winter would stretch into spring and summer, then fall, winter, and yet another spring and summer before I'd return.

Over the next eighteen months, my face-to-face collaborations with students morphed into conversations with screens. Our writing center has offered asynchronous consultations to students for years—what we call "written feedback"—so continuing that service was easy. But as face-to-face interactions became virtual, unfamiliar technologies took center stage. Remarks like: "I think you're muted," or "Can you see my screen?" punctuated every conversation. Then came the apologies over private challenges that filtered into Zoom rooms ("Sorry for the noise. My kids are fighting in the hallway"). As real life intersected with technology, I sought to navigate another novel situation: virtual spaces that required no physical labor to access but were nonetheless emotionally and physically draining—at least compared to the routine face-to-face meetings that used to structure my days. Yet, over time, new formats grew familiar, even comfortable. And despite the occasional bandwidth hiccups, we all learned what to expect.

What I didn't expect, however, was the shift in my relationships with students—particularly those I saw regularly. Technologies like Zoom turned us into everyday witnesses with front-row seats to each other's lives. While reading students' papers, I entered not just living rooms, office cubicles, or kitchen tables, but the experiences and emotions of the moment.

And like a witness in a courtroom, I am here to testify to the impact of those moments.

For example, Zoom made possible my witness of the joy of a student who had taken her citizenship oath the day before, even as that joy was tempered by disappointment over COVID-19 protocols that kept her family waiting in the car. Zoom made me a witness to the off-camera meltdown of a four-year-old who decided his student father's meeting had gone on long enough and "now" was the promised hour of the pillow fort. A few weeks later, I bore witness to more pillows, as I met with a faculty member propped up in bed with her young daughter sleeping beside her—both stricken with COVID-19. I occasionally even witnessed invisibility: conversations held with a smiling photo or a name emblazoned across a black screen. These interactions represented lives into which I was not invited, their faceless voices sometimes carrying the emotional exhaustion of loneliness or other pandemic-inspired struggles. Zoom opened a window—day after day—to witness overwhelmed students laboring to maintain a sense of normalcy in indisputably abnormal times.

And most painfully, Zoom allowed my witness of the fears of a graduate student for her grown daughter, hospitalized with COVID-19. Weeks later, I again bore witness as grief invaded her anxiety over her now orphaned grandchildren amidst a family-wide COVID-19 diagnosis—all while this student staggered under a full load of summer courses. As we reviewed her final papers, her pain bubbled over, and we cried together—our tears witnessed only by Zoom.

These experiences—and many others like them—made clear that the pandemic carried a different kind of labor into the emergency workspace of my home. During those eighteen long months, my job became so much more than writing collaboration. In the virtual spaces afforded by technology, I became—unanticipated—witness, counselor, and comforter, all the while laboring to maintain a reassuring professional face in the midst of student trauma.

Dealing with the emotions of others has always played a role in writing center work, as staff and tutors work to encourage stressed-out students. And as a personal writing specialist, my work centers on helping people tell personal—and occasionally, painful—stories in statements for scholarships, internships, or graduate school. But throughout the pandemic, a typical appointment shifted toward levels of emotional support that had never been required before. Sure, my students have always shared their personal challenges: concerns over coursework or family expectations, deadlines that loom large. For many students, finding time to write is overshadowed by the clamor of other responsibilities: jobs, children, life. And when subject matter is closely tied to students' identity, writing can be emotionally fraught.

Even in *ordinary* times.

But what I witnessed during the pandemic was something else—something deeper. Students were hurting. Though coming for writing help, they sometimes brought loneliness, worries over sickness, loss of childcare or jobs—even food insecurity and impending homelessness. Would this have happened if we'd met face to face? Maybe. But in seven years in the writing center, I had never experienced anything quite like this. The screens between us somehow seemed to make it easier for students to share private pain they might not have otherwise spoken.

With their lives upended, students' abilities to cope were often overtaxed as they and their families passed through the turbulent waters of the ongoing pandemic, while trying to continue their education and maintain some sense of normalcy. And like my students, I was also dazed by the intersecting pressures of job and family during a public health crisis that no one saw coming. Yet, for more than eighteen months, I listened. I commiserated. I smiled and encouraged. I assured students we'd all be ok.

I even offered feedback on writing.

And I ended each day depleted by the effort—my home no longer feeling like the sanctuary from work it once had. Interacting with traumatized students and attempting to support them through my own emotional labor had taken a personal toll: I grew anxious, wanting nothing more than to hide from the world and resentful that I couldn't. Combined with the fact that, during these same eighteen months, I had been writing my dissertation during every spare moment. I was an emotional wreck, no matter how much I pretended everything was fine.

In September 2021, administration called us back to campus. I returned to my office, anxious to reclaim a positive viewpoint. As classes began, my colleagues and I—masked, vaxxed, and wary—prepared to greet the students we had been assured were eager to return in-person. But as fall quarter unfolded, our writing center was quiet. We came to campus daily but continued to work primarily in virtual spaces, by student request. As 2022 arrived and COVID-19 again swept through our community, winter quarter began with a last-minute, month-long return to online instruction. While many classes continued online for the rest of the quarter—their faculty unwilling to confront the chaos of a mid-quarter return—writing center staff worked a staggered hybrid schedule: on campus four days, working remotely on the fifth. Yet, from winter through spring and summer, most of my appointments with students remained virtual. The burdens of the pandemic and accompanying social stressors persisted for us all.

Today—mid-September 2022—I am preparing for yet another fall quarter. Yet, in storying the experiences of the past two and a half years, I am beginning to realize some of what I've learned: that the objectivity writing centers often claim is not possible, not *really*. We cannot hide from students' distress. Still, much of the emotionally fraught work we do remains unwitnessed outside the walls of our centers. Which leads me to wonder: is it because we are not *speaking* that no one is listening?

Bearing witness—sharing stories of our experiences with others—opens a space to make meaning for ourselves *and* our audiences. After all, naming our trauma can be empowering. In discussing this idea with my director, she seemed surprised—at first—by my suggestion of opening such a dialogue with our student tutors. Yet, she came to agree that sharing the personal impact of our emotional labor can help us find meaning in it, both now and moving forward.

This dialogue is now part of our tutor training agenda for the year.

Reaching the end of this testimony, I feel ready to move forward, to bear witness—at last—to tiny glimmers of hope:

- That this year will be different.
- That students will find their way back into our physical space.
- That face-to-face writing groups, workshops, and consultations will come to feel "normal" again.
- That our emotional labors will lighten as we share them.
- And finally, I am reaching for the hope that I will soon bear witness to *all* these things.

Theme 6. Care Work and Sustainability

This final section displays a rich network of stories that show the ways in which communal everyday acts of care can make our work more sustainable and enjoyable, even while striving for work-life balance (Morris, "Care and Work/spaces"; Skinner and Wells, "Labor of Love"; Junaid, "What the COVID-19 Pandemic Taught Us About Writing Center Work"). At the same time, however, specific traumas often precipitate this kind of care work, whether it is the death of a family member, the loss of support structures, or even the birth of a child. Life often gets in the way of work, but, in this section, we see how our lives and our bodies can be brought into our work in novel and humane ways. These narratives show the relationality of writing center work. Of course, many of the narratives prior to this section demonstrate this phenomenon, but we felt the stories here focused on relationships more than other dimensions of practice and labor. For example, several stories in this section discuss the effects of the pandemic on writing center labor. Morris' piece explores how our labor is tied to our relationships—not just in our professional spaces but beyond. Skinner & Wells' story shares how they supported each other through motherhood, demonstrating the sort of metalabor that can make this work sustainable, enjoyable, and worth advocating for. Miley (2016) asserted "that by infusing the principles of feminist mothering into our own theorization of writing center administration, writing center directors empower writing center work and resist the neoliberal, patriarchal production of the institution" (p. 19). We see Skinner & Wells's piece as providing an example of what such theorization might look like in practice. We also see relationality and care work as deeply anti-capitalist.

There are also seemingly quotidian events that happen in our work that we don't always mark or examine but that are the mainstay of tutoring work. These experiences can also perhaps provide us with some of the most joy. Green's piece, "Mike" (this collection) details how a tutor supports and mentors a student as they consider taking a predatory multi-level marketing job. Garner's story "Keep Writing Centers Weird" (this collection) shares the serendipitous work of the "weird" writing center. While perhaps not considered "work" in the traditional sense, he tells the story of a student who shared fantasy poetry and ballads in a tutoring session. The student-produced writing beyond the university that is both moving and unique; we ought to pay more attention to these surprising, pleasurable, and moving experiences in our work.

Elliott's "Disruptive Labor" (this collection) and Bond's "Growing Like Moss" (this collection) consider how change can occur in writing centers and institutions through collaborative and sustainable actions. In particular, Bond's metaphor of moss growing into places where it is needed or where it is most successful is an apt one. It helps us to understand that while pushing boundaries (Elliott) is critical in writing center administrative work, so, too, is creating networks of allies and developing a shared purpose. As Wright (2019) has argued, coalition-building and cooperation are key strategies for resisting capitalism, and we see stories here that speak to this particular anti-capitalist approach.

Discussion Questions

- What does remote work enable that in-person work disallows? How are caretaking and family prioritized in remote work or taking breaks or leaves from work?
- How can we create supportive environments where we mutually care for one another, as Skinner & Wells share in their story?
- What types of positive and communal feelings do writing centers provide to workers and writers, alike, particularly in times of crisis?
- Why do we do writing center work? What do we take from this work that is joyful, satisfying, or pleasurable? What do we hope to take from this work?
- Have you ever been offered guidance or given guidance—as Green details in his story about advising a student against a multi-level marketing scheme—in the writing center that is above and beyond "the call of duty"? Think back to this moment and describe what was offered and how it impacted you.
- Part of the joy of writing center work is the unpredictability of it as Garner discusses in his story about keeping writing centers weird. Think back to a "weird" but enjoyable experience you have had in the writing center and share it with others. Is there a way to bottle the lightning that some sessions create for tutors and writers, alike?
- When do we need to push boundaries in our work, as Elliott does in her story? When might we need to set our own boundaries around our work?
- How do we create sustainable and collaborative writing center workplaces? Bond details some strategies but develop your own based on institutional context and need.

Chapter 33. Care and Work/Spaces: Writing Center Labor During COVID-19

Janine Morris
NOVA SOUTHEASTERN UNIVERSITY

When we held our writing center's virtual end-of-the-year celebration in April 2021, I was working from the spare bedroom at my mom's house. As long as the chair was positioned directly in front of the computer, you could avoid seeing the bed in the background; the headboard barely visible in the periphery. I never did figure out how to use the Zoom backgrounds.

When we held our writing center's virtual end-of-the-year celebration that April, it was less than a month before my mom went into Hospice. During the celebration, I feigned excitement for our graduating consultants while we waited for a family meeting with my mom's palliative care team.

Whereas COVID-19 made travel impossible for some, working remotely allowed me to be back home with my mom as she became progressively sicker, and ultimately passed away. I came back to Canada that January without booking a return flight to Florida. I knew I wanted to stay as long as possible. My flight home was the day before Canada implemented its COVID-19 testing requirement to enter the country. I waited in line at the Fort Lauderdale airport with sunburnt families carrying Disney suitcases. We weren't supposed to travel. While those cruise- and Disney-bound passengers were living as though the pandemic wasn't happening, my life felt like it was at a standstill as I waited to travel back home.

My job in my writing center is mainly administrative. Half my load is teaching first-year writing and graduate-level classes in my home department, and the other half is a faculty coordinator in our university's writing and communication center. For the writing center, my job primarily involves supporting graduate student writers by working with faculty across the disciplines and conducting discipline-specific writing workshops. I was fortunate to be able to do all of that remotely during the pandemic. No one cared that there was part of a bed in the background as long as I covered the writing content the students needed. I conducted my first workshop of the winter 2021 semester through Zoom with a group of about 130 Pharmacy students alone in the Airbnb while I quarantined before moving in with my mom.

Like for many, the COVID-19 pandemic caused me to pause and re-think my relationship with work. As a junior faculty member in my first job post-graduate school, I was used to working from home before the pandemic started. I spent many hours at the dining room table, the couch, the balcony, or the kitchen counter. But during the pandemic, the boundaries of work and home dissolved even further. The weight of being at home, being with my mom, was ever-present. It was impossible to turn off what was happening around me during the times I was "at work." Yet, being hyper-focused on what was happening around me wasn't necessarily a bad thing. I wanted to be present. My mom and I incorporated daily walks and evening time to cross stitch together. I no longer felt the need to spend my free time at my computer answering emails or catching up on work.

Being back home with my mom for five months changed my orientation to work/spaces and to the boundaries of work/home and public/private. While my writing center office was a shared space between three faculty coordinators—belonging at once to no one and to everyone—the space at my mom's was also shared between myself and family members who used the workspace while caretaking for my mom. I tried (and failed) to separate the space where I did the majority of my work from the rest of my life.

In writing center lore, the space of the writing center is often emphasized: the closet, the basement, the shiny new location in the middle of campus. The physical space is an important one. That's where connections are made and the space is where students are invited to return again and again. Consultants in my once face-to-face writing center started consulting remotely through Zoom once the pandemic began. We were lucky. We tried to keep our pre-COVID-19 expectations for connecting with students and maintaining professionalism the same: cameras on, limit background noises and distraction, avoid eating during a session, no consultations from your car. This was all easier said than done. It's hard to ignore a family member just off camera when you're working on a consultation or multitasking reading a draft while videoing with someone on your phone. The lag on Zoom can make carrying a conversation hard. While we could keep up with our number of consultations, the interactions weren't exactly the same. Our lives came crashing into our workplace, though perhaps they were never really not there. . . .

Even when we were mindful of what students were experiencing while working from home—the technological barriers, being at home with families or kids, the burnout from being on the screen for hours a day—we didn't truly change our orientations to labor. While I could work from anywhere, it felt as though I couldn't really escape work. In sharing with others, if anything, throughout the pandemic, it felt like we were always on—professor on-demand only a click away. I didn't fully realize the gravity of what it meant to work in those conditions until I was back home with my mom. How could I expect to be professional in one room when my mom was getting sicker and weaker in the next? How could I contain my life as a professional to one part of the house when life was so much bigger than the tiny laptop that made up my working life?

During the period of time I spent with my mom, I continued working as an administrator, teaching, mentoring, and supporting graduate student writers on my campus. As Clinnin (2020) writes of writing program administrators: ". . . in college settings are rarely prepared to perform the multiple forms of labor—especially emotional labor—that are necessary to safely and effectively respond to crisis" (p. 130). We aren't readily equipped to respond to crisis situations, especially when the writing program administrator (or writing center administrator in this case) is also facing their own trauma. During the pandemic, we were all called to crisis and to respond out of the blue. Clinnin (2020) recommends creating preventative self-care plans to put in place in anticipation of crisis scenarios. While impossible for me to know pre-pandemic, going forward that advice is especially useful since a crisis can strike at any time.

Throughout my mom's sickness, I worked without taking any leave. Others on my leadership team covered for me when working and caregiving became too much. So many during the pandemic weren't as fortunate. I'm thankful I was able to go home and be with my mom. However, life continues, and as the US attempts to move on from the pandemic, we need to be aware of the distinctions between our home/work spaces and to the laboring conditions we (and our students) operate in. We can't forget all that has happened and continues to happen as the world tries to lurch back to "normal." As administrators, that means respecting students' boundaries and understanding the challenges that come with being a caretaker at home and a student/worker. It means recognizing the emotional and mental labor we all operate under. It means refusing to ask them (or ourselves) to do more than necessary.

My mom passed away May 2021. I spent the summer cleaning out and selling her house with my sisters before returning to Florida. This experience made me realize how important it is to maintain work/life boundaries and hold dear the moments I have with those I love. I now have an eight-month-old and have learned yet again the importance of slowing down, closing my computer, disabling Outlook notifications on my phone, taking the good with the bad, and living in the moment. I try and extend a greater understanding and compassion to the students and consultants I work with. I encourage them to do things they enjoy and prioritize their emotional, physical, and mental well-being over their success in school or work. Especially with the graduate students I mentor, I stress the importance of taking time away from work and saying "no." Although it's a struggle, I try to avoid the constant always-on attitude and resist the need to stay connected. While the desire to return to pre-pandemic life is strong, there are some things we can't simply return to. We must remember to prioritize our health, our relationships, and the people we are outside of and away from our workspaces.

References

Clinnin, K. (2020). And so I respond: The emotional labor of writing program administrators in crisis response. In C. Adams Wooten, et al. (Eds.), *The things we carry: Strategies for recognizing and negotiating emotional labor in writing program administration* (pp. 129–144). Utah State University Press.

Chapter 34. Labor of Love: Managing the Writing Center and New Motherhood during the Pandemic

Mary Elizabeth Skinner and Jaclyn Wells
UNIVERSITY OF ALABAMA AT BIRMINGHAM

Our writing center labor story has taught us the impossibility of separating our personal and professional lives. Both working mothers, we have learned that life and work get complicated when the two collide but also that friendship and flexibility can ease the challenges of working full-time while raising children. In this essay, we reflect on how the pandemic necessitated new ways of laboring that offered surprising advantages for navigating working motherhood. Our friendship maximized these advantages and modeled working friendships for our tutors. Without minimizing the pandemic's tragedies or arguing that friendship can replace supportive labor policies, we offer some thoughts about how writing center leaders can support caregiving employees and students.

Our story begins in October 2018, when Elizabeth began working as our writing center's first full-time office manager. Jaclyn had requested this position for years to lighten her own and the tutors' loads and redirect their focus appropriately to directing the center and tutoring. While she loved her writing center work, Jaclyn often felt so overwhelmed by the day-to-day labor of the center that thinking creatively about its practices and spending time on big-picture planning was difficult. She was also lonely: As the only full-time employee in the writing center, she was often physically alone during breaks and off hours and intellectually alone without a full-time, nonstudent colleague with whom to collaborate.

A recent English graduate and former writing center tutor, Elizabeth was not new to the center, but she was new to working full-time at the university. More importantly, the newness of the position meant that Elizabeth was creating much of her job from day one. It was on day 10 or so that Jaclyn called Elizabeth into her office to say, "I'm pregnant and will be on leave this summer!" Understandably, this announcement startled Elizabeth, who felt excited but nervous at experiencing such a huge change when she had just been getting her footing in the job.

There was no reason to be nervous: By winter break, Elizabeth was a pro who had become crucial to the center's day-to-day functioning, the tutors' good spirits, and Jaclyn's renewed joy and newfound calm in her work as a writing center director. With Elizabeth and an interim director at the helm, Jaclyn went on maternity leave in summer 2019 as all parents should be able, knowing with confidence that she could ignore work and focus on healing and caring for her new baby.

That fall, Jaclyn returned to the office as a new working mom, complete with all the anxieties and exhaustion that come with the role. Elizabeth was always extremely empathetic, and for good reason: During the winter break of 2019, Elizabeth came into Jaclyn's office to say, "I'm pregnant and will be on leave this summer!" While thrilled, Jaclyn felt the same nerves Elizabeth had at Jaclyn's announcement, as she had just been getting her footing as a full-time working mom.

In early spring, spirits were high. The center successfully hosted the Southeastern Writing Center Association (SWCA) 2020 conference in February, and tutoring numbers were higher than ever. While we rarely said so directly, the subtext of our conversations often revolved around how much we had accomplished professionally when we were personally, even *physically*, in the midst of so many changes. Elizabeth found herself panting on her walks across campus, a walk she'd made 100 times before without problems. For her part, Jaclyn mastered the art of a desk nap on days when her baby had decided the night before that sleep was for suckers. During the SWCA conference, social media highlighted our personal changes, as posts included pictures of Elizabeth's very pregnant body standing at the check-in desk and the conference keynote speaker holding Jaclyn's eight-month-old daughter. We were proud of the message these posts sent: We can successfully labor at work without hiding or downplaying our labor or identity as parents.

Then came Friday, March 13, 2020. When we came to work that day, we knew it would be our last in-person for a bit, but we could never have anticipated that "a bit" would turn into a year and a half. No one even bothered to clean the dry-erase calendar at the front desk.

Of course, the pandemic created a completely new labor story for Elizabeth and Jaclyn. Both the labor itself and the context for that labor transformed overnight. Creating a fully remote writing center presented challenges, including getting to know several new technologies. In a different example, the hiring process Elizabeth had worked so hard to perfect the year prior had to be overhauled again. Further, Jaclyn and Elizabeth had to maneuver ever-changing policies and hiring freezes that left summer and fall hiring a last-minute misery.

Even with these challenges, remote work offered surprising advantages. For Elizabeth, working from home during the last few months of pregnancy proved useful as she quickly became so swollen that walking was difficult. She was grateful to be able to lay on the bed, feet propped high into the air as she worked on a video about how to use the virtual scheduling system. Without the pandemic, Elizabeth would have taken her maternity leave early, leaving her less time to recover, or try to push through the swelling, among other things. For Jaclyn, working from home with a baby was difficult but the flexibility of remote work was extremely valuable. She was grateful for the time spent at home with her daughter, who improved many a Zoom meeting by smiling and waving at the camera; she was also grateful for the occasional cat nap on the couch instead of her desk. Without the pandemic, Jaclyn may not have learned the joy of this approach to working motherhood, though we, of course, must acknowledge the immense challenges the pandemic brought for parents with older children who needed help with remote schooling and who may be less entertained by tagging along on Zoom meetings.

A few weeks into fall 2020, Elizabeth returned to the office two months postpartum. Jaclyn returned the next day, thanks to an agreement to alternate days to avoid spread. The semester felt lonely and quiet, especially since the tutors continued to work remotely. After years of a bustling writing center, it felt haunting to see an empty space and a whiteboard calendar still reading March 2020. At the same time, the hybrid work schedule helped us navigate work and family in ways we did not anticipate. While lonely, the arrangement helped Elizabeth ease back into working postpartum. Having two days at home with her baby, assisted by her mother, allowed her to continue to recover from childbirth while working full-time and continuing graduate school. For Jaclyn, the flexible hybrid schedule meant she did not need to scramble for childcare on days her daughter stayed home from daycare. While the pandemic brought a lot of pain to our world, it also upended how we labor in ways that proved advantageous to us as new working mothers.

Our friendship was also important to the success we found personally and professionally over the last three years. That we care about each other and each other's families made our work more productive and more joyful and the challenges we faced easier to solve together. Much energy is spent trying to separate the personal and professional, but we feel our time is better spent talking openly about how to be both/and—both parents and writing center leaders, in one example, and both friends and colleagues, in another. We have brought our babies to the writing center. We have declared random Wednesdays Cake Day when it seemed the staff needed cake. Elizabeth has said to Jaclyn, "Why are you here? You don't feel well. Go home," and Jaclyn has said to Elizabeth, "Your kid is sick? Go. I've got today." This attitude has trickled down to our tutors, who likewise feel comfortable telling us when they had a rotten tutoring session because of something going on in their personal lives or when they simply need a mental health day. In caring for our writing center, its staff, and each other, we embrace the mix of personal and professional that the pandemic and working motherhood have required.

Despite the challenges of working motherhood and the incalculable pain of the pandemic, we feel grateful for how both experiences have helped us embrace empathy and flexibility for caregivers laboring in the writing center as students, tutors, and center leaders. We are also grateful for how the experiences have helped us reimagine writing center labor in ways that may better support caregivers. Before the pandemic, parents working from home with their children seemed like an impractical pipe dream. Anecdotally, we know that writing center administrators often feel pressure to work from campus more than other faculty, perhaps because centers are such physical spaces. We encourage writing center leaders to take their time working from home, particularly if they have young children, and we also urge them to allow and advocate for their staff, particularly parents and other caregivers, to work from home when needed. While we cannot control broader university labor policies like parental leave, we often *can* control how labor works in our centers.

The time both of us were able to work from home with our children also brought to our awareness how important virtual tutoring is for student and tutor caregivers and parents-to-be. Giving parents virtual tutoring options makes education more accessible to those caring for children, aging parents, and others, and they offer a more comfortable option when long treks to our physical centers are challenging for pregnant bodies. Virtual tutoring also provides flexibility for caregiving tutors who find themselves with sick children or closed daycares and schools. The flexibility of virtual tutoring illustrates again how we may support students and tutors even when broader university policies are beyond our control. Even with our best intentions, liability and other concerns may limit our ability to create child-friendly spaces on campus, but virtual tutoring may step in to offer a flexible, accessible option for those balancing childcare with school, work, or both.

Chapter 35. What the COVID-19 Pandemic Taught Us About Writing Center Work: The Joys of a Tutor at the Laboratory of Academic Literacy (LLAC)

Oluwatosin Mariam Junaid
UNIVERSITY OF SÃO PAULO

Likened to a Yoruba proverb, "*Kari kapo ni nyeni*," there is joy in a cooperative effort. In writing center work, tutors and tutees work collaboratively to improve tutees' texts. However, there is little focus on the importance of focusing on tutors, who I will refer to as their "backbone." This narrative uses my experience to highlight the joys experienced in writing center work. Tutors have individual needs and material realities, which, if recognized, can bring growth because writing centers cannot thrive without efficient tutors "*igi kan ko le da igbo se*" (a tree cannot make a forest).

The COVID-19 pandemic exposed us to an unexpected reality of social distancing, contrary to human nature hardwired for connections that bring about a feeling of belonging. We relied on online platforms such as Skype, Google Meet, and Zoom for meetings, interactions, and communication to protect ourselves from the ravaging coronavirus's effect.

This new reality highlighted the importance of belonging to support groups where we share a sense of connectedness. Born into the Yoruba cultural tribe of southwestern Nigeria, I recognized the importance of belonging to communities early in life. The Yoruba people believe that as human beings, we thrive when we have the opportunity to share relatedness in which our physical, social, and emotional well-being are taken care of.

Therefore, based on my background, I naturally desire a sense of belonging within a community, wherever I find myself. As an international doctoral student at the University of São Paulo, Brazil, I research how to help students find their voices through writing. One of my main goals is to find and belong to communities where I can use my chosen field of study to positively impact the university community. The Laboratory of Academic Literacy (LLAC) provided that space and opportunity. LLAC is a writing center providing writing support through tutors and tutees' collaborative efforts in English, French, and Portuguese to staff, graduate, and postgraduate students of the university community. LACC provides *a non-judgmental* tutoring environment that embraces tutees and tutors despite their difficulties, race, gender, and personality.

However, in becoming a tutor at LLAC, one fear I had was whether LLAC recognized the importance of tutors' care and emotional well-being, which is paramount for productivity. I began to overcome this fear from the first meeting I had with the writing center's administrators and fellow tutors. I walked into a room filled with strangers and was met with smiles, hugs, and pecks on the cheeks welcoming me into the group. Everyone was concerned about my settling into the university system. They were willing to extend a hand of assistance when needed in all ramifications ranging from course registration, research, accommodation, childcare, and healthcare, among others. The reception for me was a strong indication of acceptance. I realized that, aside from tutoring, my well-being was also a priority.

I had found a village that could help me navigate through uncertainty and succeed in different facets of my academic journey, a unique characteristic of LACC. At LACC, priority is given to ensuring that tutors succeed and meet all institutional requirements. Like me, tutors at LLAC are postgraduate students. During the pandemic, we took the same courses and formed online study groups where we discussed, researched, and learned from each other. In LACC, we also publish academic papers together due to the publish or perish policies. For me, working in this environment ensured I had a balanced intellectual, work, and life balance. Knowing that I was supported and valued in my writing center work taught me the strength in vulnerability, and it improved my social confidence and interactions.

The Strength in Vulnerability

I remember receiving a message from the writing center's coordinator at the onset of the pandemic asking tutors how they were coping with our new, unexpected reality. It was a reminder that the writing center was open to helping tutors. This message made me realize that the writing center was not just a space or a building we occupied for tutoring but an idea from which everyone who embraced it could benefit.

As a mother of three young kids, I was thrown into a sea of confusion, fear, anxiety, and panic due to the pandemic. I needed to finish my studies, write my qualification report, be a mother, homeschool my kids, and conduct tutoring and research. This was a critical period in my life, but I felt embarrassed owning up to my challenges. However, the coordinator's message motivated me to speak to the director and fellow tutors about my challenges. Amazingly, this was the pathway toward finding solutions. I got advice from other mothers whose homes had also become offices, libraries, playgrounds, and schools. I received tutoring from fellow tutors willing to adjust their schedules to suit mine, which helped me navigate my responsibilities and made life manageable. The collaboration between other members of LLAC and me gives credence to the Yoruba proverb, *"Eniyan ni esin atileyin mi"* (humans are my support system).

The consequence of receiving the support I needed was that I was motivated to help tutees to the best of my abilities and ensure the success of the writing center as a whole during the pandemic. I realized there was strength in vulnerability. I have learned that a bit of thoughtfulness from writing center administrators unites tutors and makes them come out of their shells, which makes it possible for them to ask for and receive the help they need. Tutors might hold onto their challenges because of the fear of being judged, as we might feel that as tutors, we ought to be perfect writers. I have also learned to access the writing center's resources to my own benefit.

Improved Social Confidence and Interaction

Belonging to a strong and supportive writing center community has improved my social confidence and interaction skills. Weekly, I encounter different students and receive them in a warm embrace. I have learned to connect with strangers within a short amount of time and make them comfortable in my company: a skill I didn't have before becoming a tutor. My patience and adaptability level have improved because I can now adapt my tutoring style to work with students with different needs. In the past, I decided who I wanted to interact with. But being a tutor, I had to learn to accommodate everyone scheduled to be tutored by me.

During one of my tutoring sessions, I worked with a doctoral student who was gloomy, visibly nervous, anxious, desperate, and confused about an article he was writing for publication. To calm him down, before we began the session, we exchanged pleasantries about our well-being, and I discussed how interesting I felt his area of research was. I could tell that he was distracted from his anxieties and happy to share his research with me. After our discussions, he seemed more relaxed discussing the purpose of the session. At the end of the session, we became friends. I was impressed that with the subsequent sessions, he grew more confident in his writing and comfortable using the writing center space as a whole.

I was able to help this tutee because I had improved my own social skills, which grew from a place of empathy and authenticity. In the past, if I had encountered such an individual, I would have found a way of avoiding communication, due to the fear of making the individual's situation worse. But my story is different today because I communicate effectively with people from various works of life. Similarly, I realize that trust is developed when we are authentic, empathetic, and perceived as competent. These qualities in my day-to-day life have helped me mitigate loneliness. I have learned to name my emotions for what it truly is without shame or fear. I have learned to share my experiences, letting tutees know they aren't alone in their struggles.

Conclusion

My experience as a tutor makes me realize that a successful writing center is not just one that provides valuable services for only its clientele, but one that prioritizes the care of tutors. In as much as I try to put my best foot forward in everything I embark on doing, my success as a tutor springs from the fact that I feel a sense of comfort, respect, and liberty within the writing center's workplace community, which puts me in a state to engage constantly. Being part of the writing center is to belong to a community of support, full of peers and faculty aimed at seeing you succeed in all areas of life. The skills I have learned on the job are life tools that have helped me develop character, which will be relevant in my collegial, personal, and professional life.

Chapter 36. Mike

Jonathan M. Green
COTTEY COLLEGE

This story comes from my experience as a writing tutor at the Sam M. Walton College of Business's Business Communication Lab (BCL) at the University of Arkansas. As a "business communication" lab, we tutored both writing and oral communication, and we explicitly served business majors. The Walton College attracted many international students, and these students constituted a good number of our tutoring sessions at the BCL. One of my most common repeat students was a senior I'll call Mike, a man from China majoring in business management.

At the start of one of our sessions, Mike sat down with even more enthusiasm than usual—he seemed to be in a particularly good mood that day. He excitedly told me that he had secured a job interview. "That's great!" I said, giving him a high five. "What's the company?" But when I heard the name, my heart sank. As it happens, I'd interviewed with that same company not too long ago and discovered in the course of the interview that this company was, in fact, a multi-level marketing scheme—an MLM, or a pyramid scheme. Sure, the job description had been attractive enough: set your own hours, be your own boss, grow your portfolio. And their website looked pretty legit, too, with photos of people happily working together on computers, shaking hands, and exchanging files. To any outsider, especially one looking to gain a foothold in the business world, it was the perfect intro-level job. But a more skeptical applicant might have noticed that the company seemed very keen on not telling you what it was, exactly, that they did. What product or service did they provide? Amid all the vague language of *we provide quality services* and *we serve a variety of stakeholders*, there was no indication of what one would be doing on a day-to-day basis—after all, if applicants knew that they'd be spending hours on their feet, outside in the Arkansas summer, pressuring people to buy subpar products for a pittance of a commission, they'd probably look elsewhere. But my interview with the manager had told me everything: the vagueness was the point. This company preyed on young, doe-eyed job seekers—preferably straight out of college—who didn't know any better and could be taken advantage of.

As my excited smile sank into an expression of dismay, I told Mike the truth about the company. I told him that I, too, had gotten a call for an interview mere hours after sending them my résumé (which should have been the first red flag), that I had gone to the isolated, run-down building in my finest slacks and blazer, that after winding through a labyrinth of unadorned hallways, I eventually found the hiring manager, a "Mr. Little," sitting alone in an oddly empty office with only a *Game of Thrones* poster on the wall. He grew increasingly defensive as I pressed him on what exactly I would be doing if hired for this job, and it was only my wife's sage advice to *never burn bridges* that kept me from getting up from the interview and thanking "Mr. Little" for wasting my time.

I answered Mike's many questions as best I could. I explained how these "jobs" worked—how they typically required the new recruits to employ high-pressure sales tactics on their friends and families or even resort to the door-to-door approach just to make a barebones commission. And if one was devoted enough to put up with the exhausting hours and pitiful pay, one might—emphasis on *might*—make it to the next tier on the pyramid. But there would always be someone higher, someone whose earnings depended on the lower tiers, and so the very concept was predatory by design. Mike was disappointed, but he understood. I showed him some resources for finding *real* jobs, jobs that wouldn't take advantage of him, and he thanked me for the explanation. I continued to work with Mike until he graduated from the business college later that semester.

On the one hand, Mike's story offers a refreshing happy ending: in a hopeful moment of solidarity, I was able to draw on my own experience and steer Mike away from a potentially disastrous outcome. But on the other hand, it raises some important questions for us in writing center work: what drives people—including tutors and even the students we work with—to pursue exploitive jobs like this in the first place? How do these illegitimate companies manage to trick otherwise savvy individuals into applying? And what can we do as tutors to prevent them from falling into the trap?

I would argue that the first two questions go hand-in-hand. Thinking back on my own experience with the company, I had been lured by the job posting's claims that I would be able to use my communication and leadership skills, network with like-minded people, and solve challenging problems. This all sounds familiar: these same opportunities had led me to writing center work in the first place. MLM schemes prey on the same types of people who seek out and excel in writing centers: the desire to use one's communication skills, the desire to continue to develop those skills through challenging and rewarding practice, and the desire to collaborate with others and work together to solve problems. It's no surprise that someone interested in writing centers, whether as a tutor or a student, would also be interested in a job that offered these opportunities. Even worse, these companies prey on those who tend to give people the benefit of the doubt, which I think we in writing centers often do. One thing that got me into writing center work was knowing that my skills and efforts would be appreciated; that my sessions would end with a reciprocal sense of genuine gratitude. MLM schemes capitalize on optimists who can be duped into thinking that if they just push through the long hours and work hard, they, too, can reach the top of the pyramid.

As for what we as tutors can do to help, maybe the most important thing we can do is teach them how to identify these toxic jobs in the first place. After all, to read an MLM's job posting and website is to engage with a piece of rhetoric—one that is often meticulously crafted and downright nefarious in its design. Even I, a Ph.D. student in rhetoric and composition, had been hoodwinked by the slick language of the posting and the strategic visual rhetoric of the website. What chance did Mike have? We need to treat these as opportunities for serious rhetorical analysis. Rhetorical analysis is a matter of reading between the lines, and that's what we have to do with these devious texts. After all, they aren't *lying*, per se—the company does indeed "provide services," "serve stakeholders," and offer "challenging opportunities for advancement." But they certainly are leaving a lot out. We can read job materials alongside students, asking key questions such as, "What exactly would we be *doing* at this job?" "What *specific* product or service is this company known for?" "Is there any information about this company somewhere besides their website?" In my case, it wasn't until I asked the manager these questions point-blank that I realized what I was in for. We'd prefer that the students we work with—our fellow laborers—not have to get to that point, of course, and that is a matter of successfully analyzing what the company is telling them versus what they're *not* telling them. This takes practice.

But aside from this opportunity for fostering some rhetorical awareness in students, I share Mike's story because I think it represents an important component of writing center work that often goes overlooked: the work that we do with students extends beyond just dispensing writing advice. Here was a moment where I was able to advise a student on a different front than the typical assistance with definite versus indefinite articles, thesis statements, and citation guidelines. Those things are important, of course, but they weren't *as* important in this instance as being Mike's cultural informant about this unsavory part of the United States job market. As we know, tutoring sessions can be unpredictable, which is part of what makes the work so challenging yet also so exciting. We need to be in tune to what sort of feedback would be most useful to the student in front of us here and now—and that feedback might not always be directly related to writing. It might come in the form of simply warning students about the dangerous reality of United States work culture. And on that note, we need to continue to think of ways we can use our positions to foster solidarity with our fellow laborers, ways that we can advocate for them as they, too, navigate the hazardous waters of the job market.

Chapter 37. Growing Like Moss: Theorizing the Labor of Writing Center Placemaking

Candis Bond
AUGUSTA UNIVERSITY

> We think of "plants" as possessing roots, a stem (or trunk), flowers, fruit, and seeds. Most of us do not automatically think of the plants that grow on rocks, rooftops, concrete, and any other moisture-laden area; however, this opportunistic bunch, choosing many eclectic substrates, exists.... "They" are the mosses.
>
> — *Oregon State University Science, "Basic Moss Biology"*

A few months back, I lost my grandpa. As I grieved, many memories from my childhood resurfaced. Much of my time growing up had been spent in my grandparents' home. I lived with them for several years and spent countless weekends at their house after my parents and I moved out. My grandpa was a quiet, contemplative man. He wasn't much for conversation. He was also an avid smoker, but my grandma did not allow him to smoke in the house. This meant he spent a lot of time on the back porch and in the front yard, observing the plant and animal life. I used to like joining him. Most of the time, we just sat together in the quiet, but sometimes, he would tell me about the birds and plants.

I remember how he told me about the different kinds of moss that spread over the damp ground. He used to say, "See how it spreads horizontally? It just kind of shoots itself out there and latches on, and before you know it, it's taken over half the yard. It's not imposing. Most people don't notice it until it's already there." I used to love watching the moss spread itself out, lush and mossy green against the backdrop of the dark soil. Some varieties bloomed tiny flowers. These were not true mosses—they were actually succulents—but they grew in the same unruly way. My favorites were the moss-rose and purslane, which had plump succulent leaves and delicate, layered, rose-like blossoms in rich colors.

My career as a writing center administrator (WCA) had developed very similarly. The growth of my center might look haphazard to someone looking in from the outside, but it had its own kind of wayward intentionality. Through partnerships with various units, faculty, and programs, we developed relationships that moved us into new territory and helped us to reshape our identity and sense of belonging in new ways. For example, when I began my position, my center served primarily undergraduates and was staffed by undergraduate peer consultants. Yet, one of the first opportunities that presented itself was a partnership with the university's Nursing Ph.D. program and the Center for Nursing Research. At first glance, this partnership didn't make sense. It would stretch our resources and extend us into a population we weren't targeting at the time. While I had reservations, I quickly realized the faculty in the program were highly invested, and it would be a misstep to pass up the opportunity. It was fertile ground.

This partnership ended up flourishing for years. We developed robust writing support for the Nursing Ph.D. students through consultations, writing groups, and workshops, and the program director and I developed an interdisciplinary research agenda focused on graduate writing in the health sciences. This growth was the result of an organic relationship between two faculty—myself and the program director—rather than a top-down initiative. When I began my current position, I had very little access to upper administration or even my own department chairs. I think my experience is common among many WCAs. What I did have access to was students and faculty. So I focused on relationship-building and making cross-unit connections.

Sometimes the relationships I formed flourished and lasted, and new off-shoots developed out of them. For instance, out of my work with the Nursing Ph.D. program came opportunities to work with other health science graduate programs. We were also able to petition for professional staffing two years ago because of our growing commitment to graduate students, and our center now looks very different than it did five years ago. Other times, however, the relationships we formed were more one-off: they served both partners well for a brief interlude, but then we both moved on. Strong partnerships require motivation and commitment on both sides. Our center is patient and flexible; we can wait until the time is right. This opportunistic behavior is in part due to necessity. Within the increasingly neoliberal model of the university, we cannot afford to make bad investments. WCAs, in particular, often lack support and find their labor extended in unsustainable ways. Our approach to growth was an intentional effort in sustainability and a means of providing as equitable a space as possible for our staff.

Our wayfinding approach to placemaking has led our center to places it would have never found if we were viewing our growth and sense of place linearly or vertically. We grew like moss, finding niches where we belonged and could flourish, surviving and thriving by putting out our feelers, latching on, and using that growth to spur new growth. Our presence on campus very much exceeds our physical and even virtual spaces. According to Fink Fletcher (2019), "Space is location, physical space and physical geography." Place, on the other hand, is defined by social relations and "is what gives a space meaning, 'personality' and a connection to a cultural or personal identity." Massey (1994) further explains that places are not bound by physical location; they include "relations that stretch beyond" (p. 5). We have established a sense of place by growing outward and being open to changing course when resources become scarce, conditions become less than ideal, or a need no longer exists.

I mentioned the analogy of moss to my good friend within the writing center field, Joy Bracewell, who sent me an article she had recently read about this very phenomenon. The article featured Robin Wall Kimmerer, an Indigenous botanist at SUNY Syracuse (CBC Radio, 2020). During the early tumult of the COVID-19 pandemic, Wall Kimmerer asked her students, "'What would moss do?'" Her students responded with answers like "Give more than you take," "be patient when resources are scarce," and "find creative ways to use what you have" (CBC Radio, 2020). Wall Kimmerer explains, "Mosses have this ability, rather than demanding a lot from the world, they're very creative in using what they have, rather than reaching for what they don't have . . . when there are limits, the mosses say, 'Let's be quiet for a while. Abundance, openness, water, will return. We'll wait this out'" (as cited in CBC Radio, 2020). Like mosses, writing centers aim to balance their ecology. They are creative and resilient spaces within universities.

This is not to say writing centers should not be demanding, or that they should settle. Writing centers bring added value to their campuses and local community contexts, and they deserve to be recognized for their labor and contributions and supported in their work. And yet, the horizontal, opportunistic approach of moss and writing center professionals seems strategic and sustainable, not just reactionary. Although I am not romanticizing the very real lack of resources and support that most writing centers face or suggesting that WCAs stop advocating for the resources, spaces, and seats at the table they need, I do wonder if we might be missing opportunities to theorize our labor in ways that make what and how we do what we do compelling and advantageous.

Writing centers are, after all, part of larger networks. To flourish, part of our work is getting a lay of the land and being intentional about how we move within our environment. Recently, my relationship with our Nursing Ph.D. program began to break down. A new program director was appointed, and a new department was formed. Our partnership is continuing for now, but I can feel the ground becoming less stable and fruitful. This may change—we might be entering into an even richer period of collaboration. But I am open to the possibility that this may not be the case. Only time will tell. Thus, I'm also pursuing an offshoot pathway into our DNP program, where another newly appointed director seems highly invested in working with us. I felt a sense of grief at shifting my focus away, ever so slightly, from what had been one of the best partnerships of my career in writing centers; but at the same time, I see how this partnership may become a drain on our energy if it is not prioritized equally on both sides. Even if we end up completely redirecting, I am certain that the years we invested into the partnership will continue to nourish us indirectly. We gained insight, skills, and connections that will carry through to new partnerships.

Growing like moss and establishing a sense of place for myself and my center required intentional flexibility and stretching. It required creative thinking and the willingness to constantly redirect. I knew places I wanted to belong and connections that I wanted to make, but the path I took developed organically and sustainably. Giving is central to this analogy: WCAs may give more than they take, but this need not always be synonymous with exploitation. It could be a pathway toward sustainability, innovation, and growth. Writing center place-making means finding opportunities in situations that are, more often than not, outside of your full control. It means being part of a complex, shifting ecology that requires flexible but strategic movements. This kind of growth holds its own kind of potential for agency.

References

CBC Radio. (2020). Why is the world so beautiful? An Indigenous botanist on the spirit of life in everything. *Tapestry*. https://tinyurl.com/mr3mz525

Fink Fletcher, M. (2019). Everyday anthropology: Space vs. place. *The Cultural Courier*. https://theculturalcourier.home.blog/2019/02/22/everyday-anthropology-space-vs-place/.

Massey, D. (1994). *Space, place and gender*. University of Minnesota Press.

Oregon State University Science. (n.d.). *Basic moss biology*. Living with Mosses, https://bryophytes.science.oregonstate.edu/page3.htm.

Chapter 38. Disruptive Labor: The Transformational Work of Pushing Boundaries

Tiffany-Anne M. Elliott
Lincoln Land Community College

When I started working in our campus writing center as a writing center specialist in 2007, I was surprised at how little writing tutoring I did. I mistakenly assumed that having been hired as a well-paid though part-time writing tutor with benefits, I would, above all, be tutoring writing. I quickly learned that writing tutoring was reserved for faculty consultants whose writing center hours earned them a course release. At that time, it was a particular point of pride for the writing center and the department that housed it that writing tutoring was provided by full-time faculty.

The part-time writing center specialists primarily worked with students enrolled in developmental writing courses who spent one hour per week in the writing center reviewing language mechanics and taking required grammar quizzes. Our work was to provide feedback on students' practice activities in their workbooks and additional practice worksheets provided by the center. When a student was ready to take a quiz, we would administer and then grade it, offering detailed explanations for items where points were deducted. My other work included answering the phone, scheduling appointments, making photocopies, filing, shredding, and logging which chapters students had completed in their workbooks. My suggestion that the bulk of these tasks might be better allocated to a student worker was viewed as implausible.

"I feel like a receptionist," I blurted out in frustration one day. I was called into the coordinator's office where it was explained to me that grading grammar quizzes was "a form of tutoring" and "very important work." It wasn't that I thought language mechanics were unimportant. I just knew that this labor was inconsistent with writing center theory and practice. I also wanted to engage in more meaningful labor. I had a vision of what our writing center could be that far exceeded what we were. I wanted to share that vision and help make it a reality.

Dissatisfied with the limitations placed on me and wanting to bring our center into the 21st century and into alignment with standard practice in the field, I vigilantly watched for the right opportunities, and I pushed.

I pushed to abort the antiquated grammar quizzes, and while the center was slow to abandon them, faculty gradually stopped assigning them. I pushed for the creation of a mission statement and adjustments to the center's hours of operation. A new coordinator, open to these ideas, made them happen. I pushed for the adoption of electronic appointment scheduling software, which we finally adopted once other centers on campus initiated the move away from paper scheduling. I pushed for the part-time professional staff and adjunct faculty to be allowed to serve as writing consultants. Again, a new coordinator readily adopted this into practice. I pushed for faculty writing consultants to have computers at their desks to use during appointments with students, and a retiring faculty member donated funds earmarked for this purpose. I pushed for the writing center to work with digital texts. With an increase in multimedia projects in our freshman composition courses, others slowly opened to this idea. I pushed for online appointments, which we piloted unsuccessfully, but were able to implement years later when the global COVID-19 pandemic required everyone to work remotely.

This labor of pushing was long and painful. A passionate and rather impatient person, my pushing was initially aggressive and understandably not well received. The resistance I faced largely due to my age (27 and newly graduated) and gender (female) frustrated and even angered me at times. I sighed. I raised my voice. I felt beat down and ragged. I kept pushing.

For years, my questions, suggestions, and presentations of research were viewed as challenging and threatening. And not entirely without good reason. The position of faculty coordinator of the writing center offered only a three-hour course release, hardly time to inspire the person holding it to embrace much less cultivate change. The specialists and faculty consultants alike understood the problematic structure of the coordinator position, but we never gained any support in redefining that role. It was a losing battle against the very ways long-time stakeholders at the college defined our writing center's value.

I was told I was "too invested," that I "worked too much," was "making others look bad," and that I was "subversive." My ideas consistently met with opposition. The message was clear: don't rock the boat. I think what others saw was someone trying to capsize it. What I wanted was for us to work together to build a ship because the boat we were rowing was obsolete and risked sinking. This became painfully obvious years later when a new Vice President of Academic Services asked an interim dean to make some cuts, eliminating over half of our faculty tutoring hours.

By this time, however, the entire staff was enthusiastic about change. For the first time, the administration was asking us what the writing center should be and how we could most effectively maximize our resources to best serve our students. This created a stronger sense of ownership over our work and space to look at the possibilities of our labor instead of its limitations. The seeds of change I had sowed now had fertile ground to take root in our community.

Together, we pushed for full-time hours. We pushed to do more of the writing tutoring ourselves. We pushed for expanding our services. We pushed for closer ties with the newly implemented corequisite model for composition courses. We pushed for greater collaboration with departments outside of English. We pushed for an embedded tutoring program.

Something amazing was born from all that pushing. Eventually, people started listening.

The coordinator position was suspended, and a new dean was hired who made the writing center a priority. Asked to review the writing center and make some changes, he led us through a grueling, year-long formative program review process. We interviewed faculty, staff, and students across campus about their perspectives on the role of the writing center and some of the new ideas we had for serving our students. As we drew the entire campus into the conversation, others began to envision the greater potential of writing center work too. This was the beginning of large-scale shifts in institutional attitudes toward the value and potential of our center. Recognizing the opportunity for our center to redefine itself and grow, we collectively pushed even more.

We brainstormed. We researched. We collaborated with each other and stakeholders across the entire campus. A new vision of the writing center was born, and now the center is thriving. The staff are all full-time. The writing center is no longer a place for grammar quizzing. Faculty, staff, and students are less likely to view the writing center as a place to get an essay edited. There is a growing vision of the writing center as a community space for writers. The center is now associated with process and practice instead of language mechanics. It is a place where writers hone skills and build confidence. The writing center is no longer confined to its physical location either. It sets up shop in the campus commons, at our outreach centers, and in virtual spaces; the specialists visit more classrooms; and a new embedded tutoring program was successfully launched. Working together as a team pursuing a specific vision, we were attuned to and seized the opportunity for change when it presented itself, and our writing center was transformed.

I was fortunate that I worked at an institution that valued writing center work enough to pay us competitively and provide benefits even if the work was only part-time. Because of this, I had space to invest in pushing boundaries. My passion for tutoring writing, persistence in pursuing my vision, and my refusal to be defeated by outdated and entrenched ideas of writing center work were essential to the eventual transformation of our center.

A lot of writing center labor often abandoned to silence is the disruptive work of pushing boundaries. Adopting this work into our conversations about what we do is an important part of changing narratives about writing centers and writing center work. While transformation requires a team effort and institutional support, it can begin with one person pushing against existing limitations of space, resources, and mindsets. This labor can be loud, difficult, painful, and frustrating; but it is necessary. There will be resistance. You will feel exhausted, sometimes outraged, possibly even defeated. Change is slow. It requires persistence, resilience, collaboration, and teamwork. Plant the seeds of change. Tend to them patiently. Be attuned to timing and seize opportunities. Guard your time. Work within realistic boundaries. But keep pushing.

Chapter 39. Keep Writing Centers Weird

James Donathan Garner
Augusta University

"We're done early. Could we look at one of my poems?" The student fumbled around in her backpack, removing a well-loved, spiral-bound notebook.

"Sure. What's it about?" I replied, eagerly flipping my legal pad to a new page.

I was no poet, but I was a new Ph.D. student in Rhetoric & Writing at the University of Texas at Austin. First-year R&W students could work either in the writing center or in a digital writing lab. I had worked in writing centers as an undergraduate, between college and grad school, and later during my MA. Living for the first time in Austin, I thought that the familiar environs of a writing center might make adjusting to graduate school easier. Tutoring would be an easy side gig, and after five years of it, nothing could surprise me.

"Great. I'll have to sing it for you, though. It's like *Lord of the Rings*."

Okay, except that. *That* surprised me.

Before I could process what was happening, the consultee began to sing forlorn iambic tetrameter couplets in a distinctly high-fantasy idiom. Dragons roared. Lovers mourned. Soldiers clashed. A tyrannical wizard god met his end in a torrent of fire. The modest tutoring room buzzed with the expected noise of concurrent meetings, but as enthrallment and confusion washed over the room, it gradually fell silent. I don't remember how long the poem lasted. In the moment, as I scribbled furious notes to battle the unnerving feeling of having all eyes on our table, it felt like an eternity.

However long it lasted, it was, well . . . weird.

Weirdness isn't a quality that writing center practitioners often ascribe to (or want to ascribe to) our work, especially given our perennial fights for institutional legitimacy and vital funding. When we do talk about weirdness, it's generally to capture more uncomfortable events happening in our spaces (McKeehen, 2017). In fact, as much as I love writing center work enough to have devoted over a decade of my life to it, when I stop and think about it, the labor involved is itself kind of weird.

Take, for instance, our bread and butter: the one-on-one peer consultation. Two perfect strangers sit down together to discuss writing. One has more training than the other but not necessarily a lot more. The writer shares a draft that they're likely anxious about. Sometimes, that writing contains material that's deeply personal, or it's simply personal because the writer has sunk time and tears into it. If it's academic writing, the tutor probably isn't an expert in the writer's field. And the tutor has just a few minutes to build trust before the whole thing goes sideways. Peer consultations have been some of the most rewarding, exhilarating, and transformative events of my life, but—except for the most convivial extroverts—they are not normal social interactions.

By the time I reached UT, peer consultations no longer felt weird, but I'd certainly had my fair share of weird ones. As an undergrad, I once had to explain to a student why inserting frequent profanity into her sociology research papers probably caused the bright red grades slashed across her essays to be lower than she wanted ("Shit, you're right," she replied). Perhaps my favorite weird moment entailed helping a student draft a custody agreement for a shared Xbox (his friend got the console Monday through Thursday. The student I worked with got it on weekends—no question, the better deal). Of all my weird writing center moments, though, being sung a fantasy ballad at 3:30 pm on a weekday was by far the weirdest.

But I don't want to be misunderstood as complaining about weirdness in writing center labor. In fact, I think that weirdness—weirdness of a less sinister variety, which actually contributes to understanding between tutor and writer—probably occurs in writing center work more often than we stop to recognize. Call it "productive weirdness," a weirdness we should celebrate and embrace. All of these experiences—even helping a student figure out how to maximize his gaming time—were productively weird as they revealed potential and possibilities in writing center work that I wouldn't have noticed without having my comfortable understanding of peer tutoring disrupted. My tutee's own literary hero, J.R.R. Tolkien, once wrote that what he termed "fairy-stories" could show us how to look at green and be astonished again by red, blue, and yellow (Tolkien, 1983). I see productively weird moments similarly: they can be opportunities that shift our understanding or teach us something new, helping us see all of the possibilities of the writing consultation that we may take for granted.

It feels appropriate that the student sang to me in Austin, TX, known for its famous rallying cry of "Keep Austin Weird," first coined in the early aughts. From 2000 on, the slogan could be seen emblazoned on bumper stickers, t-shirts, billboards, storefronts, and more, a crucifix held aloft by small business owners to ward off the forces of capital swarming to suck the life out of the Bat City's local economy. The slogan's actual success is unfortunately debatable: tech oligarchs and real estate moguls have made a meal of the city's last remaining bits of character. Likewise, Wassenich's call for Austin to retain its weirdness has been rendered bloodless, succumbing to commodification as part of a wildly profitable marketing campaign. Nevertheless, this episode is instructive. Both the original spirit behind this rallying cry and the slogan's failure illuminate how I understand the productive weirdness that we encounter in writing center work.

Being sung poetry about immolated wizard gods while tutoring shifted my understanding of why writing centers matter. It could have been a moment to stop the student and re-explain the norms and decorum that upheld our legitimacy as an institution within the broader university system. Or just to tell her,

"Hey, this is interrupting the other sessions." But I'm glad that I didn't. When she finished her song and our conversation became lost again in the gentle hum of the other sessions, she explained that her dad, who had passed away a few years earlier, would read *The Hobbit* to her and make up melodies for the poetry. Writing (and singing) fantasy poetry gave her a way to feel close to him, and she was grateful for a place to share her work. There aren't many other institutional spaces where this could happen, but the writing center can be one.

I just had to learn to welcome the weirdness.

We collaborated on her writing weekly for the next two semesters. We discussed her coursework, her novel, and—of course—more poetry (it was a five-book cycle). She sang verses a few more times, and our discussions of her verses, of how she assembled words and images to stir the same feelings in her audience that she felt reading Tolkien with her dad, trickled into our work on her class projects and led to lots of engaging discussions about writing and genre expectations. Weird sessions can be tough, but the minor discomfort is nearly always more enriching than the ones that go perfectly according to plan. Sometimes, they may even refresh your perspective of work that had long become commonplace.

In the years since those sessions, I have moved from tutor to graduate student administrator to writing center director. If I could encourage my writing tutors in one thing, it would be to welcome those moments of productive weirdness. But productive weirdness is a tricky thing to try to capture and cultivate, especially in writing center work, which is so situated and dependent on social interactions that it can be difficult to anticipate. You can't just make these moments happen, so they're hard to prepare for. Even if we could, we would risk hollowing out what makes them special by trying to codify and replicate them. They would, like Austin's ill-fated slogan, cease to be weird.

So how, precisely, do writing center administrators and practitioners keep our centers weird without forcing it? At the risk of undermining everything I wrote in the previous paragraph, I see a few ways to hold space for the productively weird. First and foremost, productive weirdness starts with helping tutors appreciate the messy humanity that makes up our learning communities. Sessions don't always go according to plan, but we can help tutors prepare to welcome these moments by giving them the tools they need to listen actively, see the best in the writers they collaborate with, and adapt to meet those writers' needs in the moment. Relatedly, administrators can work to design and promote flexible policies and practices that grant tutors the autonomy to improvise when writers' needs conflict with our rules. Finally, writing centers can continue cultivating inclusive spaces where every writer feels welcome and confident that they belong. Without embracing the sometimes uncomfortable, sometimes joyful moments of productive weirdness, writing centers risk becoming too institutionalized and impersonal. Keeping writing centers weird means being receptive and open to every radically individual writer and every radically individual writing task that comes our way—especially when wizards and dragons are involved.

References

McKeehen, S. (2017). Critical empathy and collaborative fact-engagement in the Trump age: A writing center approach. *The Peer Review*, *1*(2). https://tinyurl.com/mrxspkp2.

Tolkien, J.R.R. (1983). On fairy-stories. In C. Tolkien (Ed.), *Beowulf: The monsters and the critics and other essays* (pp. 109–161). George Allen & Unwin.

Act III. Where We're Going: Conclusion and Call to Action

Chapter 40. Reclaiming Metalabor

> *We live in capitalism. Its power seems inescapable—but then, so did the divine right of kings. Any human power can be resisted and changed by human beings.*
>
> —Ursula LeGuin

As we read the narratives in this collection, we were struck by how many contributors describe working outside of the parameters of their jobs in order to do their jobs. If, as Arlene Kaplan Daniels (1987) formulated it, invisible work is the uncompensated, gendered, and thus unvalued work of the domestic sphere, always seeking some legitimacy, we would argue that metalabor is how it translates into the work sphere of writing centers. Writing centers—often seen as cozy "home spaces"—are liminal workspaces, and thus not always seen as valid. Rather, they are seen as "womens' work." As Daniels (1987) explained, "Where the assumption is prevalent that payment reflects skill, there is still widespread lack of recognition that the skills and education required for typical women's jobs have for so long been under-rewarded" (p. 408). We thus posit metalabor as a form of invisible work. Metalabor *is* work: it exacts a toll on the worker; it is expected of the worker, but in and of itself it is not *valued*. Take, for instance, a director collecting data and drafting reports: the data collection and reporting serve as a justification for the "work" of the center, yet it is not the actual work of the center (which is tutoring). It is, therefore, additional and burdensome work that administrators demand but do not typically recognize. Put another way, metalabor is invisible work typically performed to legitimize and facilitate paid work. It is a way to make certain kinds of labor be seen as *real* work. Despite such work being time- and labor-intensive, it is often seen as ancillary or a given; thus, it is not often explicitly included in writing center job descriptions.

Metalabor, for instance, is enacted in Lan Wang-Hiles's story when she tries to support a writing center from afar, despite not working directly in the center itself. This dimension of metalabor can also be seen in the anonymous narrative "My Writing Center Side Hustle":

> Moreover, since I've been here, our learning commons has been a one-woman show. As a result, because of my background in writing center administration and research, I've supported a few different women who have ventured to coordinate our learning commons. I've taught a three-credit writing center tutor education course in the rare semesters that we've opted to offer it. I've also conducted tutor education at a start-of-semester orientation for new consultants who were paid to attend. I've even developed plans for consultant meetings and have run or helped

run them weekly or every other week. I do all of this in addition to my official job.

Here relationality ("support"), gender, and the "unofficial" nature of the work are brought to the forefront of the story. Metalabor is not necessarily invisible to our profession: many writing administrators discuss dimensions of it both in conversation and in research. But for the larger institution, it is largely unseen even as it drives and enables much of the paid work that we are able to do. Harris also describes doing metalabor in her narrative when she lists the assorted tasks of directors:

> For a writing center director, there is data to collect; reports to write; tutors to hire, train, oversee, evaluate, and professionalize; instructors to talk to about using the center; the physical room to set up and maintain; clerical staff to hire; technology to purchase and run; a budget to keep within; perhaps social media presence to maintain; staff meetings to plan and lead; the need to be physically present for many hours in the writing center; publicity to keep the institution aware of the writing center; and planning for continuing improvement and perhaps increase of services offered. And—of course—arguments and data to convince administrators higher up the food chain that, if the threat of cutbacks loomed, the center is successful and necessary. Whew! All that is in addition to the labor of other faculty and adjuncts...

What Harris explains in the early part of her description—training, hiring, data collection, staff meetings, etc.—conforms to Daniels' description of invisible work: unseen, necessary, expected (if not valued). But when Harris describes the arguments that she has to make to administrators for the right for the writing center to even exist, she provides an example of the implicit metalabor she must perform to maintain her explicit work.

Administrative legitimacy work, however, is not the only kind of metalabor performed in and for the writing center. Metalabor can also be highly relational, and highly emotional. It can take the form of emotional labor, though the two terms are not interchangeable (Figure 40.1), despite the "drag" Caswell et al. (2016, p. 16) have described of it. Conversely, there is invisible work that isn't metalabor. Accordingly, we configure emotional labor as a form of metalabor (just as all metalabor is a form of invisible work).

The contributor who shares the story of a tutor's death—"Tragedy in the Writing Center"—captures the affective dimensions of metalabor and its invisibility: how it isn't compensated, and yet how crucial it is for writing centers when he states, "Job ads for writing center directors do not ask for someone who can look out for the emotional wellbeing of our tutors, yet it's perhaps, in some key ways, the most important part of our work" (Belkin, this collection). This sentiment is echoed in the stories of Dunsky, Chadderdon et al., Lundberg, and others demonstrating that writing center work is relational and more involved in care work than some educational spaces might realize or even allow for. The stories of jobs gone sideways demonstrate our professional ethics as they bump up against workplace expectations.

In short, metalabor permeates the stories shared in this collection: the work of advocating for fair wages; advocating for intentional training and ethical practices; resisting ever more uncompensated task creep on our duties; of making lateral career moves in the hopes of landing a position that will allow for some form of advancement; and of ensuring the well-being of tutors and administrators is nurtured despite the many circumstances acting against thriving. All of this is well beyond keeping tutoring running and helping students to produce writing. It is work for and about work—work for work's sake.

Perhaps ironically, we see metalabor—this uncompensated, invisible, and unpaid work that facilitates our visible and paid work—as the primary means of moving forward. More metalabor must be done to legitimize writing center work. But rather than continuing to do this labor invisibly in our individual institutions, we need to make this labor more visible and more communal. Metalabor—and invisible work conceived more broadly—are products of both capitalism and patriarchy. We thus appeal to our field's values of equity and fairness, freedom and democracy, and most especially of community and solidarity. Here we draw on the values inherent in what Wright (2019) explicitly identifies as central to a moral critique of capitalism. If we wish to make our labor legitimate, we must organize and coordinate in new, more visible ways. In other words, we must make others recognize our metalabor *as* labor that ought to be compensated and supported as such.

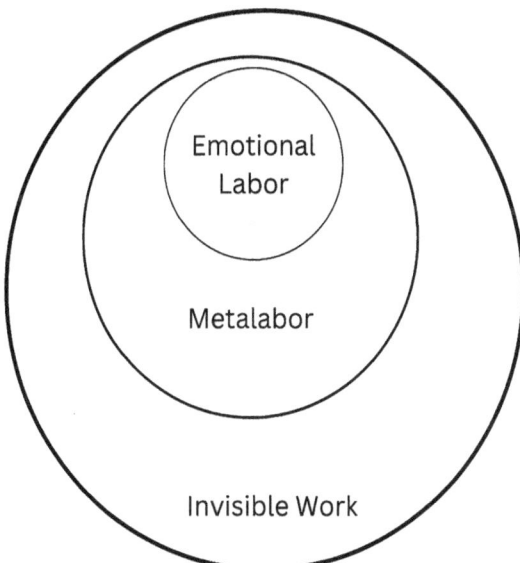

Figure 40.1. Relationship between invisible work, metalabor, and emotional labor

We acknowledge here that so much of the metalabor and so many of the drivers of the unsustainable labor conditions we see in Act II's stories are inextricably imbricated in the expanding neoliberalization of the university. To work against this labor creep is thus to work against capitalism itself.

Imagining Anti-Capitalist Futures in Our Neoliberal Moment

Many, if not all, of the themes present in the stories in Act II about contemporary writing centers have existed since the beginning of writing centers: ambiguous positioning in the institution, precarity, advocacy, joy, and excitement in the work of individual and collective mentorship about the teaching and learning of writing, negotiating identity in the workplace, dealing with trauma, and care work. Anecdotally, however, we see these concerns and consequences of writing center work becoming ever more prevalent in our current moment. Perhaps this is due in part to the COVID-19 pandemic and the financial fallout that institutions are facing from it, but we have also observed decades of defunding alongside other financial pressures. These issues also come up in conversations at conferences, in listservs, and more. There is a pattern. We intuit that the stories included in this project also reflect an acceleration in the challenges around our labor. For us, the underlying theme is that these are all responses to encroaching neoliberal and capitalistic practices in the institution. And, as some of the contributors share, very few safe harbors remain in our profession, even among tenured individuals.

While we appreciated the enthusiasm, passion, and utopian aspirations demonstrated in so many of the stories in Act II, we also worry that these same impulses have long been used against writing center workers. Passion can often act as an enabler for self-exploitation, and it can provide an alibi for the neoliberal forces driving so much of modern-day writing center work. After all, how can something directors and tutors truly believe will help students be a bad thing? We volunteer extra labor because we see a need in the community, and we worry what happens if we withhold it. As Daniels (1987) herself observed, however:

> The work of community service volunteers is useful, but that it is not paid tells others—and the volunteers themselves—that it is not needed, not really important work despite all the lip service about the value of altruistic endeavor. Calling something altruistic is a way of saying it is not work. Since it is not remunerated, and though it may be recognized as a personal benefit—as well as one for society—it is not work (405).

In the course of assembling this book, we have come to believe that as long as practitioners continue to exploit themselves and their tutors for what they feel they can provide to students, their conditions will remain the same. Worse, those students will continue to be exploited as well: uncompensated writing center support will enable them to retain/persist, to be "returns on investment," and they become still more data in service to neoliberal austerity measures. At the same time, we recognize that it is hard to leave writing center work, especially after years of investment and direction. We also know that many stay in order to protect tutors and staff from still worse possibilities. There are no easy answers here, though we offer specific guidance on unlearning internalized capitalism and on engaging in labor organizing.

Capitalism is extractive and predatory. It leans on the already precarious; it benefits from workers being on the back foot; it encourages extractive behaviors over sustainable ones. We see instances of this predatory behavior in many other industries like temporary or gig worker economies arising out of tech companies claiming to create (but not regulate) communities of buyers and providers, or in other poorly regulated industries like the ones that have developed in response to climate disaster. Here, we see a shady fast-moving industry hire precarious—often undocumented—labor to perform incredibly hazardous work, such as cleaning up physical and chemical hazards after fire, flooding, hurricanes, and other natural disasters made worse by our rapidly warming world (Stillman, 2021). Prisoners also do this kind of work, particularly fire fighting, as the "pyrocene" and climate change contribute to more damaging and massive fires (Lowe, 2021). An ever-increasing globalized economy, combined with outsourcing, lack of regulation, rampant privatization, and climate change has exacerbated many labor problems since a neoliberal economic model became common in the 1970s and 1980s.

Academia does not escape the predatory effects of capitalism. We might not want to relate education work to disaster capitalism, climate change, and the effects of neoliberal economic policies like outsourcing, temp work, and deskilling, in a world where we are sicker, poorer, and less mentally well than in previous generations. But this is *exactly* the equation we should be making. And, as with other industries that have become eroded and less regulated over time, academia has faced all kinds of crises that were enabled by short-term thinking, adjunctification, restructuring, extractive policies, and other kinds of neoliberalization. Even in academic spaces where there *is* regulation such as around medical school or other industry staffing and curricula requirements, the uneven distribution of resources punishes less regulated and protected areas of the university. Writing programs and other humanities programs bear the brunt of the managed university's resource calculus.

One result of neoliberalism is deskilling. As many of the stories in this project illustrate, institutions frequently place less value on the work that we do—especially around hiring for expertise—than our field/profession does. Consequently, writing center directors and administrators have varying degrees of preparation, training, and, ultimately, job security: tenure-line faculty with doctorates in writing studies; tenure-line faculty with doctorates in other disciplines; non-tenure line faculty with doctorates; staff with doctorates; faculty with master's degrees or master of fine arts; staff with master's degrees or master of fine arts; even faculty or staff with bachelor's degrees. Because writing centers are configured differently within various institutions, they have varying levels of authority, autonomy, and support. In many institutions (as seen in "Into and Out of the Writing Center," this volume), writing centers have been folded into larger learning commons without any consideration for the disciplinary expertise or history of our profession and are supervised by individuals with no training or knowledge of the field. This new organizational model exacerbates the deskilling of writing center labor.

Within the current economic model in higher education, writing centers and other support services are perhaps one of the hardest hit by austerity: not necessarily revenue generating or credit-offering; not necessarily shiny or novel; not necessarily full of stably-employed professional workers. And as several stories in Act II explain (e.g., Harris, Tirabassi, Whiddon, Elliott), though writing centers are a part of the institutions in which they are enmeshed, these spaces have also been collectivist, disruptive, and, as we argue, anti-capitalist. Created out of volunteerism that cuts across hierarchies (graduate students, adjuncts, faculty, non-faculty volunteers) and often with the express interest of student well-being and professionalization in mind, early writing centers filled a space in the university ecosystem that no one else wanted to or could fill and it often did so with student well-being and success in mind.

At the same time, writing centers' long-term thinking about our mission and purpose has *always* been at odds with the short-term thinking that is the logic of the managed university. Of course, writing centers and other support services perform a functional service to the well-being of students. However, as austerity measures and neoliberal logics within institutions lead to reduced support for other resources—like advising, mental health services, faculty staffing, and so on. Writing centers are also impacted by austerity, playing a catchall support role; this model of student support is perhaps why so many people are drawn to them: the work is meaningful. It helps. It's expansive, as many contributors in Act II detail like Green (this volume) or Garner (this volume). At the same time, writing centers may very well be changing and even disappearing as academic commons and other models subsume their lines and resources in an ever-more managed university model.

As one anonymous contributor in this project observed, "I have always believed that writing centers are a keen solution to one of the problems of academia and the managed higher education neo-liberal spaces: the tendency to conglomerate students in some sort of misguided industrial model and 'stack 'em deep' to 'educate 'em cheap'" ("I've Got a Secret"). Harris echoes this feeling in her story when she writes: "As an administrator near the top of the university hierarchy once told me (when I sought information about how the writing center had fared in the most recent outside review), the institution valued our writing lab because it produced 'more bang for the buck.'" The value of a writing center then lies in its meaningful work for the managed institution and its low-cost model.

What's more, much of the emotional labor performed by writing center workers can be seen as a means of reducing the alienation of students in a neoliberal schooling environment, thus enabling the institution to extract as much capital and labor as it can from those subjects. In short, unchecked capitalism hurts us and makes us feel like we have no options but to follow a path of destruction. Yet, we *do* have options. And we are in an unprecedented moment where labor rights are on the minds of workers around the country and around the world. We believe it is time to act.

While many in our field talk about how neoliberal capitalism has impacted their work implicitly through discussing active shooter situations (Clinnin, 2021), climate-change-fueled natural disasters (Schlachte, 2020), racism (Green, 2018; Faison & Condon, 2022; Carter-Tod, 2020; Haltiwanger Morrison & Evans Garriott, 2023; Morrison & Nanton, 2019), demands and emotional labor (Caswell et al., 2016; Wooten et al., 2020; Morris & Concannon, 2022), and some have discussed specifically how neoliberalism has shaped our work (Greenfield, 2019; Monty, 2019; Fels et al., 2021; Giaimo, 2023), there have historically been few field-wide, profession-wide, critiques of our labor and fewer pieces still on how to respond to these issues. At the same time, with the recent publication of a special issue of the *Writing Center Journal* on contingency (Herb et al., 2023), this project, and others, these studies are coming out more frequently and with an eye trained on labor issues, specifically, not just work issues.

Here we use Wright's (2019) framework in *How to be an Anti-Capitalist for the 21st Century* to facilitate and coordinate this action. Wright (2019) argues that combining elements from several anti-capitalist approaches (including: *smashing, dismantling, taming, resisting,* and *escaping* capitalism) becomes an overall strategy of *eroding* capitalism. Eroding capitalism is not "simply a fantasy" (p. 28) but is rooted in collective action. Given our purposes and contexts in university writing centers, we focus on it here especially:

> One way to challenge capitalism is to build more democratic, egalitarian, participatory economic relations in the spaces and cracks within this complex system where this is possible. The idea of eroding capitalism imagines that these alternatives have the potential, in the long run, of becoming sufficiently prominent in the lives of individuals and communities that capitalism could eventually be displaced from this dominant role in the system as a whole. (p. 26)

The process of eroding capitalism is gradual. Wright (2019) compared it to the transition from feudalism to capitalism, wherein practices and structures associated with the new order emerged and eventually displaced previous dominant structures. Often, these transitions occurred at watershed moments much like the ones we face today in a post-COVID-19 world wracked by the outcomes of neoliberal capitalism.

Our labor ought to be valued, legitimized, and made visible. Professional standards need to exist for the resourcing, training, and expertise, as well as compensation and social capital, of our professional workers. The very problem, however, lies in that collectivity: by determining what counts as skilled labor, many writing centers—at least as they are currently configured by their institutions—would be excluded. This paradox highlights many of the inherent class conflicts within our subfield: between research faculty and practitioners; between tenured and contingent administrators; between those with release time sufficient to contribute to professional organizations and journals and those without; between those with funding to participate in conferences and summer institutes and those without; and still more. So, on the one hand, we can't exclude less-trained or less-resourced writing centers. On the other hand, we cannot simply advocate for more standards or uniform accreditation without risking the marginalization of those members of our community. This paradox sums up the state of our field as we see it. And while we wish (and recommend) that our professional organizations take action to address deskilling, resourcing, and erosion of workplace standards, we have to confront our own attitudes about these things, as well. What purpose do our professional organizations serve? What more can they—and we—do? What are our labor values? How do we understand our work?

We believe the field is primed to have deep and complex conversations about writing center labor with several special issues, edited collections, workshops, and other events focused on this topic, as we discuss in Act I. However, we also need to engage in "deliberate, intentional action" to produce social transformation (Wright, 2019, p. 17). Given our purposes and contexts in university writing centers, we focus on action in the sections below, particularly around accreditation, field-wide standards, and through organizing and collective bargaining. However, before we move onto specific actions we encourage readers to engage in self-examination through the unlearning capitalism section and then to reimagine anti-capitalist futures for writing centers using Wright's framework as a guiding lens (this volume).

Unlearning Internalized Capitalism

While below and in the appendices we offer templates, guides, and heuristics for engaging in Wright's framework of eroding capitalism through actions that include *dismantling, taming, resisting*, and *escaping* capitalism, we recognize that not all of this work is external or even action-oriented. Some of this work is internal and requires soul-searching and self-scrutiny. It requires asking hard questions and sitting with discomfort. Our actions at work, as we have learned, do not always match up with our personally held beliefs and values. And, because much of our current economy runs on crisis mode—especially in higher education—we can be far more reactive than proactive in how we respond to workplace issues. Therefore, we include this section for folks who are perhaps just getting started on their journey to anti-capitalism. Perhaps you are sick of feeling continuously tired, or you dread going to work, or you feel trapped in your current job, or you find yourself unable to celebrate successes. You might, like Dan and Genie, be looking around at the current state of your institution and wondering how the workplace culture changed so rapidly. Or, like us, you might have considered leaving the profession altogether. Below, we offer some guidance on unlearning internalized capitalism, which is both self-protective and self-scrutinizing. We ask you to openly engage with your internalized stances toward work and to scrutinize your work behavior and values. Take care of yourself: this is long-term and likely tiring work, but it is necessary before moving towards actionable strategies. It starts with unlearning internalized capitalism (Rich, no date).

Self-Guided Questions

- Interrogate your internalized values or guiding principles about work—is there a little capitalist inside of you urging you to greater productivity and output, to "grind" or enact "hustle culture," or toward some other harmful practice(s)?
- Do you tie your value and self-worth to your work? If so, how might you uncouple selfhood and your job?
- Are you unable to rest or take breaks from work—even when you are sick, off the clock, on vacation, or otherwise not "supposed" to be working? Have you missed major social or personal events because of work?
- Do you experience deep anticipatory dread before work (popularly called "Sunday scaries") or before specific meetings or interactions? Is this dread due to typical work stressors, or does it indicate a larger more systemic issue with your job?
- Do you feel like your life would have little to no meaning if you no longer did the job(s) you are currently doing?
- Are you continuously searching for "the next thing" in your career? Do you celebrate "wins" or successes or simply move on to the next project?
- If you did not have to work, what would you do? How would you spend your time?

Actions to Take

- Name your feelings about work and recognize where they are coming from.
- Set boundaries in your work, try to say "no" more often.
- Slow your response time.
- Celebrate your professional successes.
- Take intentional time away from work (use your vacation or other paid time, and, if you do not have these things, disconnect from work after working hours).

- Seek community outside of work (friends, family, spiritual organizations, social justice organizations, etc.).
- Seek meaning outside of work in non-work pursuits (i.e., socialization, exercise, visualization, hobbies, art, music, etc.).
- Take other actions towards bettering your life and your community outside of work/productivity.

Chapter 41. What Can We Do? Adopting an Anti-capitalist Framework in Writing Center Work

As the stories in this book detail, there are many places that our field and its workers are headed. Many look towards more sustainable and labor-forward models of writing center work. Some are changing jobs or leaving the profession altogether. Others still root their work in joy and pleasure. Yet, others challenge the very notion of writing center work as it is currently configured. These narratives show that members of the writing center community are reconsidering their orientation toward work and how our centers operate: expanding to communities, countercultures, and perhaps most especially to more collectivist approaches. In particular, we see examples in these stories of several strategic logics for anti-capitalism that Wright (2019) describes in his book including: *smashing, dismantling, taming, resisting,* and *escaping* capitalism, all of which he draws upon in formulating a broader strategy of *eroding* capitalism.

Below, we explore these strategies and what they might look like in implementation, going beyond the theoretical into action: both in our everyday labor as well as in our larger efforts for advocacy and solidarity. And although we favor some approaches and paradigms over others, we do not necessarily prescribe them. That said, in this project, we elide "smashing capitalism" for reasons of moral value and our own skepticism. For one, the inherent metaphors for and appeals to violence in this more revolutionary strategy may be at odds with what we believe to be our field's values if not our own. Secondly, we feel that what amounts to a student service in the university system is frankly an unlikely place to amass the power necessary to destroy capitalism and is thus well beyond the scope of this book. Third and finally, Wright (2015) himself cautions readers that "Capitalism is not smashable, at least if you really want to construct an emancipatory future" (p. 22).

Instead, we invite readers to unlearn internalized capitalism (guidance provided in the section above) even as they imagine a world where the bottom line doesn't determine decision-making for our work. Imagine a space where outcomes might be measured differently from a Fordist model of appointments completed or students served. Imagine a space where you have an idea, initiative, or goal, and money is freely forthcoming without the need to leap through bureaucratic hoops. Imagine, in other words, a culture where capitalism—and its extractive short-term policies of harm—does not rule the day. If crisis and austerity do not dictate our work experiences, we imagine all kinds of progress that can be made. We imagine innovation and community work. We also imagine higher job satisfaction. So, in short, we don't need to labor within an extractive system in order to do good work. We don't need to always be borrowing against our own well-being—or the well-being of our workers—to do a good job. Writing centers cannot solve the ills of capitalism on their own. But they *can* be a part of the solution, and they *can* provide an example for others to emulate in collectively solving it. Beyond the everyday experiences of our individual centers, anti-capitalism work also lies in coalition building, and we believe that laying out intentional strategies in this section will help our field to assemble collective actors. Wright (2019) observes that "Strategies don't just happen; they are adopted by people in organizations, parties, and movements" (p. 28). Writing centers, while always imbricated in larger neoliberal and capitalist projects, can also be spaces where we can advocate not only for our class interests, but for our moral values in anti-capitalist efforts beyond the institutions to which we are bound.

The suggestions below are direct ways in which we can erode capitalism, perhaps not wholesale or systemically, but in our day-to-day labor and administrative work. Some of these actions are collective, some are individual, some are both. We hope you can take away from the following section useful actions and goals to make your labor more sustainable and pleasurable.

Dismantling Capitalism

Wright (2019) contrasts the strategy of dismantling capitalism with smashing capitalism. Whereas smashing necessitates a rupture of the current order, dismantling is a means of changing conditions piece by piece. Dismantling capitalism starts with rejecting privatization, embracing social programs, and encouraging state-directed reform (p. 19). While many aspects of dismantling have become unfashionable after World War II—particularly as states became more capitalist—dismantling remains a key strategy in eroding capitalism. Rather than a singular disruption, dismantling as a strategy envisions a coexistence between capitalist and alternative models until there is a gradual process of replacement from the former to the latter. It is an incrementalist model.

Some efforts may seem more likely than others. For example, writing centers often reject privatization of their services through outsourcing to for-profit corporations. Other efforts, like a state-directed reform of educational policy, seem less likely given the current political climate and taste for regulation in most sectors. Embracing more equitable, accessible programs, then, might occur as a bottom-up rather than a top-down approach. Below, we detail some of the keys to engaging in dismantling—namely, "never go it alone" and the critical importance of information gathering and sharing—and provide some ways that writing center administrators and other writing center workers can engage in dismantling actions across an institution. The point here is to reject neoliberalism through coalition building and collectivist pressure campaigns. To launch such dismantling work, one needs as much information (institutionally *and* field-wide) as possible. Knowledge really *is* power in anti-capitalist work.

The work of dismantling (as with many of these strategies) starts with building coalitions, gathering information, making allies, and networking across campus. In Act II, we see variations on this sort of work in Bond's narrative—"Growing Like Moss: Theorizing the Labor of Writing Center Placemaking"—about allowing the writing center to grow like moss, rhizomatic and purposive; not with unlimited expansion, but rather as nurturing what will be sustained and appropriate for the entity. Similarly, we see it in Tirabassi's narrative—"Advocating for Equitable Tutor Pay with Campus Partners"—where she describes collaborating with assorted campus stakeholders to ensure that *all* student worker wages were increased, not solely those of her tutors. We also see it in the work detailed by a union representative in "From the Archive of A Tutor Representative's Email Correspondences (Summer 2022)" by Anonymous. There are also times, however, where coalition fails, such as in Lan Wang-Hiles's story "Counterstory: Ignored Labor with a Writing Center." Here, a good faith but exploited actor, Wang-Hiles, works to build a community around writing center best practices but fails because a learning commons director does not see the value in this work. So, while coalitions can be built, they are often time consuming and rely on good faith investment from community stakeholders.

Since the writing center director is often the sole full-time (or benefitted, one might argue, if not full-time) employee, many of these actions might fall to them. This is not to say, however, that the writing center director cannot connect their workers with similar kinds of educational workers throughout the institution or take other actions to bring people together. In fact, it is likely that they get the ball rolling on networking and coalition building among organizations on campus that have service missions, that employ student labor, and that are public-facing. These actions help to dismantle capitalism at the institution by creating a collectivist sense of labor, sharing information about working conditions and wages, and banding together to advocate for better working conditions and wages. Such coalition building brings along other workers (like graduate students through graduate council, through student unions, student governance, etc.) in their center and, perhaps, at other tutoring and informal educational spaces on campus.

Additionally, because writing center directors arguably have access to professional organizations such as International Writing Centers Association, Council of Writing Program Administrators, and the College Composition and Communication, etc. over time, they are more likely to be able to further collect information that rejects the fast education movement which encourages poorly trained, deskilled labor with a high turnover rate. In place of this, writing center directors can deliberately invest in their workers through professional development opportunities like training, attending conferences and networking events, and conducting research work and other duties typically reserved for more seasoned, permanent, and better paid employees. This model of worker flourishing is one that many in our field already engage and that several contributors also detailed in their stories.

Yet, another way to liaise with professional organizations includes conducting information gathering among colleagues, organizations, and field-specific databases like the National Census of Writing or Purdue's Writing Center Research Project Survey about the state of the field. This can include collecting salary information for different pay rates for different kinds of administrators (faculty, professional, adjunct, etc.) and tutors (peer, graduate, professional, etc.) through AAUP Faculty Compensation Survey (https://www.aaup.org/our-work/research/FCS), IPEDs peer data (https://nces.ed.gov/ipeds/use-the-data), Writing Center Research Project Survey (Purdue) (https://owl.purdue.edu/research/writing_centers_research_project_survey.html), National Census of Writing (https://writingcensus.ucsd.edu/); collecting information on standard (and non-standard) job positions in the field; securing grants for under-resourced centers; advocating for center sponsorship and partnership between well-resourced and under-resourced centers as a kind of wealth redistribution; creating coalitions of writing centers who have similar missions and student demographics.

We find this last avenue of consideration to be a particularly potent means of expanding access. Equality, specifically equality of access, is one of the normative foundations of Wright's (2019) anti-capitalist framework. Wright (2019) contrasts equal access and equal opportunity; whereas opportunity takes a more individualistic approach (which could be satisfied, say, with a lottery), equal access emphasizes actual access to the material and conditions that would allow for a flourishing life (p. 5). In the context of writing centers, some centers are funded at levels surplus to their needs and are thus able to pursue interesting and important research projects, community partnerships, and more. But we would ask the field to imagine a way to more equitably distribute that surplus, whether by asking more established and financed centers and programs to consider developing funds through regional organizations to help struggling centers; asking those centers to consider contributing more to professional organizations' travel- and support-oriented scholarships for conferences; asking our professional organizations to facilitate more needs assessment among their member institutions; and more. Our organizations could also provide guidance and resources to advocate for more stable tenure stream positions and labor organizing.

Taming Capitalism

The focus of taming capitalism lies in reducing its harms (e.g., exploitation, wage theft, precarity, extraction) through "reforms that introduce in one way or another egalitarian, democratic and solidaristic values and principles into the operation of capitalism" (p. 21). A "more humane economic system" (p. 21) is a cornerstone of this particular action. There are many ways that we might "tame" the adverse effects of late-stage capitalism on writing center work.

As one of the narratives in this project asserts "I've got a Secret," leveraging the accreditation process may be one of the most powerful means available to writing centers to tame capitalism. Colleges and universities in the United States all undergo accreditation and re-accreditation processes. Re-accreditation processes occur on a ten-year cycle, though there are often check-ins before and after the major re-accreditation process. An accredited institution maintains education standards, which impacts qualification for federal monies, acceptability of transfer credit, and student enrollment.

The process of accreditation (https://sacscoc.org/accrediting-standards/re affirmation-process/) is labor-intensive and involves many different internal and external committees. This process can be (and often is) a sign and a result of encroaching neoliberal logics on education. For instance, Moore et al. (2016) shared assorted concerns around the shift to larger scale assessments and accreditation, including big data, the increasing prominence of private educational assessment companies and their role in facilitating standardized assessment, and the shift from accountability to comparability between universities. That said, several case studies such as those in *Reclaiming Accountability* (O'Neill & Crow, 2016) demonstrate that large-scale accreditation-supported initiatives can be a site to leverage productive change for both programs and institutions. We see this shift, too, as a) a means to leverage resources to writing centers and thus improve working conditions, and b) a way to represent our expertise and praxis to accreditors and retain some autonomy in accreditation processes. In short, if we more purposefully integrate our work into some of the instruments of accreditation, we may receive the support to do what we have already been doing; if we fail to, we may be subject to the regulation and mandates without such support—our metalabor thus remains invisible.

The Southern Association of Colleges and Schools Commission on Colleges (SACSCOC) provides an interesting template to consider. SACSCOC accredits Southern colleges and universities in the United States. For the reaffirmation process, SACSCOC requires the creation of an institutional committee of faculty, staff, and administrators. That committee develops a quality enhancement plan (QEP) which is then shared with the entire institution. Students are also involved in this accreditation process. After an initial off-site review of the compliance certification, which results in a report, an on-site committee is created, which includes nearly a dozen administrative and faculty members from other institutions. They review different elements of the QEP, as well as core requirements and standards (related to things like the clarity of financial policies, the preparedness of faculty, the success of student support services, etc.). The on-site committee also creates a report and a response to the QEP. These materials are then, in turn, reviewed by SACSCOC Board of Trustees (BoT), who put forth a recommendation to reaffirm accreditation. This, in turn, is shared with the executive council, who recommends action to the BoT, who then finalizes their decision.

The process of accreditation and reaffirmation—a process specific to SACSCOC—aims to create a kind of consensus among an institution's community for the focus of an assessment and implementation plan (say, for improving outcomes from first year writing). There are several opportunities for a writing center administrator to become involved. From the initial QEP and reaffirmation planning committee, to the on-site visit, there are many chances to share research and assessment outcomes about the writing center that otherwise might not see the light of day. Furthermore, putting peer writing tutors in front of the on-site committee is a critical way to demonstrate the work of the writing center.

At the same time, accreditation is perhaps one of the places where we can advocate for recognition of our work alongside changes to how that work is done. Arguing for best practices and workplace standards for student support work, for example, can help to impact how accreditors evaluate the work of a writing center. If not up to par, this is a chance to advocate for more resources, better and more ethical practices, and, of course, regional standards for sustainable and regulated tutoring.

Advocate Through Accreditors

- Involve your writing center in your institution's accreditation process (https://www.chea.org/regional-accrediting-organizations).
- Provide research and assessment about the writing center to your institution's re-accreditation committee.
- Develop—through regional affiliates or main professional organization—workplace guidelines for best practices in tutoring work that includes basic resourcing requirements.
- Below, we share a template (Appendix B) that individual writing center directors can share with their regional accreditation board advocating for how the writing center ought to be assessed in the accreditation process.

As a note, we are not the first people who have asked for the International Writing Centers Association (IWCA) to develop worker and workplace standards for writing centers. An open letter shared in summer 2020 with the organization demanded a statement on the Black Lives Matter (BLM) movement and the treatment of BIPOC people in writing center work. Another open letter demanded COVID-19 policies for academic workers. Still other individuals have advocated for research and response to erosion in our field's tenure stream job market. In the end, the COVID-19 workplace policy was never formalized, and the open letter on BLM and anti-racism work in writing centers became part of a larger initiative that, ironically, did not create a workplace statement or set of standards. Similarly, the job market work was sidelined despite researchers' findings that traced and predicted a drastic fall off in tenure stream academic writing center administrator positions. In over three decades of operation, IWCA has passed only seven position statements, most of which we feel do not address the material realities of our work or put forth best practices and standards that regulate our field. In comparison, Council of Writing Program Administrators and Conference on College Composition and Communication both include position statements that directly address workplace issues like bullying, contingent labor, evaluating writing program administration labor for promotion and tenure, etc. College Composition and Communication has an entire section of their website devoted to working conditions. Yet, these other organizations—though they are also involved in writing center work and likely represent writing center administrators who also do other administrative work—do not include any statements specific to writing centers. Our working conditions, then, seem to matter less than others working in writing studies, which, we argue, is a canary in the coal mine issue. If stable writing center administrator positions continue to disappear, this will likely have a domino effect on other writing administrator positions, such as writing program directors, WAC/WID directors, etc. Therefore, we need to put forth field-specific standards for writing center administrators but, also, other workers.

Advocate for Field-Specific Standards

- Identify some of the greatest workplace challenges currently facing writing center workers (e.g., precarity, poor payment, confusing or unclear hiring lines, mental health concerns, healthcare policies, privatization, and outsourcing issues).
- Put forward position statements specifically addressing the challenges currently impacting workers and working conditions as well as ways to address these issues.
- Provide workshops, seminars, and other field-wide conversations around job negotiation strategies, creating memoranda of understanding (MOUs), clarifying hiring lines, and, even, guidance on developing field-specific positions and job ads.
- Create a list of best practices for the hiring and labor of writing center workers, just like WPA provides for WPAs, and for writing instructors.
- Develop a writing-center-specific certification and external review wing, much like the WPA consultant-evaluator panel.

Finally, professional organizations that are run on volunteer labor may not necessarily be the ideal spaces to advocate for workplace standards and aggressive worker advocacy. Other disciplines often hire and compensate the leaders of professional organizations and journal editors, which changes the production cycle, the balance of paid and unpaid labor, and the general functioning of these organizations. At the same time, however, most workers turn to unions and collective bargaining for sustained workplace advocacy and support. We place the action of labor organizing in the section below (resisting), however, one can argue that early trade union development responded to early capitalism, attempting to both tame and resist worker exploitation. So unionization efforts can fall into both of these categories.

Resisting Capitalism

Dismantling capitalism, like taming capitalism, as Wright (2019) explains, requires high levels of cooperation and coalition-building. Each approach seeks to use state, or, in our context, institutional power to regulate the negative outcomes of capitalism. That is, to dismantle or tame the influence of neoliberalism in our institutions or writing centers, we must rely on the apparatus of the institution itself.

In contrast, resisting capitalism "seeks to affect the behavior of capitalists and political elites through protest and other forms of resistance outside of the state. We may not be able to transform capitalism, but we can defend ourselves from its harms by causing trouble, protesting, raising the costs to elites of their actions" (Wright, 2019, p. 22). Resisting thus lies outside of existing or proscribed state/institutional structures. This strategy may involve smaller-scale organizing within the institution or through individual acts of resistance.

Unionization is one such means to resist capitalism. While some of the effects of the labor movement also seek to tame capitalism through regulation, we feel this model—because of its grassroots action often outside official institutions—should be discussed in this subsection. Yet, because of the erosion of the labor rights movement from the 1970s until quite recently, academic unionization is the kind of work that takes place in fits and spurts. As labor historian Mattson (2000) notes, there is a strange relationship between academics and their work. At the same time that there was a movement of unionization happening in the late 1990s and early 2000s among graduate students at Yale, New York University, University of Maryland, and University of Washington and adjunct workers at Miami Dade Community College and state colleges across New Jersey, there was also resistance to unionization from tenured faculty. Arguing that academic labor still followed a guild model where apprentice workers like graduate students become more trained and better paid as Assistant- and then tenured-professors, many secure academics have assumptions about academia that are anti-union, even as they profess otherwise progressive politics (Mattson, 2000, pp. 5–7).

Academia works on "paternalistic and individual training" (Mattson, 2000, p. 6). Yet, with the adjunctification of the academic workforce—60 percent when Mattson (2000) was writing and closer to 71 percent more recently (Culver & Kezar, 2021)—this medieval guild model of academic labor falls apart. Instead, as Mattson (2000) noted, a small number of secure people sit at the top of the workforce hierarchy while the bottom three quartiles struggle to make ends meet. This very issue actually led to guild worker reform in the mid-19th century as more apprentices and journeymen realized they would never become master craftsmen (p. 6). While Mattson (2000) identified a movement taking place in 2000, this, of course, did not foresee the anti-union policies put into place during the second decade of the 21st century, such as right-to-work legislation in two dozen states and a Supreme Court Ruling that eroded unions through ruling that they cannot require workers to pay fees thereby prohibiting required member fees.

The academic labor movement has struggled to develop and articulate a sense of class consciousness for decades. We see this in TT faculty failing to adequately support unionization, but even more so failing to organize unions of their own. We posit that this is due to a lack of class consciousness among many—not all—in tenure-stream academic positions, particularly those outside of the Writing and Rhetoric field, which are still dominated by a small and select group of elite institutions (Flaherty, 2022). This struggle is further demonstrated and commented upon in several of the stories in Act II. For example, in "Writing Center as Life Raft," an anonymous contributor notes "Narratives have more power for people who are working class, who come from nothing and have nothing, and who have had to carefully learn the 'rules' and how to navigate the system." Both Giaimo in "Boundless" (this collection) and Witt in "'Fucking Up' and Listening in the Writing Center" (this collection) share similar stories of struggling with class consciousness and the implicit rules and narratives that underwrite this system in the workplace.

Beyond the assumptions around a guild-like model of labor that requires years of investment, subjugation, and, ultimately, reward, there are also structural and legal barriers that prevent tenure-track faculty from either seeing their work as labor or seeing themselves as part of a labor class that needs union support. One systemic enactment that separates tenured and tenure track faculty from their fellow academic workers is the 1980 Supreme Court Yeshiva ruling (Lieberwitz, 2013), which made it illegal for tenure track and tenured faculty at private universities and colleges to form a union as they are classified as managerial. This kind of stratification of academic workers impacts both how these workers are classified (and the benefits and protections they are given), but, more insidiously, they create worker factions by separating out those with power from contingent workers. Despite recent drives to unionize adjunct and non-tenure track faculty at private institutions like Bates College (Neumann, 2021), it is still rare to have tenure and tenure-track faculty support for such drives. Additionally, institutions with money and power, like Northeastern University, have vigorously fought the formation of a graduate student union (Bernstein, 2017). In Act II, one anonymous contributor ("From the Archive," this collection) details some of the laborious work of union advocacy and representation for contingent workers, describing the ways in which management freezes these workers out of decision making around their center and jobs. Wall-to-wall organizing of different types of workers in the university—like the recent strike at Rutgers in 2023—appears to be one of the more efficacious ways to organize in higher education.

Despite local and often federal antagonism towards unionization, there have been a number of high-profile drives in the past few years that were likely spurred by the pandemic. Workers at an Amazon warehouse in Staten Island (Weise & Scheiber, 2022), at Starbucks locations in Buffalo, Rochester, Ithaca, Kansas City, and Manhattan—among many other sites—have all voted in favor of forming a union (Molla, 2022). In academia, between 2013 and 2019—years when some of the most repressive state and Federal rulings against unions and workers' rights were passed—188 faculty unions were certified or recognized (Flannery, 2020). This momentum has only gathered steam during the COVID-19 pandemic (Wakamo, 2021) as working conditions have deteriorated and real wages have dropped significantly alongside major institutional restructuring, hiring freezes, and other workforce planning decisions that took away jobs from many academic workers across the United States.

In a lot of ways, we have come a long way since 2000, largely because academia is so broken. The majority of academic workers will never be on the tenure track. Graduate students who traditionally went into professional academic higher ed teaching careers now regularly talk about alternative academic careers and union drives. And the COVID-19 pandemic has clearly demonstrated that our administrators care more about the bottom line than worker or student safety. We know that collective bargaining can resist the extractive effects of capitalism through advocating for and securing better wages, workplace conditions, benefits, democratic governance, and a host of other worker-forward interventions. So, whenever possible, we urge readers to consider unionizing as a critical piece of the regulation work that is involved in resisting capitalism. Below, we include advice for unionization and collective bargaining, including a guide (Appendix C) to running a union drive.

Unionization and Collective Bargaining

- Work with local American Association of University Professors and union chapters to assess working conditions and gauge interest in forming a union.
- Consider enrolling (individually or as a group) in one of UC Berkeley Labor Center's workshops (https://laborcenter.berkeley.edu/workshops-leadership-schools/), which include multi-day intensive training, or course-based models that range from 200 dollars to 1,500 dollars and cover anywhere from 1 to 20 people, depending on the program.
- Consult with lawyers on the feasibility of forming a union.
- If faculty at private universities and colleges, consider alternative options like a minority or members-only union.
- Connect with local teaching and service unions (e.g., National Education Association, American Federation of Teachers, or Service Employees International Union) to undertake a union drive (Appendix C) that excites, educates, and organizes adjuncts, professional staff, and other non-tenure track faculty.

- Encourage student workers to unionize (Perkins, 2022).
- If you already have union representation, ask to join the bargaining committee as a representative.

Escaping Capitalism

We acknowledge that a great deal of what we outline above will no doubt result in still more metalabor for writing center workers. We would add the caveat, however, that this work is necessary to ultimately reduce the sorts of metalabor less in line with our values. We offer a final set of strategies that would help reduce this less-meaningful sort of metalabor through what Wright (2019) describes as *escaping* capitalism, which is an effort "to try to insulate ourselves from the damaging effects of capitalism, and perhaps escape altogether its ravages in some sheltered environment" (p. 23). Existing scholarship and practices in writing centers already echo many of the values and work of escaping capitalism. One can see parallels, for example, between the sorts of sites we seek to foster on campus and Wright's (2019) description of how "Workers cooperatives attempt to create workplaces organized around principles of democracy, solidarity and equality, free of the alienation and exploitation of capitalist firms" (p. 23). Although there are inherent power differentials between directors and tutors (and other paraprofessionals involved in writing center work), the ethos of writing centers is often embedded in democratic and egalitarian practices within our spaces. Even beyond the culture and practices we may foster within our centers, there are strategies for escaping capitalism for individuals, such as pleasure activism, so-called quiet quitting, setting firm boundaries, or even leaving.

Pleasure Activism

While leaving and quiet quitting (or drawing hard boundaries around work) are very much in the cultural zeitgeist with the Great Resignation, we believe that this other, less discussed, strategy of pleasure activism is one that merges social justice with practices found in Zen Buddhism like non-attachment and loving-kindness to subvert oppression. Additionally, strategies like leaving or quiet quitting are also included in pleasure activism, as we detail below in the "pleasure principles" brown (2019) created below.

In Act II's collection of stories, several talk about how community care and the flexibilities of work and mentorship help workers to thrive in their positions. For example, Anand discusses the importance of a mentor in shaping professional and personal development ("Thank you for Carrying Me Through, Thank You for Your Labor"). Molly Ryan details the process of coming out as queer over and over again to support others in the writing center in "Coaching Queerly: Healing in Writing Center Work." Mary Elizabeth Skinner & Jaclyn Wells in "Labor of

Love: Managing the Writing Center and New Motherhood during the Pandemic" discuss how work sharing and flexible work schedules help them to take parental leave. Another example of how intentional work policies can be enacted to support one's work-life balance comes from this collection's "Care and work/spaces: Writing center labor during COVID-19," where Janine Morris shares caring for her terminally ill mother during the COVID-19 pandemic. Here, flexible work policies allow Janine to return to Canada to care for her dying mother without fear of job loss or missing work. Finally, Oluwatosin Mariam Junaid finds joy in tutoring work and the fellowship of shared practice during the COVID-19 pandemic in "What the Covid-19 pandemic taught us about writing center work: The joys of a tutor at the Laboratory of Academic Literacy (LLAC)" (this collection). Here, the joys of the work and the gifts that this field can give us are facilitated by mutual aid, community care, flexible work policies, mentorship, and pleasure-centered work.

According to maree brown (2019), pleasure activism is "the work we do to reclaim our whole, happy, and satisfiable selves from the impacts, delusions, and limitations of oppression and/or supremacy" (p. 11). While brown (2019) discussed pleasurable activities that might seem separate from intellectual (or even paid) work such as food, fashion, humor, the erotic, the arts, "passion work," she also recognizes that there are "policies and power dynamics inside of everything that makes us feel good" (p. 11). brown (2019) also recognized that pleasure in a capitalist society is bound with precarity, oppression, and scarcity. In engaging in pleasure activism—particularly focusing on "those most impacted by oppression"—we can tap "into the potential goodness in each of us [even as] we can generate justice and liberation, growing a healing abundance where we have been socialized to believe only scarcity exists" (brown, 2019, p. 11). Pleasure activism, then, in a real sense can combat the deleterious effects of toxic work culture like workism, burnout, bullying, and racism. In embracing the collective and focusing on abundance (rather than scarcity) and "passion work" (rather than optimization) we can be more joyous and satisfied, even as we "bring about social and political change" (brown, 2019, p. 12).

Pleasure activism includes practices that can be applied, as brown (2019) has noted, to one's work life as much as one's social life. Some of these—like saying "no" to say "yes" later, or moderation is the key, are themes that are echoed in many of the stories in this book. Others like "riding the line between commitment and detachment" or "we become what we practice" are strategies that have analogues in Zen Buddhism and mindfulness work (p. 12). Engagement in specific consistent behavioral and thought practices, and practicing non-attachment are keys to spiritual practice. They can also teach us important lessons about how we approach work and the limiting factors beyond the self at work. All of this, we hope, will help people to have more healthy work lives and, also, leave room for more positive feelings like contentment, joy, and, hopefully, pleasure.

Pleasure activism, however, is inherently political and concerned with the work of social justice and liberation, particularly anti-racist work and racial liberation; it is not hedonistic, despite the use of the term pleasure. As maree brown (2019) noted: "pleasure is not one of the spoils of capitalism. It is what our bodies, our human systems, are structured for; it is the aliveness and awakening, the gratitude and humility, the joy and celebration of being miraculous" (p. 13). brown (2019) observes a natural abundance in the world and pleasure activism taps into that abundance. Yet, even the concept—not just the practice—of pleasure is denied to so many of us because it is so often the purview of those who are wealthy, able, white, and straight enough to enjoy it. Returning to the collective, and combining it with pleasure activism, one can imagine alternative work (and social) spaces that tap into positive feelings while orienting towards social justice. Many writing centers are already trying to do this work, though we do not explicitly characterize it as pleasure or joy.

So, for different people, expression of pleasure activism might look quite different and have vastly different implications and outcomes. For our BIPOC colleagues, pleasure activism might be a matter of life or death, as Neisha-Anne Green (2018) detailed in her International Writing Centers Association keynote when discussing Black Lives Matter activists facing burnout and struggling with suicidal ideation or navigating her own dangerous experiences with racism in the workplace. For our white colleagues, this might include engaging in pleasure activism that is oriented towards racial justice and liberation; work that centers joy but also justice. This might include new workplace policies that protect and support workers, celebrating workers—especially BIPOC workers. It might include reimagining the work of the writing center as one that is both justice-oriented AND pleasurable, perhaps even occurring outside the university or college.

We often talk about a love of work, but really we mean pleasure and passion as they relate to work but also extend outside labor and production, as maree brown (2019) identified. Untangling our feelings about work and how we situate ourselves in our work (or do not) helps to build healthier and joyous connections to our work, even as it also helps us to escape the more toxic effects of late-stage capitalism such as exploitation and oppression. This approach allows us to alter our relationship to work to one that is meaningful, socially just, and outside the typical bounds of neoliberal institutions.

Pleasure Principles (adopted from maree brown, 2019, p. 12)

- What you pay attention to grows.
- We become what we practice.
- We feel pleasure when we make decisions and live into them.
- When we are happy, it is good for the world.
- The deepest pleasure comes from riding the line between commitment
- and detachment.

- Make justice and liberation feel good.
- Your "no" makes the way for your "yes."
- Moderation is key.

Quiet Quitting, Work to Rule, and Drawing Hard Work Boundaries

The term *quiet quitting* has gained traction in popular discourse in the wake of the COVID-19 pandemic although the term itself is somewhat controversial. As a recent article in the *Guardian* characterizes it:

> Rather than working late on a Friday evening, organizing the annual team-building trip to Slough or volunteering to supervise the boss's teenager on work experience, the quiet quitters are avoiding the above and beyond, the hustle culture mentality, or what psychologists call "occupational citizenship behaviors." (Tapper, 2022)

In short, *quiet quitting* generally refers to the trend of people consciously (quietly) refusing to go above and beyond the existing and explicit expectations around performance and productivity in their work, or, specifically, working only to one's contractual obligations.

That said, even the term itself is couched in capitalist ideologies. Ed Zitron, publisher of the labor-focused newsletter, *Where's Your Ed At*, explained in an interview with *National Public Radio* that "The term 'quiet quitting' is so offensive, because it suggests that people that do their work have somehow quit their job, framing workers as some sort of villain in an equation where they're doing exactly what they were told" (Kilpatrick, 2022). Workism—or work as a spiritual pursuit above most other elements of one's life—is associated with so many industries has become an object of increasing scrutiny, leading many to wonder if their work and the focus on it is in line with their actual values. While we acknowledge the controversial nature of the term, we invite readers to consider its rhetorical potency and the term's reclamation as a form of resistance itself.

Quiet quitting is an opportunity to examine our priorities as laborers: what is essential to our work, and what is ticking boxes? What can be done minimally or de-emphasized to make room for the sorts of labor we see as meaningful and that will lead to flourishing? Being mindful and purposive about that prioritization may also free up the time and emotional reserves necessary to do the sorts of metalabor we describe in other forms of eroding capitalism. Rather than seeing quiet quitting as a neglect of our duties, we see it as a call to quietly escape some of the more panoptic and regulatory forms of neoliberalism that have intruded on our work—a call to be able to define and pursue our duties on our terms.

Another—more pro-worker—term for quiet quitting is *work to rule*, which is a coordinated union action where workers follow their contracts to the letter and perform their duties and nothing more. This kind of approach ends up being disruptive because it slows down productivity—even though the workers are doing their jobs—because it demonstrates all the ways in which job descriptions and duties have been encroached upon and how additional duties creep into everyday work. In performing work to rule, workers (and unions) educate management on how it is only by the largess of workers, and perhaps because of their precarity, that work gets done at the speed and quality that we often come to expect. Unlike quiet quitting, which negatively connotes a worker's choice to only perform the core duties of their job, work to rule is an empowering action often used during contract negotiation. It brings to the fore the fragile ecosystem of a workplace where fewer workers are expected to perform double or even triple duty because of cutbacks, efficiencies, or understaffing. Work to rule, however, need not be coordinated by a union—though collective worker action packs more of a punch to productivity. It can be done individually and, as opposed to quiet quitting, openly as a way to advocate for job position changes, additional staffing, and other workplace interventions.

So while many of the stories in this book discuss establishing work boundaries and work boundaries that are transgressed, work to rule can function as a guiding framework for setting firm, explicit boundaries around work and duties. Below, we share some practices common in work to rule that can be adopted even without collective action, though through collective action it is likely that more workplace demands will be met . . .

Guide to Work to Rule

- **Ensuring** that job descriptions are up-to-date and accurate, so that laborers perform only the essential and core functions of the job.
- **Knowing** what your contract says and sticking to it.
- **Refusing** additional uncompensated service, teaching, or administrative tasks.
- **Setting** hard work/life boundaries, with work taking up roughly 8 hours per weekday and no more.
- **Refusing** to respond to email during non-work hours or paid or sick leave.
- **Resisting** pressure to attend unpaid social or off-hours events.
- **Asking** for additional compensation to undertake additional work.
- **Making** use of vacation days, sick leave, and paid time off.
- **Refusing** to take on additional tasks without them being added to job descriptions.

We suspect that many directors post-pandemic have begun to interrogate their work-life balance and setting firmer work boundaries, as Johnston's story "The First Year: A New Director's Experience" shares, "What is more challenging is advocating for myself. That's the part I'm continually working on. I'm making appointments across campus with administrators to advocate for increased funding. I'm learning to be loud. I'm learning to say no" (this collection). Boundary-setting can be intimidating for workers, and it may mark workers as difficult or uncooperative. That said, we wonder what would happen if you said "no?" Would the potential loss of capital force the institution to see the center differently—to see *you* differently?

Leaving

Finally, we want to observe that leaving the job is an option for those seeking to escape the labor conditions inherent in writing center work in our contemporary climate of neoliberalism and austerity. "From Dream Job to Unsustainable" (Anonymous, this collection) and Cheatle in "Moving On to Move Up" (this collection) share two different types of leaving—leaving the profession entirely or engaging in hyper-mobility within the profession to secure a more sustainable position. Though it may seem obvious, leaving a job can be one of the most empowering choices one can make. We've spoken about the Great Resignation at several points in this book, but it bears repeating here: once workers realized that their work was not compensating them what they were worth and began resigning en masse, *wages and benefits increased dramatically* (Bruner, 2022). Indeed, given the expanded opportunities in the private sphere as a consequence of the Great Resignation—or reshuffling as some have found most moved into other positions, eventually—higher education will have to compete if they wish to retain competent workers.

And though it may sound heretical, we ask: should a field that is sustained by exploitive practices be sustained? If administrators are not willing to adequately resource and support an apparatus that we know to provide them a return on investment through retention and other measures, why are we enabling it? Why are we taking on so much extra, uncompensated labor to perpetuate this system? In addition to some of the stories shared here—which detail the decision to leave or being forced to leave their jobs—we personally know of several friends and colleagues who have left the profession since we began this project, either leaving academia entirely or moving into other academic areas: some into administration and others returning to teaching. We do not yet know, however, if the positions they have left will be resourced or supported at the levels they were before or if those will be configured differently. We can only hope, at this point, that leaving may "move the needle," so to speak, on what is an acceptable job in our field.

Beyond the collective implications of leaving the job, leaving can also be the right, moral choice for individuals. Though workism has cultivated a disdain for so-called quitters and has glorified "hustle" culture, we ask here what it means for the dignity of the individuals toiling within these systems. Is alienation from one's labor a necessary prerequisite for the right to exist? If the Great Resignation has taught us anything, it is that there are alternatives that might lead to flourishing. Wright (2019) speaks of "flourishing," as follows:

> I use the idea of human flourishing as a way of capturing an all-around sense of a person's life going well. A flourishing life is one in which a person's capacities and talents have developed in ways which enable them to pursue their life goals, so that in some general sense they have been able to realize their potentials and purposes. It is easy to see what this means when we think of a person's health and physical condition: a flourishing life is more than just the absence of disease; it also embodies a positive idea of physical vitality that enables people to live energetically in the world. Similarly, for other aspects of one's life, flourishing implies a positive, robust realization of one's capacities, not just an absence of grave deficits. (p. 5)

If writing center work does not enable its workers to flourish—to "live energetically" and with a "robust realization of [their] capacities" (Wright, 2019, p. 5)—it is logical and just to leave it. We remain optimistic that if enough workers were to leave, such a migration may prompt administrators and institutions to adapt and to adequately compensate and support writing center practitioners as a whole, enabling them to flourish in that work.

That said, we also acknowledge that leaving isn't an option for all laborers. Debt has become an increasing prerequisite for pursuing a college degree, and college degrees are generally required to work in college writing centers. Accordingly, as Daniel (2022) has detailed, "For the average borrower, financial immobility and reduced choice . . . are typical consequences of this debt system" (p. 61). Leaving may not be an option for all laborers, but we hope that other tactics of dismantling, taming, resisting, and escaping may mitigate some of the labor conditions that would otherwise compel someone to leave.

So, ultimately, to further unpack the complexity of whether to leave, we believe it is critical to not only listen critically to co-workers and to administrators who encourage staying "for the good of others." You should also listen to yourself: to engage in radical honesty ("Radical Honesty," 2021) where you perform an honest assessment of feelings, experiences, attitudes, and needs about your work. Removing defensive stances from the equation is helpful in this process, as is closing out the "noise" of other signals outside of yours and your family's. If after engaging in radical honesty about this work and what keeps you in it and where you hope to be in the future, you decide to leave, we hope you feel acceptance in this conclusion.

Concluding Thoughts

We believe that the stories in this collection demonstrate that writing centers are very good at supporting students in environments with limited funding, but perhaps they are less prepared to support themselves. Individually, we do not always have the agency to determine budgets. Individually, we cannot often successfully argue for tenure lines, for more stability, or for better pay. Writing center administrators are also often powerless in the face of shifting reporting lines or institutional positioning. And though writing centers can assert their value in terms of continuing to teach writing through individualized peer support, without collective action, we will remain contingent in many of the ways described at length in this project, both individually and as a field.

But what if we treated ourselves as a collective? What if we spoke, wrote, and acted collectively? What if we worked together to enact the creation of good jobs? What if the profession worked to standardize expectations around salaries? What if we lobbied collectively and were more vocal, more outspoken, and more aggressive? What if we collaborated to anticipate and counter the latest fiscal "crises" and austerity measures? What if we took agency by collectively seizing power? What if we unlearned our internalized capitalist logics?

In "Invisible Work" Daniels (1987) wrote about the fundamental shift when women entered the paid labor market, changing both the home and communal spaces like churches. Institutions, then, are not simply maintained by this invisible work but are also drastically altered when communal, unpaid, and often overlooked work is withheld:

> Changes in institutions bring to light not only the earlier work required for their maintenance but also the work implicated in creation of new institutional forms. If we examine changes closely, we can see what has been added or taken away in our society by the presence or absence of efforts that we have come to take for granted. We appreciate and want the efforts that make our institutions more workable though we wouldn't credit most of it as work. (412)

Withholding labor through strikes is one such strategy to bring unpaid and invisible work to the forefront of our discussions about our institutions. There are, however, more large-scale protests such as mass walkouts that bring attention to labor equity issues from a population standpoint rather than an industry-specific one. For example, in 2020 essential workers across the United States walked off their jobs to support Black lives (Treisman, 2020). The walkout was organized by 60 labor unions as well as social justice organizations. The 1975 Icelandic women's strike—organized by women from political parties as well as Feminist organizations—urged women to walk out of their paid and unpaid (domestic) work to protest unequal pay and violence towards women. This protest put Iceland at the forefront of gender equity policy and rights (Hofverberg, 2022). Recently, in late October 2023, there was another walk-out of women and non-binary people in Iceland, still in protest of equal pay and sexual violence ("Why are women in 'feminist paradise' Iceland striking?" 2023).

Here, we see two very different kinds of labor organizing, but the Iceland walkout explicitly addressed how invisible work—particularly in the domestic space—was necessary for the functioning of the country. When women walked out, they left their children, their cooking, their chores, all of which underpin the fabric of the paid economy and the work of men. Interestingly, the 1975 strike was known as the long Friday and the country ran out of sausages, because men chose a simple and fast meal to cook for their children. The walkout, then, caused mass shortages, work stoppages, and general disruption on a national scale; it also paved the way for gender equity policies and many contribute the strike to the election of Iceland's first female Prime Minister five years later (Hofverberg, 2022). Imagine if every writing center participated in a national walkout in the United States. How many hundreds of thousands of students would fail to receive support? How many thousands of faculty would be denied professional development and support? Mass protest could help bring our invisible work, our emotional labor, our metalabor to the fore. It might, as other education workers have done through withholding grades while striking for better pay and workplace conditions, create a kind of painful but incredibly visible absence in the ecosystem of higher education. Imagine what a world without writing centers would be like for the institutions we serve.

Of course, in addition to direct action, we believe we need more research to inform, document, and support our collective efforts. More research on invisible work, emotional labor, job creep, and metalabor would be useful in making this often-unseen labor more visible and thus valued. If we were able to systematically name, for instance, how we use affect and emotion in our sessions and in our administration, we might be better equipped to train—and be compensated—for that work. We also wish to continue and encourage research on intersectionality, labor, and writing center work. We wonder, for example, how laborers experience disability and access fatigue (Konrad, 2021) and how this fatigue compounds with the other metalabors of administrative work. We wonder similar things about the emotional tax levied on BIPOC workers and how those workers encounter it in writing center spaces. We hope to see research by those who have taken radical labor steps: what are the results of those steps? What are the costs? What further opportunities have availed themselves? These are only a few of the areas of inquiry we imagine for anti-capitalist writing center futures.

We also hope future work will unpack our histories—particularly, how writing centers were formed and how they currently run. We see many models of writing centers that were created decades ago and under drastically different circumstances than workers in the managed university currently face. In examining our histories, we might learn more about how decisions that were made in the past still shape our work currently, and whether or not these models are still sustainable or require similar or more (or somehow less) metalabor.

Finally, as many of the writing center directors who were there at the start of our modern iteration in the 1970s start to retire and—sadly—die, the field loses histories that would otherwise teach us more about our field's origins and the establishment of modern-day writing centers. We believe there have been significant changes in the gender, class, and race make-up of our field, yet in many ways we are currently an overwhelmingly white, female-identifying profession. If current trends in higher education apply to our field, we suspect that male-identifying workers perhaps move more easily into and out of more stable administration positions than their female and non-binary counterparts (Whitford, 2020). The gender dynamics of our field, then, must be interrogated more systemically. We are especially interested in how the profession—and its pipeline into tenure track and more stable positions—has changed over the past 60 years or so and how gender has played a role in that shift.

We still have so many questions about our collective future, the future of higher education, and the state of our workplaces. We also have a lot of dreams and wishes. Many of these are reflected in the stories in Act II and in the guidance in Act III—imagining a different way, a better way forward into the future. And while conversations around these topics often feel personal and risk further marginalizing already-marginalized members of our community, we assert that these conversations might empower those same members and give those who experience less precarity an opportunity to step into advocacy roles. Ultimately, these conversations might lead to our ability to flourish in this work. This is an unlearning process, made more meaningful by storying and, of course, by writing. The next step, however, is action; we are more powerful as a collective, when we act *together*.

References

AAUP (2022). Forming a Union Chapter. https://www.aaup.org/chapter-resources/forming-new-union.

AlJazeera. (2023). Why are women in 'feminist paradise' Iceland striking? *AlJazeera*. https://www.aljazeera.com/editorial/2023/10/24/why-are-women-in-feminist-paradise-iceland-striking.

Associated Press (2022). University of California workers end strike after approving contracts. *National Public Radio*. https://www.npr.org/2022/12/24/1145415255/university-of-california-end-strike-approve-contract.

Associated Press (2023). Thousands of U.S. workers are on strike. Here's a rundown of major work stoppages. *Time*. https://time.com/6320913/thousands-u-s-workers-strike/.

Bamberg, M. & Georgakopoulou, A. (2008). Small stories as a new perspective in narrative and identity analysis. *Text & Talk, 28*(3), 377–396.

Bawarshi, A. & Pelkowski, S. (1999). Postcolonialism and the idea of a writing center. *The Writing Center Journal, 19*(2), 41–58.

Beck, J. (2018). The concept creep of emotional labor. *The Atlantic*. https://www.theatlantic.com/family/archive/2018/11/arlie-hochschild-housework-isnt-emotional-labor/576637/.

Berg, M. & Seeber, B. K. (2013). The slow professor: Challenging the culture of speed in the academy. *Transformative Dialogues: Teaching & Learning Journal, 6*(3), 1–7.

Berg, M. & Seeber, B. K. (2016). *The slow professor: Challenging the culture of speed in the academy*. University of Toronto Press.

Bernstein, H. (2017). Graduate student workers rally for union recognition. *The Huntington News*. https://huntnewsnu.com/49746/campus/49746/.

Brentnell L., Dixon, E. & Robinson, R. (2021). The hidden and invisible: Vulnerability in writing center work. In G. N. Giaimo (Ed.), *Wellness and care in writing center work*. PB Pressbooks. https://ship.pressbooks.pub/writingcentersandwellness/chapter/title-here-3/.

brown, a. m. (2019). *Pleasure activism*. AK Press.

Bruner, R. (2022). The great resignation fueled higher pay—Even for those who didn't switch jobs. *Time*. https://time.com/6143212/us-wage-growth-record-high/.

Burns, P. K. (2023). "We have to continue to teach this university a lesson": 3 Rutgers faculty unions vote to ratify contract, but say "unfinished business" remains. *National Public Radio*. https://whyy.org/articles/rutgers-university-union-agreement-ratified-workers/.

Camarillo, E. C. (2022). An idea of a writing center: Moving toward antiracism in asynchronous sessions. *WLN: A Journal of Writing Center Scholarship, 46*(7–8), 19–27.

Card, K. G. & Hepburn, K. J. (2023). Is neoliberalism killing us? A cross sectional study of the impact of neoliberal beliefs on health and social wellbeing in the midst of the COVID-19 pandemic. *International Journal of Social Determinants of Health and Health Services, 53*(3), 363–373.

Carter-Tod, S. (2020). Administrating while Black: Negotiating the emotional labor of an African American female WPA. In C. A. Wooten, J. Babb & K. M. Costello (Eds.), *The things we carry: Strategies for recognizing and negotiating emotional labor in writing program administration* (pp. 197–214). Utah State University Press.

Caswell, N., McKinney, J. G. & Jackson, R. (2016). *The working lives of new writing center directors*. Utah State University Press.

Chase, S. (2011). Narrative inquiry: Still a field in the making. In N.K. Denzin & Y.S. Lincoln (Eds.), *The SAGE handbook of qualitative research* (pp. 421–434). SAGE.

Clark, I. L. (1993). Portfolio evaluation, collaboration, and writing centers. *College Composition and Communication, 44*(4), 515–524.

Clinnin, K. (2020). And so I respond. In C.A. Wooten, J. Babb & K.M. Costello (Eds.), *The things we carry: Strategies for recognizing and negotiating emotional labor in writing program administration* (pp. 129–144). Utah State University Press.

Clinnin, K. (2021). In the event of an emergency: Crisis management for WPAs. *WPA: Writing Program Administration, 45*(1), 9–30.

Cohen, D. & Mikaelian, A. (2021). *The Privatization of everything: How the plunder of public goods transformed America and how we can fight back*. The New Press.

Conference on College Composition and Communication (2022). *CCCC Position Statements*. https://cccc.ncte.org/cccc/resources/positions.

Council for Higher Education Accreditation (2020). *Regional accrediting organizations*. https://www.chea.org/regional-accrediting-organizations.

Council of Writing Program Administrators (2022). *WPA position statements and resolutions*. https://wpacouncil.org/aws/CWPA/pt/sp/statements.

Culver, K. C. & Kezar, A. (2021). The impacts of 2020 on advancement of non-tenure track and adjunct faculty. *National Academies*. https://nap.nationalacademies.org/resource/26405/6_The_Impacts_of_2020_on_Advancement_of_Contingent_Faculty-Culver_Kezar.pdf.

Daniels, A. K. (1987). Invisible work. *Social problems, 34*(5), 403–415.

Daniel, J. R. (2020). Burning out: Writing and the self in the era of terminal productivity. *Enculturation: A Journal of Rhetoric, Writing, and Culture, 30*.

Daniel, J.R. (2022). *Toward an anti-capitalist composition*. Utah State University Press.

DeBacher, S. & Harris-Moore, R. (2016). First, do no harm: Teaching writing in the wake of traumatic events. *Composition Forum, 34*. https://compositionforum.com/issue/34/first-do-no-harm.php.

Delgado, R. (1989). Storytelling for oppositionists and others: A plea for narrative. *Michigan Law Review, 87*(8), 2411–2441.

Degner, H., Wojciehowski, K. & Giroux, C. (2015). Opening closed doors: A rationale for creating a safe space for tutors struggling with mental health concerns or illnesses. *Praxis: A Writing Center Journal 13*(1), 27–37.

Denny, H. (2005). Queering the writing center. *Writing Center Journal, 25*(2), 39–63.

Denny, H. C., Mundy, R., Naydan, L. M., Sévère, R. & Sicari, A. (Eds.). (2019). *Out in the center: Public controversies and private struggles*. Utah State University Press.

Driscoll, D. L. & Perdue, S. W. (2012). Theory, lore, and more: An analysis of RAD research in The Writing Center Journal 1980–2009. *The Writing Center Journal, 32*(2), 11–39.

Driscoll, D. L., Perdue, S.W. & Rafoth, B. (2017). *Embracing bold new frontiers: Writing centers as sites of production*. Conference on College Composition and Communication Annual Conference, Portland, OR, United States.

Driscoll, D. L. & Wells, J. (2020). Tutoring the whole person: Supporting emotional development in writers and tutors. *Praxis: A Writing Center Journal, 17*(3), 16–28.

Dugarova, E. (2020). Unpaid care work in times of the COVID-19 crisis: Gendered impacts, emerging evidence and promising policy responses. Paper presented for UN Expert Group Meeting 'Families in development: Assessing progress, challenges and emerging issues, Focus on modalities for IYF+30. https://www.un.org/development/desa/family/wp-content/uploads/sites/23/2020/09/Duragova.Paper_.pdf.

Emmelhainz, N. (2020). Tutoring begins with breath: Guided meditation and its effects on writing consultant training. *WLN: A Journal of Writing Center Scholarship, 44*(5/6), 2–10.

Faison, W. & Condon, F. (Eds.). (2022). *Counterstories from the writing center*. Utah State University Press.

Fels, D. (2017). The risks of contingent writing center directorships. In Kahn et al. (Eds.), *Contingency, exploitation, and solidarity: Labor and action in English composition*, (pp. 119–131). The WAC Clearinghouse; University Press of Colorado. https://doi.org/10.37514/PER-B.2017.0858.

Fels, D., Gardner, C., Herb, M. M. & Naydan, L. M. (2021). Contingent writing center work. *The Writing Center Journal, 39*(1/2), 351–380.

Flaherty, C. (2021). Faculty salaries dip this year. *Inside Higher Ed*. https://www.insidehighered.com/news/2021/04/13/faculty-salaries-decreased-year.

Flaherty, C. (2022). Prestige hiring across academe. *Inside Higher Ed*. https://tinyurl.com/mrx343zm.

Flannery, M. E. (2020). "We stepped up and fought back": Behind the explosive growth of new faculty unions. *National Education Association*. https://tinyurl.com/2j33v5rs.

Forbes. (2021). Radical honesty: How to build trust in a dispersed workforce. *Forbes*. https://www.forbes.com/sites/servicenow/2021/12/09/radical-honesty-how-to-build-trust-in-a-dispersed-workforce/?sh=624f9b922053.

Geller, A. E. & Denny, H. (2013). Of ladybugs, low status, and loving the job: Writing center professionals navigating their careers. *The Writing Center Journal, 33*(1), 96–129.

Giaimo, G. (2020). Laboring in a time of crisis: The entanglement of wellness and work in writing centers. *Praxis: A Writing Center Journal, 17*(3), 3–15. https://www.praxisuwc.com/173-giaimo.

Giaimo, G. (Ed.) (2021). *Wellness and care in writing center work: A WLN digital edited collection*. Digital Edited Collections: An Imprint of WLN.

Giaimo, G. (2022). Is it enough? An interrogation of the wellness turn in writing centers. In Morris, J. & Concannon, K. (Eds.), *Emotion and affect in the writing center* (pp. 272–288). Parlor Press.

Giaimo, G. (2022). Continuing to labor in a crisis: Counternarratives to workism culture. *Praxis: A Writing Center Journal, 19*(2), 3–9. https://www.praxisuwc.com/192-giaimo.

Giaimo, G. N. (2023). *Unwell writing centers: Searching for wellness in neoliberal educational institutions and beyond.* Utah State University Press.

Giaimo, G., Brooks, M., Smith, T., Dixon, E., Faison, W. & Caswell, N. (unpublished). IWCA-sponsored survey on social justice and working conditions. *Conference on College Composition and Communication.*

Green, N. A. (2018). Moving beyond alright: And the emotional toll of this, my life matters too, in the writing center work. *The Writing Center Journal, 37*(1), 15–34.

Greenfield, L. (2019). *Radical writing center praxis: A call for ethical political engagement.* Utah State University Press.

Greenfield, L. & Rowan, K. (Eds.). (2011). *Writing centers and the new racism: A call for sustainable dialogue and change.* Utah State University Press.

Grimm, N. (1996). The regulatory role of the writing center: Coming to terms with a loss of innocence. *The Writing Center Journal, 17*(1), 5–29.

Guay, A. M. (2023). Comfort, contingency, and writing center work: An essay in three illusions. *The Writing Center Journal, 41*(1), 7–16.

Haltiwanger Morrison, T. M. & Evans Garriott, D. A. (Eds.) (2023). *Writing centers and racial justice: A guidebook for critical praxis.* Utah State University Press.

Haltiwanger Morrison, T. M. & Nanton, T. O. (2019). Dear writing centers: Black women speaking silence into language and action. *The Peer Review, 3*(1). https://tinyurl.com/ycxstjbd.

Haswell, R. H. (2005). NCTE/CCCC's recent war on scholarship. *Written Communication, 22*(2), 198–223.

Healy, D. (1991). Tutorial role conflict in the writing center. *The Writing Center Journal, 11*(2), 41–50.

Healy, D. (1995). Writing center directors: An emerging portrait of the profession. *WPA-LOGAN-, 18*, 26–43.

Herb, M.M., Naydan, L.M. & Gardner, C. (Eds.). (2023). Contingency and its intersections in writing centers [Special issue]. *Writing Center Journal, 4* (1).

Hochschild, A. R. (2013). *So how's the family? And other essays.* University of California Press.

Hofverberg, E. (2022, March 8). Kvennafridagurinn – The day Icelandic women went on strike [Blog post]. *Library of Congress Blogs.* https://blogs.loc.gov/law/2022/03/kvennafridagurinn-the-day-icelandic-women-went-on-strike/.

Iantosca, T. (2020). Imagining the new community: The writing center's hidden antagonisms after the neoliberal turn. Im@go. *A Journal of the Social Imaginary,* (16), 151–173.

International Writing Centers Association (2018). *Position statements.* https://writingcenters.org/position-statements/.

Isaacs, E. & Knight, M. A bird's eye view of writing centers: Institutional infrastructure, scope and programmatic issues, reported practices. *WPA, 37*(2), 36–67.

Jackson, R. L. (2008). Resisting institutional narratives: one student's counterstories of writing and learning in the academy. *Writing Center Journal, 28*(1), 23–42.

Janus v. American Federation of State, County, and Municipal Employees, Council 31. (2018). Oyez. https://www.oyez.org/cases/2017/16-1466.

Jiang, X., Salgado, A. R. & Glass, C. (2022). Peri-pandemic graduate writing mentorship. *Praxis, 19*(3). https://www.praxisuwc.com/193-jiang-et-al.

Johnson, S. (2018). Mindful tutors, embodied writers: Positioning mindfulness meditation as a writing strategy to optimize cognitive load and potentialize writing center tutors' supportive roles. *Praxis: A Writing Center Journal, 15*(2). https://www.praxisuwc.com/johnson-152.

Kail, H. (1983). Collaborative learning in context: The problem with peer tutoring. *College English, 45*(6), 594–599.

Kervin, C. E. & Barrett, H. E. (2018). Emotional management over time management: Using mindfulness to address student procrastination. *WLN: A Journal of Writing Center Scholarship, 42*(9/10), 10–18.

Kilpatrick, A. (2022). What is 'quiet quitting,' and how it may be a misnomer for setting boundaries at work. *National Public Radio.* https://www.npr.org/2022/08/19/1117753535/quiet-quitting-work-tiktok.

Kjesrud, R. D. (2015). Lessons from data: Avoiding lore bias in research paradigms. *The Writing Center Journal, 34*(2), 33–58.

Konrad, A.K. (2021). Access fatigue: The rhetorical work of disability in everyday life. *College English, 83*(3), 179–99.

Leary, J. (2023). What Is Neoliberalism? An Economic and Political System Devoted to the Free Market. *Teen Vogue.* https://www.teenvogue.com/story/what-is-neoliberalism.

Lerner, N. (2009). *The idea of a writing laboratory.* SIU Press.

Lewis, T. (2019). Longmore lecture: Contexts, clarity & grounding. *Personal Blog and Notes from February 19, 2019 Longmore Lecture at San Francisco State University,* https://www.talilalewis.com/blog/longmore-lecture-context-clarity-grounding.

Lieberwitz, R. L. (2013). Navigating troubled waters at the NLRB. *Academe, 99*(6), 10–15.

Lowe, J. (2021). What does California owe its incarcerated firefighters? *The Atlantic.* https://www.theatlantic.com/politics/archive/2021/07/california-inmate-firefighters/619567/.

Mack, E. & Hupp, K. (2017). Mindfulness in the writing center: A total encounter. *Praxis: A Writing Center Journal, 14*(2). https://www.praxisuwc.com/mack-and-hupp-142.

Mahala, D. (2007). Writing centers in the managed university. *Writing Center Journal, 27*(2), 3–17. https://doi.org/10.7771/2832-9414.1627.

Mannon, B. (2021). Centering the Emotional Labor of Writing Tutors. *The Writing Center Journal, 39*(1/2), 143–168.

Martinez, A. Y. (2016). Alejandra writes a book: A critical race counterstory about writing, identity, and being Chicanx in the academy. *Praxis: A Writing Center Journal, 14*(1), 56–61.

Martini, R. H. (2022). *Disrupting the center: A partnership approach to writing across the university.* Utah State University Press.

Mattson, K. (2000). The academic labor movement: Understanding its origins and current challenges. *Social Policy, 30*(4), 4–10.

Mayo, R. & Dixon, N. E. (2021). Navigating and adapting writing centers through a pandemic: Justifying our work in new contexts. *The Peer Review, 5*(2), https://tinyurl.com/32wba9hs.

McKinney, J. G. (2005). Leaving home sweet home: Towards critical readings of writing center spaces. *Writing Center Journal, 25*(2), 6–21.

McKinney, J. G. (2013). *Peripheral visions for writing centers.* Utah State University Press.

Mesle, M. (2021). Why we celebrate Labor Day: Two of the little-known heroes of Pullman. *National Parks Conservation Association.* https://www.npca.org/articles/2991-why-we-celebrate-labor-day-two-of-the-little-known-heroes-of-pullman.

Micciche, L.R. (2018). From the editor. *Composition Studies, 46*(2), 10–11.

Molla, R. (2022). How a bunch of Starbucks baristas built a labor movement. *Vox.* https://www.vox.com/recode/22993509/starbucks-successful-union-drive.

Monty, R. (2019). Undergirding writing centers' responses to the neoliberal academy. *Praxis: A Writing Center Journal, 16*(3). https://www.praxisuwc.com/163-monty-et-al.

Moore, C., O'Neill, P. & Crow, A. (2016). Assessing for learning in an age for comparability. In Scherer, W. et al. (Eds.), *Reclaiming accountability: Improving writing programming through accreditation and large-scale assessments* (pp. 17–35). Utah State University Press.

Morris, J. & Concannon, K. (2022). *Emotions and affect in writing centers.* Parlor Press.

Morrison, T. H. & Nanton, T. O. (2019). Dear writing centers: Black women speaking silence into language and action. *The Peer Review, 3*(1). https://thepeerreview-iwca.org/issues/redefining-welcome/dear-writing-centers-black-women-speaking-silence-into-language-and-action/.

Moseley, A. (1984). From factory to workshop: Revising the writing center. *The Writing Center Journal, 4*(2), 31–38.

Murray, D. (2003). Zen tutoring: Unlocking the mind. *The Writing Lab Newsletter, 27*(10), 12–14.

Navarro, V. (2020). The consequences of neoliberalism in the current pandemic. *International Journal of Health Services, 50*(3), 271–275.

Naydan, L. M. (2017). Toward a rhetoric of labor activism in college and university writing centers. *Praxis: A Writing Center Journal, 14*(2), 33–40. https://www.praxisuwc.com/naydan-142.

Neumann, D. (2021). Bates College staff launch union drive in response to low pay, high turnover. *Beacon.* https://mainebeacon.com/bates-college-staff-want-to-unionize-due-to-low-pay-and-high-turnover.

OPEIU (2022). Step 10—Start the Contract Campaign. https://tinyurl.com/373jebtt.

Owens, K. H. (2020). Handling sexual assault reports as a WPA. In C. Wooten, J. Babb, K. Costello & K. Navickas (Eds.), *The things we carry: Strategies for recognizing and negotiating emotional labor in writing program administration* (pp. 115–128). Utah State University Press.

Parker, M. & Jary, D. (1994). The managed university. *Management Research News*, 17(7/8/9), 56–57.

Perkins, K. (2022). Unionization is catching on among undergraduate student workers. *National Public Radio*. https://www.npr.org/2022/06/07/1103569564/unionization-is-catching-on-among-undergraduate-student-workers.

Perry, A. (2016). Training for triggers: Helping writing center consultants navigate emotional sessions. *Composition Forum, 34*. https://compositionforum.com/issue/34/training-triggers.php.

Polkinghorne, D. E. (1995). Narrative configuration in qualitative analysis. In J. A. Hatch & R. Wisniewski (Eds.), *Life history and narrative* (5–23). London: Falmer.

Quinn, R. (2023). Despite national pushback, West Virginia will cut faculty, programs. *Inside Higher Ed*. https://www.insidehighered.com/news/faculty-issues/shared-governance/2023/09/15/despite-national-pushback-wvu-will-cut-faculty.

Rich, D. (n.d.) Feeling burned out? Internalized capitalism may be to blame. *Clarity Therapy NYC*. https://www.claritytherapynyc.com/feeling-burned-out-internalized-capitalism-may-be-to-blame/.

Robillard, A. (2021). From isolated stories to a collective: Speaking out about misogyny in English departments. *Peitho*, 23(2). https://tinyurl.com/3he9x589.

Scheper-Hughes, N. (2000). Ire in Ireland. *Ethnography*, 1(1), 117–140.

Schlachte, C. (2020). Shelter in place: Contingency and affect in graduate teacher training courses. In C. Wooten, J. Babb, K. Costello & K. Navickas (Eds.), *The things we carry: Strategies for recognizing and negotiating emotional labor in writing program administration*, (pp. 145–160). Utah State University Press.

Sharer, W., Morse, T. A., Eble, M. F. & Banks, W. P. (Eds.). (2016). *Reclaiming accountability: Improving writing programs through accreditation and large-scale assessments*. Utah State University Press.

Spohrer, E. (2008). From goals to intentions: yoga, Zen, and our writing center work. *Writing Lab Newsletter*, 33(2), 10–13.

Stillman, S. (2021). The migrant workers who follow climate disasters. *The New Yorker*. https://tinyurl.com/3bb95mnx.

Sull, D., Sull, C. & Zweig, B. (2022). Toxic culture is driving the great resignation. *MIT Sloan Management Review*, 63(2), 1–9.

Tapper, J. (2022). Quiet quitting: Why doing the bare minimum at work has gone global. *The Guardian*. https://tinyurl.com/2b42n3ux.

Terkel, S. (Ed.). (1974). *Working: People talk about what they do all day and how they feel about what they do*. The New Press.

Thompson, I., Whyte, A., Shannon, D., Muse, A., Miller, K., Chappell, M. & Whigham, A. (2009). Examining our lore: A survey of students' and tutors' satisfaction with writing center conferences. *The Writing Center Journal*, 29(1), 78–105.

Travis, D. J. & Thorpe-Moscon, T. (2018). *Day-to-day experiences of emotional tax among women and men of color in the workplace*. Catalyst. https://www.catalyst.org/wp-content/uploads/2019/02/emotionaltax.pdf.

Treisman, R. (2020). Essential workers hold walkouts and protests in national 'Strike for Black lives.' *National Public Radio*. https://tinyurl.com/244ey5rk.

Wakamo, B. (2021). The pandemic is sparking a wave of union drives on college campuses. *Institute for Policy Studies*. https://tinyurl.com/4mk9wn3n.

Wang, I. K. (2022). Our theories of race will not save us: Towards localized storyings of race, colonialisms, and relationships. *Praxis*, 19(1), 47–57. https://www.praxisuwc.com/191-wang.

Webster, T. (2021). *Queerly centered: LGBTQA writing center directors navigate the workplace*. Utah State University Press.

Weise, K. & Scheiber, N. (2022). Amazon workers on Staten Island vote to unionize in landmark win for labor. *The New York Times*. https://www.nytimes.com/2022/04/01/technology/amazon-union-staten-island.html.

Whitford, E. (2020). College presidents' cabinets still far from gender parity. *Inside Higher Education*. https://tinyurl.com/3uhmju7f.

Wooten, C., Babb, J., Costello, K. M. & Navickas, K. (2020). *The things we carry: Strategies for recognizing and negotiating emotional labor in writing program administration*. Utah State University Press.

Wooten, C. A., Fitzpatrick, B., Fernandez, L., Goldenthal, A. M. & Matthews, J. (2022). Drown[ing] a little bit all the time: The intersections of labor constraints and professional development in hybrid contingent faculty experiences. *Academic Labor: Research and Artistry*, 6, 1–26.

Wright, E. O. (2015). How to be an anticapitalist in the twenty-first century. *Journal of Australian Political Economy*, 77, 5–22.

Wright, E. O. (2019). *How to be an anticapitalist in the twenty-first century*. Verso Books.

Wynn Perdue, S. K., Driscoll, D. L. & Petrykowski, A. (2017). Centering institutional status and scholarly identity: An analysis of writing center administration position advertisements, 2004–2014. *Writing Center Journal*, 37(2), 265–293.

Appendix A. Email to Workshop Participants

Subject: Writing Collective Debrief
June 20, 2022

Hello All,

It was great talking with so many of you today about your stories and story ideas. Below are some resources and advice that came up during our conversation which we hope will help you as you complete your stories.

- Framing your narrative around specific memories, incidences, or experiences is important to setting the scene for your story. Some good ones that came up today included: doing a job you never thought you would do (drilling a desk, moving a tutor out of their apartment, managing a fight between two tutors over clothing choice).
- When you are writing about an experience that has been written about before, try to find models to see how others write about that experience.
- Use "artifacts" like email topic chains, quotes from letters, writing feedback, etc. to "frame" your narrative. These can be useful signposting guides for readers.
- Don't overexplain the day-to-day stuff. We all struggle with staffing (more or less), we all struggle with burnout (more or less), we all go above and beyond in our work (more or less). How do YOU specifically do these things, be specific, show us, don't tell!
- Try not to academicize your writing. You want to cite, cool, but do so using an APA style which includes paraphrase over direct citation and do it briefly. Cite and then move on to your ideas!
- If you have a unique setting (one person mentioned a creepy abandoned children's hospital room as their office), use it! Place us in the moment.
- Use examples and then introspect. It is ok to deconstruct your experience but again try not to over-explain things!
- *It is OK to use composite approaches when telling a story. This means putting together several conversations, several experiences, and then creatively restructuring them to make your point. Lots of memoirs create wholesale dialogue. Unless a person has a recorder/records everything (looking at you Alison Bechdel), it is likely that some of that is creatively constructed.

*Of course, this being said, there should be "truth" to your story. Don't tell other people's stories without their permission, try not to represent yourself outside of your identity/experience, and try to stick to the facts as they are creatively engaged with :)

Cheers, Genie and Dan

Appendix B. Letter to Accreditors

To Whom it May Concern,

I reach out to you today to advocate for the work of [YOUR WC NAME HERE] at [YOUR INSTITUTION HERE], and to request for our writing center to be included in discussions of assessment, accreditation, and success per the criteria of your organization at [YOUR INSTITUTION HERE].

Assessment of writing centers and their relation to larger programmatic assessment has been an ongoing topic in rhetoric and writing studies research. Writing centers also have a long and well-documented history of contributing to several indicators typically associated with student success, such as

- Retention (Bell and Frost, 2012; Kilmer, 1993; Lerner, 2003; Rapp and Fritschze, 2002; Roberts, 1988; Simpson, 1988; Waldo, 1987)
- Improved performance in first-year writing classes (Deiderich & Schroeder, 2008; Lerner, 1997; Lerner, 2003)
- Transfer of writing knowledge between contexts (Bromley et al., 2016; Hill, 2016; Weissbach & Pflueger, 2018)
- High-impact practices such as conducting original research through shared intellectual experiences per Council of Undergraduate Research (https://www.cur.org/) and American Association of Colleges and Universities (https://www.aacu.org/trending-topics/high-impact), 2022
- Student professional development via training and research (Giaimo & Turner, 2019; Hughes et al., 2010)

Our own efforts at [YOUR INSTITUTION HERE] echo many of these indicators. For example, [SHARE SOME STATS/OUTCOMES HERE].

Given our contribution and ability to assist [INSTITUTION HERE] in meeting your organization's criteria for accreditation, we ask to be more fully incorporated into assessment and accreditation processes and to have a say in those processes. We believe that being fully instantiated into the assessment and accreditation processes offered by your organization would enable us to better address student success and provide us the sort of visibility and resources necessary to contribute even further.

We welcome any opportunities for conversation, correspondence, or other ways to engage with you on these important matters. We look forward to working with you.

Sincerely,

[YOUR NAME HERE]

References

American Association of Colleges and Universities (2022). *High Impact Practices.* https://www.aacu.org/trending-topics/high-impact.

Bell, D. C. & Frost, A. (2012). Critical inquiry and writing centers: A methodology of assessment. *Learning Assistance Review,17*(1), 15–26.

Bromley, P., Northway, K. & Schonberg, E. (2016). Transfer and dispositions in writing centers: A cross-institutional, mixed-methods study. *Across the Disciplines, 13*(1), 1–15.

Council of Undergraduate Research (2022). *Main page.* https://www.cur.org/.

Diederich, N. A. & Schroeder, S. J. (2008). Effect of writing centers and targeted pairings on students repeating first-year composition. *Learning Assistance Review, 13*(2), 17–26.

Giaimo, G. N. & Turner, S. J. (2019). Session notes as a professionalization tool for writing center staff: Conducting discourse analysis to determine training efficacy and tutor growth. *Journal of Writing Research, 11*(1), 131–162.

Hill, H. N. (2016). Tutoring for transfer: The benefits of teaching writing center tutors about transfer theory. *The Writing Center Journal, 35*(3), 77–102.

Hughes, B., Gillespie, P. & Kail, H. (2010). What they take with them: Findings from the peer writing tutor alumni research project. *The Writing Center Journal, 30*(2), 12–46.

Kilmer, W. (1993). Explaining and justifying writing centers: One MORE example. *The Writing Lab Newsletter*, 5–7.

Lerner, N. (1997). Counting beans and making beans count. *Writing Lab Newsletter, 22*(1), 1–3.

Lerner, N. (2003). Writing center assessment: Searching for the 'proof' of our effectiveness. *The Center Will Hold*, 58–73.

Rapp Young, B. & B.A. Fritzsche. (2002). Writing center users procrastinate less: The relationship between individual differences in procrastination, peer feedback, and student writing success. *The Writing Center Journal, 23*(1), 45–58. https://doi.org/10.2307/j.ctt46nxnq.7 .

SEIU Faculty Forward (2022). *Transforming Higher Education.* https://victories.seiufacultyforward.org/2016/.

Simpson, J. (1991). The role of writing centers in student retention programs. In R. Wallace (Ed.), *The writing center: New directions* (pp. 102–109). Garland Publishing.

Roberts, D. H. (1988). A study of writing center effectiveness. *The Writing Center Journal 9*(1), 53–60.

Waldo, M. L. (1987). More than 'first-aid': A report on the effectiveness of writing center intervention in the writing process. *Issues in College Learning Centers, 5*, 12–22.

Weissbach, R. S. & Pflueger, R. C. (2018). Collaborating with writing centers on interdisciplinary peer tutor training to improve writing support for engineering students. *IEEE Transactions on Professional Communication, 61*(2), 206–220.

Appendix C. Playbook for Unionizing

The American Association of University Professors (AAUP) provides a great set of guides on union organizing that range from the basics to specific steps to forming a union.[1] Below, we distill this information in a kind of playbook for both gauging the possibility and interest in forming a union, undertaking a drive, and, if successful, handling contract negotiations. Because there are many concerns that academic workers bring to the fore that range from wages and position descriptions to issues of faculty governance and academic freedom, it is important to note here that every campaign might turn on a different group of issues that mobilize people. It is also important to note that the messiness of coalition building cannot be fully captured in single playbooks but that "wall-to-wall" unions that bring together all kinds of academic workers (graduate students, adjuncts, non-tenure track, tenure track, and staff) are an exciting and inclusive way to justify and run a union drive.

Recruit: Start by identifying leaders on campus. These folks might include newer and more seasoned workers. However, the core leadership group of a union is key to a successful drive. So, choosing people who can generate consensus around the larger group and who have broad appeal will likely be necessary. Also, if there are current governance structures, such as a faculty or staff council, it is important to consider whether or not to turn to specific individuals in those groups to recruit leaders. This initial group of recruited leaders becomes the campaign committee. Typically not elected until the union is recognized, this group is tasked with organizing and inspiring a larger group of people to join the campaign or drive. The American Association of University Professors suggests that this organizing committee do the following two tasks:

1. Create a full list of organization members with their names, positions, and contact information.
2. Further recruiting leaders from across the college or university to represent membership. They suggest a broad representation on the organizing committee of 1 "member for every ten to twenty future members" (AAUP).

Consult: Many organizers take the step of contacting either an appropriate (i.e., teacher's union) or local union organizer in order to connect, learn about local initiatives, and learn from on-the-ground organizers who advise union campaigns. And while there might be the option of creating an independent union, joining a national union gives the chapter resources and access beyond what one might gain as a small independent union. In this model, the national organization

---

1. This playbook is adapted and expanded from the American Association of University Professors' "Forming a Union Chapter" (https://www.aaup.org/chapter-resources/forming-new-union).

often engages with the local chapter on things like a union drive and, later, contract negotiation and collective bargaining. So, choosing the right union to join can involve some vetting, community-wide discussion, and, of course, research. Below, we provide databases and organizations that have aggregated information about labor unions in the United States. While some academic institutions choose to join teacher unions (e.g., American Federation of Teachers or the National Education Association). However, adjunct faculty, graduate students, and full and part-time faculty have successfully unionized through the service workers union (Service Employees International Union, 2022). So, in addition to conducting local research and hands-on person-to-person engagement around working conditions, key issues, unionization support, and other on-the-ground concerns, the organizing committee also needs to research and eventually vet national unions to determine if they want to join them and become a chapter or if they want to form an independent union.

Campaign: Before starting a campaign or drive, it is critical that the organizing committee is both representative and, also, that the folks they recruit are on board with unionization. Typically, a union drive is not made public until there is broad support for unionization. The campaign starts with education work by the OC to the college population. This can take the form of educational materials, information meetings, one-on-one meetings with individuals, and, perhaps, more public meetings about worker concerns, such as a town hall meeting. If part of a national union, an organizer from outside the institution should also be able to help support the campaign and, perhaps, offer resources for the organizing committee.

The American Association of University Professors suggests the development of the following to start to campaign:

- Talking points
- Database or file for tracking visits to community members
- Training organizers in basic questions and concerns about unions (such as dues)
- Check-in meetings among the organizing committee to share "roses and thorns" or positive and negative outcomes from organizing work
- A plan to keep the work sustainable and enjoyable

Before going public, the organizing committee needs to lay out its main goals and concerns–based on their meetings with workers–to promote "unifying support" and have majority support for unionization (AAUP).

Gathering signatures and going public: Once majority support has been secured, the organizing committee begins a card signing drive. This is a very public moment in the campaign and one that is likely to be plagued by misinformation, intimidation, and stalling tactics. In this moment, it is critical to document the drive, keep up momentum with public gatherings and celebrations of card signing, and combat misinformation with media and on-the-ground counter information campaigns.

In the public phase of the campaign right before and during voting:

- Maintain a list of "yes," "no," and "unsure"/"unclear" votes for the union
- Continue to meet with people one-on-one during the drive
- Clarify and explain how to fill out the ballot (perhaps with a sample ballot with a "yes" vote for the union)
- Develop a clear system to track who has voted and who still needs to vote (see resources below)
- Circulate clear information about where, when, and how to vote
- Establish poll watchers from the organizing committee to document any intimidation, obstruction, or misinformation tactics during the vote

After the Vote: If the vote passes, take time to celebrate with the organizing committee and union supporters. Also, as soon as possible, communicate the results of the vote to participants in the drive (and in the community at large) in order to control messaging. After taking some time to regroup and rest, a new committee (perhaps with members of the organizing committee) needs to be formed to participate in contract campaign negotiations. Again, a representative from the national union might be able to provide support or resources during this time. It is also likely they will have a representative on the bargaining committee.

The Contract Campaign (from Office and Professional Employees International Union):

- Requires information gathering and data
- Survey members about key issues and concerns
- Organize a contract bargaining team
- Keep members informed about the creation of the contract and key issues
- Continue to engage community members and allies
- Continue to recruit members and promote the contract campaign
- Develop new leaders and recruitment strategies
- Celebrate your victories

Resources to Get started

- Union base provides connections to union organizations around the country (https://unionbase.org/)
- Center for Union Facts has compiled a comprehensive database about US-based labor unions (https://www.unionfacts.com/cuf/)
- Action builder (https://www.actionbuilder.org/) is an organizing tool developed in partnership with the American Federation of Labor and Congress of Industrial Organizations (AFL-CIO); it helps organizers to track union drives through digitized versions of wall charts, assessments, membership lists, etc.

- American Association of University Professors (AAUP) union chapter resources (https://www.aaup.org/chapter-resources/union-chapter-resources)
- National Labor Relations Board (NLRB) (https://www.nlrb.gov/about-nlrb/rights-we-protect/the-law/employees/your-right-to-form-a-union)
- American Federation of Labor and Congress of Industrial Organizations (AFL-CIO) (https://aflcio.org/formaunion)

It takes a lot of work and continuous engagement (and pressure on the institution) to engage in a union drive. At times, this work can be intimidating, frustrating, and seemingly pointless. If anyone has ever sat through a faculty council meeting or a department meeting, we know how many voices there are in the room and how few of them take up the majority of air time. Creating a union (or even establishing an AAUP chapter as an alternative to current governance structures) can help to dramatically improve working conditions and worker rights. So, while this work can take years, it is also something that we writing center folks are already trained to do. We are trained to do research and assessment, to communicate our results, to convince people to engage in best practices or ethical practices, and to connect people from disparate places in the university. We are also continuously engaging in marketing and information campaigns even as we train a rotating group of people in the work we do. And, we often write *a lot* and quickly. In a lot of ways, organizing is quite similar work. So, in addition to considering the advice above, think about what unique strengths you bring to organizing work from your writing center and other academic work. As one of the stories in this collection shares, this work helps benefit the most precarious workers among us, but, also, it is about creating community and connections and, crucially, sharing information about what workers are entitled to based on collective bargaining. It is empowering and necessary work

Contributors

Anonymous ("From Dream Job to Unsustainable"). This contributor worked in higher education for over a decade and focused their scholarship and presentations on topics related to first-year composition, the intersections of writing centers and learning commons, and training graduate assistants to teach composition. The Contributor is no longer in higher education, but remains connected to—and will forever be supportive of—writing centers and the labor of those who direct them.

Anonymous ("Into and Out of the Tutoring Center"). The author of this chapter has worked in writing centers and taught English for more than thirty years at a variety of institution types. The author has also been involved in writing center professional communities throughout their tenure, serving in various leadership positions.

Saurabh Anand is a Rhetoric and Composition Studies Ph.D. student at the University of Georgia, where he serves as an assistant director of the writing center. His essays have appeared in the *Writing Center Journal, Praxis: A Writing Center Journal*, and he received the 2024 Scholar of Dream Award and the 2023 Future Leader Award by the International Writing Center Association.

Libby Anthony is Associate Professor of English and Director of the Writing and Study Skills Center at the University of Cincinnati, Blue Ash College. Her research interests include craft rhetorics, writing center theory and pedagogy, and study abroad.

Vincent Belkin (Pseudonymous) is Associate Professor of English at a small Midwestern liberal arts university and has been the director of its growing writing center for 13 years. They have won numerous teaching awards, and their scholarship has primarily been on linguistic justice and Critical Language Awareness.

Candis Bond is Director of the Center for Writing Excellence at Augusta University, where she is also Associate Professor of English. Her research interests include dimensions of writing center labor, writing in STEM, WAC/WID, and higher education leadership. She has published scholarship in journals such as *Writing Center Journal, WLN: A Journal of Writing Center Scholarship, Praxis: A Writing Center Journal, Southern Discourse in the Center*, and *The Peer Review*.

John Chadderdon is a professional writing tutor at SUNY Buffalo State University, where he helps students across disciplines refine their writing practices. He is also a local musician and has served as a contributing editor on the *Elm Leaves Journal* Blackout edition.

Joseph Cheatle is Assistant Professor of English and Director of the Writing and Communication Center at Oxford College of Emory University. He is the co-editor of the edited collection *Redefining Roles: The Professional, Faculty, and Graduate Consultant's Guide to Writing Centers,* published at Utah State

University Press. His work has appeared in *Writing Center Journal, Praxis, Kairos, Southern Discourse in the Center,* and the *Journal of Writing Analytics.* And he is a recipient of the IWCA Research Grant for his project "Organization Theory and Writing Centers."

Eva Dunsky is an adjunct professor of first-year writing at Baruch College and the School of Visual Arts; in addition, she has worked in the writing centers at Barnard College, Columbia University, and Fordham University. She also writes fiction and criticism, and translates from Spanish and Catalan into English.

Tiffany-Anne M. Elliott is Academic Support Programs Coordinator at Lincoln Land Community College where she oversees the peer tutoring, study group, math center, and embedded support programs. Before moving into her current position, she worked in the campus writing center and taught freshman English for 15 years. She is currently earning her Ed.D. in Leadership and Innovation from Arizona State University where her research focuses on embedded tutoring.

Genie Nicole Giaimo is Associate Professor of Writing Studies and Rhetoric at Hofstra University, where they serve as the writing center director. Their research has appeared in *Praxis, Writing Center Journal, TPR, Journal of Writing Research, Kairos, Journal of Writing Analytics, Journal of Multimodal Rhetorics,* and several other peer-reviewed journals in rhetoric and composition. They are the author of *Unwell Writing Centers: Searching for Wellness in Neoliberal Educational Institutions and Beyond* (2023) and the editor of *Wellness and Care in Writing Center Work* (2021).

James Donathan Garner is Associate Director of the Center for Writing Excellence at Augusta University. His essays have appeared in in *Praxis: A Writing Center Journal, Rhetorica,* and *The Journal for the History of Rhetoric.*

Jonathan Green is Assistant Professor of English and Director of the Writing Center at Cottey College, a small women's liberal arts college in Nevada, MO. His research focuses on how writing can be thought of and taught as a practice-able, improvable skill similar to sports or music.

Rebecca Hallman Martini is Associate Professor of English and Director of the Jill and Marvin Willis Center for Writing at the University of Georgia. Her book, *Disrupting the Center: A Partnership Approach to Writing Across the University* (USUP 2022), won the 2024 CCCC Advancement of Knowledge Award. Other works have appeared in *WPA, Writing Center Journal, Across the Disciplines, WAC Journal,* and *Computers and Composition.* She is the founding editor of IWCA's journal, *The Peer Review,* and serves as associate publisher for accessibility and sustainability with the WAC Clearinghouse.

Muriel Harris is Professor of English (emerita) at Purdue University and Director of the Writing Lab (retired), where she and several graduate students started the Purdue University Writing Lab. She also initiated the Purdue OWL and the journal *WLN: A Journal of Writing Center Scholarship,* the first in the field of writing center studies. Her publications, in addition to her textbooks, have appeared in numerous journals and as chapters in book collections, and she has been a keynote speaker, a workshop leader, and a presenter at regional, national, and international conferences. Her CV is available at https://wac.colostate.edu/docs/wln/cv.pdf While she is gratified to have spent her academic life involved in writing centers, which she views as extraordinary, effective sites of learning, her proudest accomplishment continues to be her children and grandchildren.

Maggie M. Herb is Associate Professor of English and Director of the Writing Center at SUNY Buffalo State University. She is also co-director of the Western New York Writing Project. Her scholarship has appeared in *Writing Center Journal*, *Praxis*, and several edited collections.

Elijah Hundley is a peer writing tutor and graduate student at SUNY Buffalo State University, where he is pursuing a Master of English.

Olivia Imirie is Instructor of English at Wor-Wic Community College teaching first-year and developmental writing. She has presented research at the International Writing Center Association conference on collaborations between college and secondary school writing centers.

Silk Jade (Pseudonymous) is a writing center administrator at a public research university. This university serves many students as multilingual and first-generation college students. Her research interests include writing tutors' and student writers' growth at the writing center, writing and writing tutoring pedagogy, professional development of peer writing tutors, issues and strategies in academic writing, transnationalism and translingualism, instructors' feedback, and faculty-student mentorship. Her studies have come to fruition in dozens of publications, including peer-reviewed journal articles and book chapters in these fields. Among those publications, over one-third are co-authored with her students and tutors.

Allie Johnston is Assistant Professor of English at Austin Peay State University, where she teaches composition and rhetoric courses. She also serves as the university's first writing center director. Her research focuses on writing center studies and multimodal curriculum in first-year writing programs.

Megan Keaton is Associate Professor of Rhetoric and Composition at the Pfeiffer University, where she serves as Writing Center Director and teaches composition courses. She has published articles in *Praxis: A Writing Center Journal*, *Southern Discourse in the Center*, and *The CEA Forum*, and she has a chapter in the edited collection, *Teaching through the Archives: Text, Collaboration, and Activism*.

Daniel Lawson is Professor of English at Central Michigan University, where he serves as the writing center director. He has published on rhetoric, media studies, and writing centers. His writing center work has appeared in venues such as *WLN*, *Praxis*, and *TPR*. He has served as the President of the Michigan Writing Centers Association and as an at-large board member of the East Central Writing Centers Association.

Neal Lerner, Professor of English at Northeastern University, teaches undergraduate and graduate courses in writing and the teaching of writing. He is the author or co-author of eight books and over 40 peer-reviewed articles and book chapters on the history, theory, and practice of learning and teaching writing, including *The Meaningful Writing Project: Learning, Teaching, and Writing in Higher Education* with Michele Eodice and Anne Ellen Geller. His most recent book is *Reformers, Teachers, Writers: Curricular and Pedagogical Inquiries*.

Margaret Lundberg is a professional writing specialist in the Teaching and Learning Center at the University of Washington Tacoma, where her portfolio includes personal narrative and mentoring graduate writers. A later-in-life returner to higher education, her research interests lie in memoir and life writing, and the (re)construction of student identity among mature women who return to higher education. She has published a novel, *Life in Continuous Present*, inspired by her work with a 19th-century diary, as well as several shorter works, including poetry and autoethnographic essays. She is also Editor-in-Chief of *Access: Interdisciplinary Journal of Student Research and Scholarship*, housed in the Digital Commons.

Oluwatosin Mariam Junaid is a doctoral candidate at the University of São Paulo Brazil(USP) where she researches academic literacies with a focus on academic writing and writing for publication purposes. She is also a writing tutor at the Laboratory of Academic Literacy (LLAC-USP). In this capacity, she provides guidance to students in navigating the complexities of academic writing. She has published several book chapters and articles. Beyond academia, Oluwatosin finds joy in diverse interests like reading, singing, writing, culinary pursuits, and engaging in community outreach initiatives. Also, she actively participates in endeavors aimed at positively impacting her surrounding environment.

Anne McMurtrey possesses more than 20 years of writing center expertise. She served as a tutor at the University of Idaho and coordinator at Washington State University before directing the University of Utah Writing Center for the past decade. Additionally, she ensures tutor quality at eTutoringOnline.org.

Janine Morris is Associate Professor of Writing at Nova Southeastern University, where she serves as a faculty coordinator of the NSU Writing and Communication Center. Her co-edited collection, *Emotions and Affect in Writing Centers*, was published by Parlor Press in 2022. Her recent essays have appeared in *Composition Forum*, *Southern Discourse in the Center* and *Peitho*, along with several edited collections.

Molly Ryan (she/her) teaches First-Year Writing at Virginia Tech, where she also serves as the Director of the Graduate Academy of Teaching Excellence. Broadly, her work explores critical pedagogy in the writing classroom, empathetic teaching philosophies, and administrative matriculation. Her work has appeared in *Kairos*, *The Sandbox*, and elsewhere.

Mary Elizabeth Skinner received her Master of English at the University of Alabama at Birmingham where she also taught composition and tutored in the University Writing Center. She currently teaches middle school composition and literature and is a freelance tutor for middle and high school students.

Katherine E. Tirabassi is the Director of the Center for Research & Writing, Professor of Communication, and Affiliate Faculty in English at Keene State College in southwestern New Hampshire. She teaches professional communication, creative writing, research methods, and a tutoring training course, and coordinates an internship program for students in Communication/Philosophy and English. She has presented and published her research on writing center studies, civic engagement, archival research, composition pedagogy, and 16th-century French writer Marie de Gournay. In 2021, Dr. Tirabassi was awarded Keene State's Distinguished Teacher of the Year Award and, in 2023, the Faculty Distinguished Service Award.

Lan Wang-Hiles is Associate Professor of English at West Virginia State University, where she teaches writing center tutor training courses frequently. She has published her studies as journal articles and book chapters by the *Journal of Second Language Writing, NYS TESOL Journal*, MLA Style Center, Michigan University Press, Springer, *Multilingual Matters*, WAC Clearinghouse, Brill, and IGI Global. She is Chair of the Non-Native English-Speaking Writing Instructors (NNESWIs) Standing Group for the Conference of College Composition and Communication (CCCC), the Newsletter Editor of the Program Administration Interest Section (PAIS) for the TESOL International Association, and a board member to represent Higher Education of the West Virginia TESOL.

Jaclyn Wells is Associate Professor at the University of Alabama at Birmingham, where she directs the writing center and teaches composition and professional writing. Jaclyn is co-author of *Partners in Literacy: A Writing Center Model for Civic Engagement*. Her work has also appeared in *College Composition and Communication*, the *Writing Center Journal*, and other journals and edited collections.

Scott Whiddon is Professor of Writing, Rhetoric, and Communication and Writing Center Director at Transylvania University in Lexington, Kentucky, with work featured in *Praxis: A Writing Center Journal, WLN: A Journal of Writing Center Scholarship*, and elsewhere. His efforts in writing centers earned the 2018 Martinson Award for Excellence and the 2022 SWCA Achievement Award. He is also an active musician.

Ryan Patrick Witt has worked with writers—as a faculty member and tutor—at institutions in the western, midwestern, and northeastern US over the span of his now 20-year journey working in higher ed. His writing and scholarship have appeared in the *Journal of Policy Practice and Research, Barrow Street, What We Wish We'd Known: Negotiating Graduate* School, and *Talking River*, among other venues. He currently directs the First-Year Seminar program and the Writing Center at the College of Idaho, and when he's not working, he enjoys cooking, fly fishing, writing and reading poetry, and spending time with his wife and daughters.

www.ingramcontent.com/pod-product-compliance
Lightning Source LLC
Chambersburg PA
CBHW060555080526
44585CB00013B/569